Communing with the Divine

BOOKS BY BARBARA Y. MARTIN AND DIMITRI MORAITIS

Change Your Aura, Change Your Life:
A Step-by-Step Guide to Unfolding Your Spiritual Power

The Healing Power of Your Aura:
How to Use Spiritual Energy for Physical Health and Well-Being

Karma and Reincarnation:
Unlocking Your 800 Lives to Enlightenment

Communing
WITH THE *Divine*

A CLAIRVOYANT'S GUIDE
TO ANGELS, ARCHANGELS,
and the
SPIRITUAL HIERARCHY

Barbara Y. Martin & Dimitri Moraitis

JEREMY P. TARCHER/PENGUIN
a member of Penguin Group (USA)
New York

JEREMY P. TARCHER/PENGUIN
Published by the Penguin Group
Penguin Group (USA) LLC
375 Hudson Street
New York, New York 10014

USA • Canada • UK • Ireland • Australia
New Zealand • India • South Africa • China

penguin.com
A Penguin Random House Company

Most Tarcher/Penguin books are available at special quantity discounts for
bulk purchase for sales promotions, premiums, fund-raising, and educational needs.
Special books or book excerpts also can be created to fit specific needs.
For details, write: Special.Markets@us.penguingroup.com.

Library of Congress Cataloging-in-Publication Data

Martin, Barbara Y.
Communing with the divine : a clairvoyant's guide to angels, archangels,
and the spiritual hierarchy / Barbara Y. Martin and Dimitri Moraitis.
p.   cm.
Includes bibliographical references and index.
ISBN 978-0-399-16774-4
1. Angels.   2. Spiritual life.   I. Title.
BL477.M3645   2014
202'.15—dc23   2013050134

Printed in the United States of America
1   3   5   7   9   10   8   6   4   2

BOOK DESIGN BY TANYA MAIBORODA

Dedicated to
the Lord of Wisdom Light
and the spiritual hierarchy
that is bringing forth
the New Age
for humanity

CONTENTS

of Wisdom Light (Lord Christ) • Divine Light under Archangel Michael •
Divine Light under Archangel Gabriel • Divine Light under Archangel Uriel •
Divine Light under Archangel Raphael • How the Holy Ones Work with You
during Meditation • Calling on the Higher outside Meditation and Prayer

LIST OF ILLUSTRATIONS

ACKNOWLEDGMENTS

We're eternally grateful to the Holy Ones who came particularly close during the writing of this book so that their inspiration was effectively transmitted through these pages. All our books are the result of divine inspiration, but as this was a book about the Holy Ones, they were particularly close to the writing process. They are life's great mystery and support.

We thank all the students and supporters of Spiritual Arts Institute. Everyone at the institute is helping in their own way to get the word out on this important work. Special thanks to Neil and Anna Mintz, Melinda Noble, A. J. Le Shay, Megumi Yamada, John Harrison, Ray and Jane Barger, Juliana Nahas, Joel Morris, Caridad Acosta, Patricia Bowman, Marisa Lenci, Fred and Stephanie Richards, Mark Hafeman, Marvette Saucer, Ariste Reno, Karen Higgins, Janine and Matthew Hannibal, Martin and Jacqueline Roos, Trisha Kelly, Jan Van Ek, Nancy Green, and Kathy Hsu for their support. Our gratitude to Barbara's family: Vasilli, Ria, Ken, and Amanda. And to the Moraitis family: George, Philip, Ann Marie, Ellen, Anne, and Julia and in memory of Dimitri's mother, Christine.

Thank you to our agent, Simon Warwick-Smith. We have worked with him for many years and he has been instrumental in the publication of our books. Our thanks go to Joel Fotinos at Penguin/Tarcher for his support. It is wonderful to work with a publisher who has such respect for and understanding of metaphysics. Thanks to Andrew Yackira for his wonderful editorial work as well as shepherding the book's publication. Our thanks go to the marketing and production staff at Penguin. We wish to say thanks to Nita Ybarra for her excellent cover design. This is the fourth book cover she has done for us. Each cover beautifully reflects the mood and feel of the book. We thank Howard David Johnson for his masterful illustrations. He did an excellent job in bringing to life Barbara's visions of the Holy Ones in a way never seen before.

PREFACE

IT HAS BEEN such a joy to be part of the writing of this book. I knew from the beginning that delving into the spiritual hierarchy was going to be a monumental task as there were so many facets about celestial beings to consider. While this book is meant to encourage people to include the divine ones in their life and spiritual work, there is also a strong inspirational element to better appreciate the depth of spiritual support each of us receives. With all the books we have worked on together, the Holy Ones come close to support the writing. Yet with this writing, they came particularly close, almost on a daily basis, to make sure the book was an accurate reflection of their inspiration. This proximity gave me a new understanding and appreciation of the divine. It felt as if we were working hand in hand as the Holy Ones shared insight after insight into their workings.

As always, I am amazed at Barbara's skill as a teacher and clairvoyant. From the beginning of working together, her connection to the divine was a dominant feature of her teaching. She has the most profound understanding and extensive experience of celestial beings of anyone I have ever met. Yet with this book, new things were revealed that showed that no matter how much one may know or have experienced in metaphysics, there are always new mountains and vistas to cross. That's what makes the spiritual journey so mysterious and exciting.

I was surprised at the depth and extent of the material the divine was willing to share in a book designed for the general public. Many insights presented were previously reserved only for the advanced student. Yet now the divine was willing to openly share many celestial keys. This can only mean that more people than ever are ready for this knowledge and the awareness it brings.

During the writing of the book, there was the question of how to reconcile varying beliefs of the divine with the metaphysical understanding presented in these pages. We made a strong effort to show that despite various cultural nomenclatures, it is the same spiritual hierarchy for all humanity. We honor the various religious and metaphysical traditions, yet recognize we are all part of the same family of God.

Another unique experience during the writing of this book was the administrative change that was going on within the hierarchy itself. The divine ones are not static; they are dynamic and unfolding with even greater spiritual splendor. There has been a stepping up of divine support in the last few years, so it made the timing of this writing particularly relevant.

On a personal note, the writing of this book coincided with one of the most important turning points in my personal spiritual development. The Holy Ones brought me to a spiritual plateau I never imagined possible. It was a wellspring of unfoldment that was the result of years of preparation. Words are hardly adequate to express my gratitude to the divine for all they have done and are still doing. I am profoundly grateful to Barbara for shepherding me to this spiritual place in my life. She is a teacher in the truest and most profound sense of the word. The only way

I can begin to repay the blessings given is to be of service to the divine in helping others.

For those of you who doubt such spiritual transformations are possible, they are. And if you doubt that celestial beings such as angels exist, they do. We have a loving support more wonderful than we can imagine. May this book offer you fresh inspiration in your spiritual journey.

In Light and Love,
Dimitri Moraitis

INTRODUCTION

I IS MY great pleasure and honor to offer this book on the spiritual hierarchy. Of the clairvoyant gifts I have been blessed with, I count my connection with the Holy Ones as my most essential. From the first experience of seeing an angel at age three, the Holy Ones of Divine Light have been my constant companions and support personally, professionally, and spiritually. I have been a metaphysical teacher for more than forty years now. I am primarily known for my work with the auric field and have taught thousands to better themselves by working with their aura and spiritual energy. Yet behind all metaphysical work are the Holy Ones. I simply could not do my spiritual work without their constant support.

I will relate several of my experiences with the Holy Ones in the following pages, but let it be said that seeing celestial beings, or the Higher as they are also called, is by no means a prerequisite to working with them. Just as I tell people you do not need to see the aura to work with it, you don't need to see the Higher to work with them. The Higher work lovingly with every soul whether you see them or not. These divine ones are the unfailing partners in all your life's pursuits. Your success depends on their help. They are intimately aware of you. In many ways, they know you better than you know yourself. They know your purpose, your strengths and weaknesses, and what you are capable of. They are doing all they can to get closer to you and help you fulfill your purpose. As you learn to work in greater harmony with the divine ones, your life becomes more beautiful and fulfilling. And such a relationship eventually leads to the great mystical union.

The ancients spoke of this gift of communing with the Holy Ones as *theophany*—conversing with the divine. In this book, the goal is to strengthen your ability to converse with the Higher. I do not mean this in a psychic or mediumistic sense, or as a wishful or delusional fantasy. I mean learning how to better connect with the celestial beings through the mystical part of your nature.

I cannot promise that by the time you finish reading this book you will have developed your direct connection to the Higher. That must unfold in its own time as you climb the spiritual ladder. What I can say is that if you are earnest in your spiritual endeavors, you will draw a great deal closer to the Holy Ones and feel their influence more directly.

This study of the divine is based on my own direct clairvoyant experiences and observations over a lifetime. Some of these visitations have been so personal that I have kept them to myself until now. It is by the urging of the Holy Ones themselves that I am sharing some of these experiences to illustrate that you too have the potential to commune with the divine.

From the time I was young, the Holy Ones would present themselves so I could become familiar with them. I learned that there were many types of celestial beings and each had their own special gifts and talents.

Sometimes they would come in the most unexpected ways. One time when I was around eight years old, I was trying to find my father to give him a message that someone had called. My father was a Greek Orthodox priest and he was in a meeting at the church. To understand this story, I need to interject that my dad loved to tell us children stories of the various saints. I felt particularly drawn to the story of Saint Spiridon—how he was orphaned as a boy in the mountains of Greece and raised himself to become a shepherd, how he became a priest and then a venerated bishop, his incredible kindness and wisdom, his amazing spiritual gifts to manifest things in service to God, and how through an act of divine intercession he helped preserve the icons in the Greek Church, among other wonderful acts of service.

Well, on this day, I went in the church looking for my dad. The church was empty and there was a full-panel icon of Saint Spiridon near the entrance. To my utter amazement, Saint Spiridon himself emerged from his icon! He smiled at me, and I smiled back. His aura was absolutely magnificent, resplendent in golden light. Unfortunately, he left a moment later, but I just stood there in awe trying to take this all in. As with all experiences with the Higher, there was no fear or apprehension, just an amazing sense of wonder. I eventually found my father but needless to say did not share with him the visitation I had!

I had my first education regarding the spiritual hierarchy when I was eleven years old. Even though I was having celestial visitations, for the most part I did not understand who these beings were. I knew they were of a divine nature, but when they came they did not communicate much. They would come in time of need or simply make themselves known, but beyond the beauty and majesty of their presence, I did not yet really understand whom I was dealing with.

At age eleven, I was living in Kansas City, Missouri, with my family and was taking acting lessons with a well-known teacher, Dorothy La Moss. She ran one of the top theater stock companies in the Midwest.

It turned out she was a Hermetic scientist and very clairvoyant. She recognized my spiritual gifts and gave me my first lessons in metaphysics. This was a revelatory and exciting time, as she helped me put my many spiritual experiences in better perspective. Every Saturday for the next year, I met with her and she taught metaphysics. She allowed me to read from some of the sacred handwritten texts that she had on the Hermetic sciences—which I found out were the most ancient and enduring of all the metaphysical arts.

During this time I learned to better appreciate my clairvoyant talents. One of the gifts Dorothy gave was a greater understanding of the aura and how to interpret the colors of the aura. As part of this training, I received my first structured teaching on the spiritual hierarchy. The Hermetic term for the spiritual hierarchy was "The Greater Beyond." The Hermetic scientists talked about how essential the Higher was, what they were all about, how we needed to learn about them, and how helpful they were to us.

When I was a teenager, my clairvoyant gifts with the aura increased and so did my ability to commune with the Holy Ones. At this point I was having steady interactions with the Higher, and they were now conversing and teaching me many things. I learned how to work with the Divine Light for myself and others and how it is the Holy Ones who bring the Divine Light to humanity. They emphasized that there was a divine path to walk and encouraged me to stay with my spiritual work. At that time, I was trying to pursue a "normal" life and not metaphysics. They gently emphasized how important the spiritual life was.

When I reached my twenties, my personal experiences with the Holy Ones unfolded even more dramatically. Without my asking for it, I started having extraordinary celestial visitations with aspects of the spiritual hierarchy I did not even know existed. It was a time when the heavens seemed to open up and I was shown firsthand the breadth and scope of the spiritual hierarchy. Unfortunately, there was no one I could share these experiences with, so I kept these life-changing moments private.

That changed when I met my spiritual mentor and compatriot Inez Hurd. Inez was a metaphysical teacher working in Los Angeles. She was an extraordinary soul with advanced spiritual skills and abilities. She had a dramatic early life. Her father, who was born of Austrian aristocracy, married a commoner, and this led to a conflict with the established order to the point that they ended up killing her mother and wanting to kill him. Her father fled the country and took Inez to the United States to live with an aunt. Feeling that Inez was not safe with him there, he left for South America, where he was eventually killed. Inez was raised in Kansas by her aunt. Eventually they moved to Los Angeles, where she married into the Hancock family. That marriage did not last, but she then met Frank Hurd, married him, and had two children. It was a happy marriage but tragedy followed when her son died in a car accident and Frank died of an illness.

When Inez was still in her late twenties, she ate some tainted lettuce and almost died from food poisoning. That night, when it wasn't clear if she would live, she prayed to God to spare her. She said if she lived, she would dedicate the rest of her life to God. She had already had many clairvoyant experiences but had not yet pursued the spiritual life directly. Now her life's purpose became very clear. Of course, she lived and the spiritual work became the central focus of her life.

She trained for many years to develop her clairvoyant talents, which were considerable. She was adept with the aura and had an exceptional connection to the spiritual hierarchy. The Holy Ones brought through her an extraordinary revelation of the mystical work she termed "Christos Wisdom." This nondenominational mysticism became the core of her work and the focus of my teachings as well. Since that time, the Holy Ones have given me an expanded understanding of this grand system of spiritual study. The metaphysical interpretation of this study is known as *the Kingdom of Light Teachings* and is part of a universal teaching being given to humanity at this time. While knowledge from the Hermetic sciences is part of this book, the Kingdom of Light Teachings is the spiritual foundation for the knowledge imparted about the hierarchy. This is the focus of all of our teaching work.

Inez trained me to systematically work with the hierarchy. By the time I finished my training, I was able to converse with the Holy Ones seamlessly. This was a needed skill both personally and as a spiritual teacher, as all true spiritual teachers are, to a large degree, acting as emissaries for the Holy Ones. My love for and relationship with the Holy Ones has deepened ever since. I have never taken them for granted. Every time I have the honor to work with them, it is a blessed experience.

Many of the experiences with the Holy Ones I will share in this book took place on this side of life, but some took place in the spirit worlds, or inner planes, as they are also called. As part of my work with the divine, they would take me to these inner worlds for training and blessings. We are all connected to the spirit worlds even while in a physical body, but we generally do not bring back conscious memory of these experiences unless that skill has been developed. In the inner worlds, the Holy Ones are generally even more grand and splendid.

The writing of this book has also been a blessing in that my coauthor, Dimitri Moraitis, has actually reached that place of building his own direct communion with the divine. This book is a testament to what is possible if you are steadfast and determined.

It is wonderful to hear others tell stories of their spiritual experiences.

But if you somehow feel that such experiences are not meant for you, take heart in knowing that the Holy Ones are a part of your life, and that you too are capable of reaching that place of communing with the divine.

In Divine Light and Love,
Barbara Y. Martin

PART 1

Our

Invisible

Support System

CHAPTER 1

WHAT IS THE SPIRITUAL HIERARCHY?

*Every blade of grass has its angel that bends
over it and whispers, "Grow, grow."*
—THE TALMUD

ALL SEEKERS OF truth yearn for the mystical experience. In search of this experience of eternity we travel down many roads. The artist searches for this mystical union in the ecstasy of creation, the scientist in the throes of a new discovery, the lover in the rapture of the beloved, the parent in the tenderness of the child. In the midst of your search, the very divine presence you seek is already with you. It is in you, surrounds you—it loves, guides, and inspires you.

In this journey, there may be times when you become discouraged. You may feel that your search for the divine is a delusion—that there is no spiritual road to walk upon. Yet even here, the divine is with you, patiently holding the lamp of truth until the clouds of doubt and despair pass by and you can once again begin the journey refreshed and reinvigorated.

Ultimately your search will bear fruit, as it has for countless souls through the ages. All aspects of your life will fall into place, the veils of matter will drop away, and the soul can experience the divine presence for itself, free and unencumbered.

In this remarkable journey, you do not walk alone. Working with you in every facet of your life is your indispensable partner to success—the spiritual hierarchy. Many think of the hierarchy in terms of angels and archangels. As extraordinary as these Holy Ones are, they are part of a larger network of celestial beings known as the spiritual hierarchy. Whether on a grand scale or in moments of intimate inspiration, you have always had a special connection to the divine. You are not meant to walk blindly through life without understanding. God has given you the tools to operate with full awareness and spiritual knowing, but you have to build this awareness through the way you live your life.

In these pages I will attempt to describe the Holy Ones from my own clairvoyant experiences over the course of a lifetime. I hope to clear up misunderstandings and confusion concerning angels, archangels, and other celestial beings. I will urge you to work more closely with the Higher and make them a greater, more intimate part of your life. It is a most sacred relationship. By understanding how sacred the Higher is, you can better understand how sacred you are.

I also hope to give you an accurate, understandable picture of how the hierarchy is organized. I will attempt to illustrate what they look like, their duties, and how we are part of the hierarchal order of life. This book is meant to be practical and will offer some of the most effective tools and techniques to work with the divine.

THREE DEFINITIONS OF THE SPIRITUAL HIERARCHY

Every society has had its belief in divine support. Angelic beings have been a running theme throughout the Bible as messengers of God. The Qur'an has made belief in angels one of the six articles of faith. The Indians speak of devas, dynasties, and divine incarnations. Taoists have their pantheon of gods and divine ones. The gods and sacred beings of ancient Mesopotamia and Egypt played a central role in those societies. The Orphic and Elysian mysteries, with their mythology of the gods, were indispensable in the development of classical Greek culture and its golden age. In more recent times, mystics such as Helena Blavatsky, Max Steiner, Alice Bailey, Rudolf Steiner, and others helped reawaken an understanding of the spiritual hierarchy. Today, with the blossoming spiritual renaissance, many are taking a closer look at our relationship to the Holy Ones.

Whether religious or secular, the concept of invisible spiritual beings is part of humanity's cultural heritage. They are a source of comfort, solace, and inspiration. Countless sages and mystics have claimed direct contact with these Holy Ones. And the ancient spiritual training centers of the world—the mystery schools and ashrams—shared a common goal of helping the aspirant achieve a direct connection to the divine.

Today, with the material scientific perspective, some look at the subject of the spiritual hierarchy as outdated myths or folktales. To them, angels and archangels are not relevant or a worthy subject for the modern mind. Yet this is the furthest thing from the truth. As we better understand the physical world we live in, it becomes even more essential to understand the spiritual roots that support and sustain our physical life.

Of all the aspects of metaphysical study, the spiritual hierarchy can be one of the most difficult to approach in a clear and levelheaded way. Part of our challenge in understanding the spiritual hierarchy is that there is much confusing and conflicting information, depending on which system you follow. Various religious and metaphysical schools have their own interpretation of the hierarchy order, and sometimes these schools will be in apparent conflict or even antagonistic to each other. This is often due to centuries of less inspired hands reinterpreting ancient revelations. The approach in this book will be syncretistic. As the Rig Veda states, "The One Truth the sages call by many names." By understanding the common thread that runs through the various spiritual systems, we can better appreciate how the Holy Ones are universal for all of us.

There are three ways to define the spiritual hierarchy that we will explore in this book:

- A network of celestial beings under God
- The hierarchal order of life
- The hierarchy of Divine Light

A Network of Celestial Beings under God

The spiritual hierarchy is the administrator of God's divine plan. They are responsible for carrying out the various duties of creation. This holy order ranges from advanced souls in the human kingdom to glorious angels, archangels, and planetary leaders. We will pay particular attention to angels and archangels, yet there are other aspects of the Higher that exert an enormous influence as well.

These Holy Ones have been on the spiritual path for a long time, many for eons, and have evolved enormously. They work to uplift humanity and form the evolutionary link connecting us to God. These exalted beings work on different levels of unfoldment, which is why it's called a hierarchy, yet all work in perfect harmony with one another. Together, they form the evolutionary chain that links all life from the simplest amoeba to the most radiant archangel. We need these great beings as they are our link to God, and God works through these wonderful beings, guiding and steering the entire process of evolution.

Just like us, the spiritual hierarchy is going through its own evolution. The Holy Ones are developing their potential and drawing even closer to the divine source. The ancient writer Pseudo-Dionysius, in his book *The Celestial Hierarchy*, spoke of the hierarchy as:

> . . . a holy order and knowledge and activity which, so far as is attainable, participates in the Divine Likeness. . . . The aim of Hierarchy is the greatest possible assimilation to and union with God.

As part of their development, the Holy Ones are responsible for helping their younger brothers and sisters in light—humanity. They do this out of love and genuine service. In fact, every kingdom in nature has its own guiding hierarchy. There is a hierarchy that works with the animal kingdom, another for the plant kingdom, and yet another for the mineral kingdom. There is even a hierarchy that works with the planets and solar system. For the most part, we will focus on the hierarchy that is directly connected to humanity's development, as we interact with this divine order every day.

The Hierarchal Order of Life

In broader terms, there is another way to look at the spiritual hierarchy, and this is as *the spiritual order of life*. One of the great metaphysical secrets is that everything in life has consciousness. This consciousness exists to varying degrees of development. For example, in ascending order, we have the more primitive aspects of consciousness in the form of plants or animals followed by human consciousness. From the human levels we move up to the varying degrees of celestial consciousness. This hierarchal order is without beginning or end. Looking at life in this way, you and I are part of the hierarchal order of life right now.

This great chain of life is the key to your relationship with God. When you pray to God, God reaches you by working through the varying degrees of divine intelligence, and this means working with spiritual beings more developed than yourself. The spiritual hierarchy *is* your pathway to God. The closer you draw to the spiritual hierarchy, the closer you draw to God.

As part of the hierarchal order of life, you and I are playing an indispensable part in the creative process. There will be times when you may resist participation in this process, but this is only temporary as the natural order of life is inherently creative, eternally moving upward and yearning for greater expression.

The Hierarchy of Divine Light

You can't talk about the spiritual hierarchy without talking about Divine Light. The Holy Ones are responsible for sending spiritual energy to humanity. Each of us has an auric field. Your aura is the individual expression of the universal life force. Every day, you build up or diminish the power of your aura through the way you live your life. And each day, the Holy Ones bless you with Divine Light. Through meditation, you can call on the light directly and this brings you closer to the Holy Ones, who are the administrants of that Divine Light. So by including the Holy Ones in your light meditation, you can greatly enhance your aura and connection to the celestial beings. Working with spiritual energy and the hierarchy will be one of the primary tools we use in this book.

I can clairvoyantly see this connection with the Higher in the auric field. When a person has developed a strong, intuitive connection with the spiritual hierarchy, wonderful, sparkling-type energies of various colors are seen around the circumference of the auric field as well as around each of the chakras, or energy centers. It's an inspiring sight. White light is also seen coming down from above the head, indicating a strong connection to the inspirational flow of the Holy Ones. And often a deep–royal blue ray comes from the heart center, indicating a devotion and dedication to the divine. Such a soul not only is in tune with the spiritual hierarchy but is accepting and implementing the inspiration given.

In addition to the intimate connection of the Holy Ones to Divine Light, there is an actual hierarchy of light. This hierarchy of light is the energetic foundation upon which every aspect of creation lives. This holy light issues from God as Primordial Light and divides into many spectral rays, each with its divine attribute yet ultimately part of one divine encompassing power and attribute. The various celestial beings embody a station in this divine order of light, and that is what gives the Holy Ones their unique power. This is true for us as well. As we build our light rays and take our place in the divine order of things, we are imbued with a divine power ray as part of this hierarchy of light.

THE KEY TO FULFILLING
YOUR LIFE'S PURPOSE

When I was in my early thirties, I had a remarkable interaction with the spiritual hierarchy that reaffirmed just how powerful an ally they really are. It was a time when my spiritual life was unfolding beautifully, but it was a difficult time in other ways. I was a single mother, raising two children, working a low-paying job at a hotel in Santa

Monica, California, and taking care of my mother. My sister had been helping a great deal but had just gotten married, and even though she was doing her best to contribute, there was a lot of financial pressure.

One night I had a dream that I crashed my car while I was driving to work. It left such a strong impression that I did not want to go to work the next morning, but I went anyway, against my better judgment. On my way to work, I was driving through an intersection when a woman driving on the adjacent street did not see that the traffic light had turned red and went through the intersection at full speed, hitting my car broadside, hard. My car flipped over, injuring my back and legs and causing whiplash.

For nine months, I could not work and had to sleep on a board while my back healed. The experience put me in an even more serious financial bind. Now out of work, I was barely getting by. Disability insurance helped but was not enough to cover my expenses.

As the months progressed, I did not know what I was going to do. I had been praying for guidance, but on this one day I was praying fervently, specifically asking for an angel of business to guide me. During my prayer, I was suddenly taken out of my body and to a beautiful place on the other side. The Holy Ones had taken me out of my body many times before for instruction, but this was one of the first times they had taken me to the other side directly related to a personal prayer request.

I found myself by a river where there was a magnificent Grecian-like temple. They took me into the temple building and to an ornate room filled with books. I found myself in front of an impressive-looking desk. The room looked like an office but not like any office you would find on earth. I was thrilled to be there. I knew how much the angels could help and was anticipating the arrival of this divine assistance.

Then a man appeared in the room behind the desk. He looked like a businessman in a sharp blue suit, commanding and prosperous. He had brown hair and blue eyes. He had a serious demeanor, but not severe, more like he did not want to waste time.

He was standing and said, "Can I help you?"

In my mind, I was expecting an angelic being with flowing robes and rays of light emanating. In my naïveté I blurted out without thinking, "But you're not an angel!"

He smiled, amused at my remark, and said, "I'm not?!"

Suddenly radiating flows of shimmering light were coming out of him. The whole room flashed into light and I was almost overwhelmed by the angelic power he radiated. Clearly he had taken on the semblance of a businessperson so I would feel more comfortable. I thought to myself, "Boy, did I goof big-time!"

A moment later the light energy subsided and he once again looked like a normal businessman. I did not know what to say next, so I simply said, "I misunderstood."

He replied sincerely, "I'd like to help you."

"I'm very concerned about the financial problems I'm having right now." I started to go into my story, but he gently interrupted.

"I don't need details. I know what it's about. It's good you are here because you have handled the problem incorrectly and need to accept what I'm telling you now. I'm not going to go into details, but I'm going to give you the light. Then you'll know what to do to resolve your situation."

A beautiful golden ray of light came out his heart center and went into my heart center. I immediately felt enlightened and uplifted. I understood what he meant in that I was not fully using the spiritual knowledge and power necessary to help in my situation. I now knew things were going to be okay.

After a moment of this blessing, the angel said, "Now you're able to resolve your situation with the light."

He kept emphasizing working with the light. I realized it wasn't his job to solve my problems for me but to give me the power and confidence to solve my own problems. I was not living up to my potential. I had been given so much insight by the Higher, and here was an opportunity to put that knowledge to use, yet I wasn't doing that or wasn't doing that enough. I was so grateful to this angelic being. The very fact that he took the time to help was so reassuring and made me realized how much the Holy Ones care for us.

I would have liked to stay there longer, but it was clear he had other pressing things to do and needed to go. I simply said, "Thank you so much!"

"I was glad to have helped," he said, and with those words he was gone, although I continued to feel his light and love.

Once I was back in my body, I followed his advice and did my part by working diligently with the light. Then the miracles began to happen. About a week later, some people I had been working with at the hotel heard of my financial situation and unexpectedly donated money to help. It was a substantial amount. When some other friends heard what was going on, they pitched in financially too. Those contributions carried me through until I could start working again.

My back seemed to heal faster now. Before long, I was ready to work and found a better-paying job at a local school helping with scholarships. I wanted to gradually pay back the people who had shown such kindness, but they refused. That experience taught me to always work with the light and the Holy Ones in every situation. Perhaps one of the most extraordinary aspects of the spiritual hierarchy is how much our lives are in their hands.

The spiritual hierarchy is silently helping and encouraging at every phase of your life, from the moment you are born to the day you pass on. They were there when you had your spiritual awakening; they are there in your time of trial and testing. They are patiently there as you go through your mistakes and missteps. In tragedy or triumph, these great celestial ones are there for support. You are truly never alone in your spiritual journey. I have seen the Holy Ones working in hospitals, healing the sick, and in jails, supporting those who are imprisoned there. They bless you during the day at your job or at home when you're relaxing. They are there when you are making a difficult decision— to uplift you if you are feeling depressed or sad. They celebrate joyful times such as graduations, marriages, and other life-changing moments. They are strongly with you in the throes of inspiration and creation. The Holy Ones are the fountainhead of all of humanity's achievements. All great inventions, artistic creations, and inspired ideas were brought to humanity with the cooperation of the spiritual hierarchy. They even help you when you travel. And of course, they are there in meditation and prayer.

As is the central theme of this book: *The spiritual hierarchy IS your pathway to God.* They are the means through which you achieve your life's purpose and reach your highest spiritual potential. You can't do it without them. They are there to help you evolve and remind you that you are not alone in life's journey—this is a cooperative effort. They are already working with you regardless of your awareness of them, but when you work in harmony with them, you greatly amplify their ability to help you.

The benefits of working with the spiritual hierarchy are enormous.

Think of them as your best friends, your greatest support. By working with the Higher, you will forge an enduring, unfailing, everlasting friendship. The Higher will always be there for you. While you may not understand all aspects of how they work, you'll know that regardless of what is going on, you have support.

The Holy Ones see you in the highest possible light and hold you to your highest ideal even if you do not see yourself in that way. They are patient and loving whether you are working toward your divine destiny or making every mistake in the book. They are always ready to forgive and have infinite patience. They will let you make your mistakes because you have to do your own growing, but they will urge you upward, showing you the next step in your growth.

By including the Holy Ones in your life, you'll develop a deeper devotion to God. In an age when many people are not sure what they believe, you will act with unwavering conviction and demonstrate strength and courage. You will have a dynamic faith that God is a real and active part of your life.

Of course, the Holy Ones are not God, yet they are unquestionably God-like. They have traveled farther down the spiritual path than you or I, yet they are still evolving. They possess tremendous spiritual knowledge, power, and awareness—yet they are not omniscient or limitless in their abilities. They do not want to be worshipped, but rather recognized as elder brothers and sisters in light and wisdom. Yet make no mistake—they are truly filled with the sacred power of the divine and must be approached with reverence, love, and respect. They are not our servants to do our bidding and service our appetites. The Holy Ones are there to help bring out the best, highest, and most spiritual part of our nature.

You Don't Need to See the Holy Ones to Work with Them

With such a powerful support system, the single biggest question asked regarding the Holy Ones is: Why can't we see them? If the Holy Ones are there, why are we not more aware of them?

In this age of self-reliance, blind forces of nature, and material rationalism, the idea of an intelligent invisible support system might seem far-fetched. When it comes to the topic of the Holy Ones, humanity's barometer can swing from one extreme of stubborn skepticism to the other extreme of blind hysteria. Our goal is to take a careful, balanced, *sober* look at an extraordinary part of life and to realize that to put our attention on the spiritual hierarchy is a worthy study, as it brings us in contact with an intelligence greater than ourselves.

To see the Holy Ones is within the power of every soul to achieve. However, it does require dedicated effort, training, and development. Operating in nonphysical dimensions and at such a high level of vibration makes it a daunting challenge to directly tune into them, but it can be done. Clairvoyance is a natural by-product of your spiritual evolution. As you develop yourself spiritually, at the right time, your clairvoyance will open and you will be able to experience the Holy Ones directly.

It is to our great benefit that there are times when the divine makes a special effort to give humanity glimpses of the Higher regardless of where we are in our spiritual development. There have been countless stories of people having visions of angels and other celestial beings. True, some of these are wishful fancies, yet others are genuine, life-changing experiences.

The truth is, it does not matter if you do not *see* the Higher to benefit from working with the divine. Seeing them is not what is expected of you. What is asked of you is to work with them through faith, trust, intuition, and intelligent application. By employing all your talents and gifts, all your consciousness and awareness, the contact is made. The Holy Ones see you. They love you dearly, and as you work with them in loving cooperation, there will come that day when you behold the Holy Ones more directly.

By reverently invoking them in the name of God, you are cultivating a more mature understanding of the divine life and invoking the spiritual powers connected to the spiritual hierarchy, which will have a tremendous uplifting effect and quicken your spiritual progress. By calling on their help, you are drawing in their power, and this has the effect of bringing you closer to them, which means closer to the divine.

I had a very dedicated student, Lois, for many years. We were very good friends. She was smart and diligent in her spiritual studies and meditations. Yet she would complain that she could not see the Divine Light—she could not see the Holy Ones, nothing. Yet she knew the spiritual work had value and saw the positive effects in her life. Well, one day, during her meditation, quite unexpectedly, she had an angelic visitation. An angel of love presented herself to Lois, smiled, and gently kissed her on the cheek. Lois was profoundly moved. Yet it did not surprise her—rather, it confirmed to her that the Holy Ones were there all along.

The tools you will use to start working with the Higher are your intuition, inspiration, and intellect. You need to develop these tools to effectively work with the Holy Ones. As we shall see, your intuition and inspiration are the driving part of your ability to connect with the Higher. They are the divine part of your nature that can tune into the Higher right now for your own personal development. As you develop and trust your intuition and inspirational nature, you will naturally develop a stronger rapport with the Higher. These are the keys that open the door to the mystical experience.

Yet intuition and inspiration do not work alone. Your intellectual/rational nature plays a strong part in your evolution. Too many people on the spiritual path throw common sense out the window, and this totally goes against the true mystical path. Intuition without the steady hand of reason can lead to irrational and superstitious behavior. The line between what is real and what is imaginary can easily become blurred. Without reason, aspiring souls can lose the compass guiding them to enlightenment. Attempting to discover the divine only by the intellect is a fruitless endeavor, however, as enlightenment is not an intellectual process. Such attempts only lead to uninspired, closed-minded, and rigid behavior. Blend these powers in their proper order, with intuition and inspiration leading the intellect, and you have the road map to spiritual success.

CHAPTER 2

GOD AND
THE HOLY ONES

I can of mine own self do nothing . . .
the Father that dwelleth in me, He doeth the works.
—JESUS THE CHRIST

YOU CAN'T TALK about the spiritual hierarchy without talking about God. It is a sad irony, with so much interest in spirituality, that the subject of God can be touchy. I've had students say things like, "I love working with spiritual energy, but why does Barbara have to bring in all this God stuff?" As if God had nothing to do with Divine Light or spiritual evolution! Many people treat the Holy Ones in the same way. They enjoy calling on angels for help, yet fail to fully acknowledge the divine source from which the angels draw their power. Many times, people call on the spiritual hierarchy as if they were servants to grant our every wish. And of course that is not why they are there. These people mistakenly think that they can work with these celestial beings for their own sake, perhaps in the same way you and I might interact with each other. And while there is a most beautiful relationship going on with the Holy Ones, we need to have a clear, mature picture of how we relate to them.

Our personality's ego gets in the way of fully connecting with the divine. We can think we're bigger than life. I remember a successful psychiatrist who came to one of my classes for a short time. She was a tall, attractive blonde and was well known for her work. She was charming but had quite an ego. During this particular session, I turned to the subject of God and remember her becoming irritated, and soon she blurted out in a defiant tone, "I don't believe in God. *I'm* God!" Now she didn't say this in a cosmic sense. Rather she was affirming the mistaken belief in the supremacy of her own intellect. Clearly her life of celebrity made her feel she was better than the rest of us. I reassured her, "There is a God and it's not you!" Needless to say, she did not return to class.

To effectively relate to the Holy Ones, you need to first align yourself with the divine source from which the celestial beings draw power. This means developing a better understanding of how you relate to the divine source we call God. The subject of God is so vast that we could spend the rest of this book on this subject of subjects and just scratch the surface. Yet let us paint a few broad strokes as illuminated by the Kingdom of Light Teachings.

The first step in understanding God is to better understand ourselves. "Who am I?" is one of the great philosophical questions of the ages. Metaphysics teaches that you are not your body. You are not even your personality. You are an immortal soul. Your soul is an individualized spark of life. This life is eternal—without beginning or end. Your soul, in some form, has always existed and always will.

This spark of life is divine in nature. It is part of the sea of life the mystics call the "unknown root" of all existence. When God and the Holy Ones look at you, they do not first see the body or persona—they see the immortal spark of life that is the real you. This is the part they can relate to and encourage.

It is one of the greatest moments in your evolution to discover and identify with the immortal you. This means that despite the many missteps and mistakes in life, God and the divine always see you in the highest light. They always bring out the best in each of us. They have always forgiven any mistakes and are always there to help. So first recognize that you are worthy of God's love and attention and worthy of the divine support of the spiritual hierarchy. The same life that is in you dwells in the Holy Ones and is part of God.

Yet as divine as the soul is, each of us is going through a process of unfolding greater spiritual power and expression. With every life experience, you are becoming more splendid in your divinity. This is the essence of creativity. Life is inherently creative, so you are inherently creative.

From this impersonal unknown root that is the essence of our soul comes all the spiritual laws of life that operate at every plane of existence. The ultimate source of this principle is beyond human understanding even though we are an indispensable part of this experience right now.[1] This unknown root is what the Chinese call the Tao. The Hermetic philosophy expresses this beautifully in the Kybalion:

> Under, and back of, the Universe of Time, Space, and Change, is ever to be found The Substantial Reality—the Fundamental Truth.
>
> That which is the Fundamental Truth—the Substantial Reality—is beyond true naming, but the Wise men call it THE ALL.
>
> In its Essence, THE ALL is UNKNOWABLE.

---

[1] Because of the difficulty in defining the unknowable infinite principle as part of our understanding of God, some metaphysical schools have attempted to speak in terms of what God is not. The idea of this approach is that by clearing the mind and consciousness of erroneous ideas and concepts, you pave the way for the truth to be more clearly discerned. The mystic school of Christianity spoke of entering the realm of God as a "Divine Darkness," that one is so dazzled by God's light that it actually appeared as a type of spiritual gloom.

The Kybalion goes on to say that to attempt to define or speculate on this unknowable infinite ALL is "as but the childish efforts of mortal mind to grasp the secret of the Infinite."

Yet this does not mean we are not meant to move in greater rhythm with the unknown root. On the one hand, we are as divine as we will ever be, yet at the same time we are in the process of becoming a greater expression of this unknown root. Taoist philosophy teaches about "coming back to the Tao" or raising our consciousness in greater harmony with the ALL.

Out of this infinite impersonal principle comes a supreme definable presence. *The supreme definable expression of the unknown root is what we call God.*[2] Whereas, by definition, the unknown root is not comprehensible, God *is* comprehensible. God is the macrocosm of the unknown root, and your soul is the microcosm. As vast and infinite as God is, we are all meant to know and experience God directly. God is a loving, divine intelligence with a cosmic mind and heart and a glorious celestial body. Each of us, and all creation, lives, moves, and has its being in this cosmic body of God. God intimately works with each of us. Every day, we receive from the mind and heart of God. It is through God that we experience all that life is in its beauty, power, and majesty.

Within the God expression of the unknown root, all superlatives that we know apply to God. God is omniscient, omnipotent, and omnipresent. God is the creator of all there has been, is, and shall ever be. He is infinite and unlimited. He[3] is ALL THERE IS.

---

[2] The word *God* comes from a proto-Germanic word, *uðan*, and it shares a common root in the Sanskrit word *guðan*, meaning "to call, to invoke." This definition is very much in line with the metaphysical interpretation of God. The Holy Ones teach that the word *God* has tremendous power and meaning. I often see white light in the aura when the word *God* is spoken with reverence and sincerity.

[3] The masculine is used in the ancient original nongendered sense of the word.

It is God who gave birth to this expression of life. We were born into this human experience in the womb of God. It is God who sustains us, and it is God to whom we shall ultimately return once we finish our pilgrimage through creation. We are His children, fashioned from His own spirit and spirit-substance. This means that we were born out of the highest degree of love and intelligence. God gave of *Himself* to give us expression in the infinite sea of life.

So, the first way to connect with God is through love. Love God. Love God as a child loves a parent. Praise Him with every part of your being. Express that love through all your activities and through service to others, which is the greatest form of loving God. Then through your love, use your mind to *understand* God, so you can express the intelligence that fashioned you. Learn about God and apply your knowledge and wisdom so that you can know God with your mind as well as your heart.

In addition to being His child, you are also His vessel of spiritual expression. God works through you for His greater glory as you permit that expression to flow. So you must open yourself to God—not to humanity's conception of God, but to the direct flow of God's power working in and through you. You are the one who stands at the door to your own consciousness and permits or refuses God entry into your life. The choice is always yours, and you will manifest your destiny according to the spiritual choices you make.

Do not be fooled by the atheist who will tell you God is not there or the agnostic who will tell you it doesn't matter if God is there or not. God is very real, and He is at the core of your life, whether you are aware of that or not. You are meant to relate to God every day of your life as the divine is relating to you. And this is the purpose of the spiritual hierarchy—to be the agent of that intimate interaction.

Hold to your highest ideal of the divine. As you strive to unite with God, the beauty of life will unfold, and you build your immortal connection to the spiritual hierarchy.

THE ONENESS OF LIFE

This brings us to an important concept in your relationship to the divine, and that is the concept of *Oneness*. The Oneness is a term used for the all-inclusive unity of God.[4] When you ask to become one with God, you are uniting with the divine, creative good that is God.

The unifying principle of all life, from the simplest atom to the greatest celestial kingdom, is the Oneness. As part of God, everything in life is part of the unity and Oneness of life. We are all interconnected. This means that all things in creation draw their life from the same spiritual source. There is no power apart from that source. "My Father and I are one," the Christ taught us. This is the law and the essence of life. There is no such thing as a power *outside* that One. There is only the one unifying principle and how we relate to that principle. Some resist the Oneness and therefore move themselves further from the divine origin, while others flow with the spiritual rhythm and draw closer to the divine source. Yet regardless of our attitude, awareness, or perception, we still are part of the One.

The idea is to build your *conscious awareness* of this Oneness, so you can connect and draw more fully from this unifying source. The way to unite with the Oneness of life is to unite with God. The closer you draw to God, the more you are a channel of that spiritual power. When you

---

4 Please note that the Oneness is not the same thing as the ALL spoken of by the Hermetic sciences. The ALL or the unknown root is the underlying *cause* of all things. The Oneness is the *unity* of life.

perceive yourself as a separate individual without any connectedness to others or God, you restrict and choke the spiritual supply you can receive. One of the biggest jobs you do on earth is to learn how to recognize the unifying spiritual principle in everything around you and in all your activities and exchanges. You cannot know God as long as you believe there to be a force opposed to God.

In physical life, we too often see ourselves as separate and therefore disconnected. You can say to yourself, "I am here and you are there, so that means we are separate." In this perception of life, it becomes hard to recognize that both draw life from the same source. When we find ourselves thinking in this narrow-minded point of view, we need to step back to gain a greater perspective. You cannot take your limited physical perceptions too literally. There is a greater reality going on at all times.

Philosophic schools call this principle of Oneness *monism*. Monism asserts that everything in the universe is part of a primordial substance. In this way, there is a fundamental unity in creation. There is not a separate material and spiritual life. Both are part of the same spectrum of life but operating at different frequencies. With this philosophy, there is not a primordial good and evil. There is only the Good, which is harmony, and discord or resistance, which can be expressed as Evil.

Some may ask how Oneness can exist if clearly there is much diversity in life. First let's be clear that the Oneness does not mean "the sameness." We are each unique and individualized. Creation clearly has dynamics and polarity—there is light and shadow, heat and cold, day and night. Metaphysics is saying that what underlies all this diversity and polarity of manifested life is the same unifying principle.

In addition, some spiritual schools teach dualist philosophies as a way to illuminate certain truths as a stepping-stone to even greater under-standing. For example, the long-held belief of a primal good and evil is a way to teach morality to a soul who needs the lesson of accountability in life. Once this lesson is learned, then the greater truth of the unifying principle is revealed and the aspiring soul will be ready to receive such illumination in the spirit it was given.

The ancient Greeks used the term *henosis*, meaning "oneness," to ex-press the unity of life. Pythagoras, the ancient Greek mystic and math-ematician, was a major proponent of the Oneness, which he termed the *monad*. In his mystical numeration system, everything in life and all numbers add up to the number one, as everything was derived from the number one, or monad. And out of the one came everything else.

The Oneness is essential because it points to the unifying principle in all inspired metaphysical and religious training. If everything is part of the One, the varying spiritual beliefs must have a common root when properly understood. This syncretistic approach is essential to our mod-ern understanding of spirituality and to the mature understanding of the Holy Ones.

Do your best to get into the Oneness, as the divine can truly be re-vealed to you in that Oneness. There is an entire art to bringing your life into the unity of life. As you live in harmony with the eternal laws of life, that harmony brings you into the divine Oneness. As you pursue your purpose and spiritual potential, you draw closer to the Oneness of life. As you express compassion, tolerance, and love, you begin to recog-nize the divine that dwells in everyone and everything; that brings you closer to the divine Oneness. And as you strive to love the divine—love God—to the best of your conception of that divine, you draw closer to the great Oneness of life.

MEDITATIVE PRAYER TO TUNE INTO THE DIVINE ONENESS[5]

Heavenly Father/Holy Mother God, down-ray unto me the pure white light to fill my consciousness with the divine Oneness. I ask to tune into the unity of life and feel part of the great whole of life.

GOD'S INTERMEDIARIES

So how do you bring together your relationship with God and the Holy Ones? Some feel that one should *only* pray to God and God alone. While the spiritual hierarchy may be acknowledged, all attention must go to God, and anything else is sacrilegious.

As we have just explored, God is the cornerstone of all spiritual practice. Yet acknowledging or praying to God alone does not complete the full spiritual picture. Just as you need the earth below your feet or the air you breathe, you need the Holy Ones. Remember, even if you are not aware of it, when you pray to God, God answers your prayers through the spiritual hierarchy. By including the Holy Ones, you are simply acknowledging a process that is already going on. The goal of metaphysics is to help you evolve your soul and become a *conscious* participant in the spiritual processes of life. And the only way to build your conscious knowing is to start by acknowledging and participating in the actual dynamics of the spiritual life.

Think of God like a trillion-watt power station—and you are a twenty-watt lightbulb. It's too much for your consciousness to take the full power of the trillion watts directly. The energy needs to be stepped

---

[5] Throughout this book, meditative prayers are offered to connect directly with the divine. Please see chapter 15 for a description of the meditative process.

down to a level that you can accept. The spiritual hierarchy represents that stepping down in vibration to a level you can work with. As you expand your power you can slowly take more spiritual power. This filling of your spiritual cup is the key to your spiritual ascent.

The beauty of working with the Holy Ones in your journey to God is that they are filled with the God presence. They *know* God exists. It's not a question to them. They have long passed the human stage to find God. Their evolution is to get to know God more deeply and delve into the divine mystery more fully. They worship God at every turn. I have seen them in conclaves where they sing holy praises and get into profound prayer to commune with the divine. Through their God-knowing, the celestial beings draw their life, power, and great joy.

When they come around you, they bring this God power and knowing with them. This is why being in the presence of the spiritual hierarchy is so wonderful and life-changing. Their presence brings you close to your divine source. As they are powerful and exalted, they are also eternally humble, as they know their place in the divine plan and know how much more there is for them to learn and develop. So they do not want you to worship them, but to honor them as the divine emissaries they are. At the same time, it is true that some aspects of the Higher are so evolved that they seem like gods unto themselves, but even these Holy Ones look up to their divine source.

The bottom line is, if you want to be successful in your work with the Holy Ones, God needs to be the centerpiece of your spiritual work. The two are part of the same process. In all the exercises and meditative prayer work we will do in this book, put God first. This way, you will complete the connection process with the Holy Ones.

THE DIVINE EXPERIENCE

This brings us to a fundamental question. Can God be experienced while in a physical body? We can definitely experience the Holy Ones, but what about God?

Yes, you can experience God, but you need to understand how. You are in the midst of the divine this very minute. God's signature is in every aspect of creation. Yet the understanding of God has to be awakened in you. The only reason you are not consciously aware of God at this moment is that you are in a process of evolution. Your soul is slowly unfolding its spiritual *potential*. As you realize your potential, you become more and more *self*-aware of the whole of life. From the beginning, you have always been conscious, but you have not always been *self*-conscious. You are building your self-conscious awareness through the many experiences of life. Eventually, these experiences will lead you back to God as a fully developed Eternal Being of Light.

On this journey back to your celestial Home, you can experience what the mystics call "the God Within." This experience is not the same thing as your union with the divine when you complete your spiritual pilgrimage. The experience of the God Within is meant for you here in physical life as a culminating experience of a long period of spiritual development and training in your journey to enlightenment. Every soul, at the right time, is meant to have this experience. Every genuine mystic through the ages has had this experience. Such a moment is not the end of your journey. Yet from this point onward, you can truly say you know God is.

I wish to share with you an experience I had related to the God Within. This experience is so personal that I have not spoken of it until now. At that time in my life, I was in the early stages of my career and had developed many of my spiritual talents. I was teaching classes, and people were excited about what they were learning. Even though I was coming into the full maturity of my work as a teacher, I knew that something was missing—a pinnacle of competence not yet reached. My greatest desire was to reach this spiritual zenith I could not quite fully define. I was ardently delving even deeper into the spiritual mysteries and connecting with the Divine Light in an even more profound way.

From a very early age, I've known that there is God. I felt God especially through the angels. They came with so much divine power and vitality. Their very presence told me there was a greater holy power at work. And of course, Holy Ones have seen God! So their very presence cannot help but make you feel close to God. But the experience I'm about to share now was very different.

One day while in meditation, I unexpectedly found myself in one of the deepest states of meditation I had ever been in. I felt the Holy Ones making their connection but soon recognized that I was stepping into an experience of a whole different order.

Soon I found myself in a place I cannot begin to describe—*place* is not really the word. *Presence* would be a better word. This was not exactly a clairvoyant experience, because it was not so much that I was seeing or hearing something spiritually. It was not really a sensory experience, yet I was very aware. It was not even a mental experience, although my mind was keenly awake and alert. The closest word I could use to describe the experience would be *beingness*. I was in the beingness of life. I know this is a vague description. I wish I could describe it in clairvoyant detail with light rays and auras, but, again, this was something different. I lost all sense of where I was or what led up to that moment.

In that moment, I was in what could only be called the God experience. There was no communication in the sense of a voice or thought.

Yet it was unmistakably God revealing a part of Himself directly. There were no words, ideas, visions, or even feelings, no time or place. It was a level of experience that went beyond those things, even though those are part of God and led me to that moment. In such a presence, you are in the flow of the Creator, and that Creator is your life within and the life without. You are in the midst of infinity—at Home and profoundly at peace.

I could not say how long this experience lasted. It was not long in terms of physical time, but the effects were life-changing. Without realizing it, this was what I had been searching for. It was a new awakening, a culminating moment in a lifetime of many dramatic spiritual moments. It brought me into an unwavering conviction of who I was as a spiritual being. Any lingering questions I had regarding my life and work were gone. There was no question in my mind about my connection and relationship to God.

As one might expect, my love for God deepened enormously after this experience. I did develop one interesting character trait: I would become righteously indignant when others put down or didn't believe in God. It felt like a personal slap on the face and a complete negation of the very wellspring of life.

I share this with you to offer personal testimony that God is real. The divine is the fountainhead of your life. You are truly on the earth to glorify God. Embrace the glories of life—its creativity, intelligence, love, joy, and everything that makes life worth living. The spiritual hierarchy is an expression of life's eternal love and grandeur. Every facet of the hierarchy is like a precious facet of the divine. Their life is dedicated to the infinite glory and creative power of God.

You don't need to wait until you have such an experience to make God your priority. Embrace the divine now to the best of your ability with your heart, mind, and soul. As you meditate and work with the Divine Light and the Holy Ones, you are building your bridge to immortality. If you work with everything that God has given you, you will live your life as it was meant to be lived.

Take inventory of your devotion and dedication to God. If it is strong, ask how it can become stronger. If it is not so strong, start rearranging your life to make God center stage. Find the divine in everything you do, in the midst of your life's activity. Take time to be still and contemplate—time for solitude and repose, as well as time for activity and action.

THE HIERARCHY OF GOD

As this chapter is about your relationship to the Holy Ones and God, I would like to share a few more insights into the nature of the divine by looking at *the Hierarchy of God*. Within the Oneness, there is in fact a hierarchal order to God. It may seem strange to speak of God in this way, yet many spiritual philosophies talk about aspects of God in attempting to bring order to the vastness of the divine. God is not static or inert, but dynamic and unfolding in even greater glory as reflected in all aspects of creation. This unfolding process is part of the expression of life. We can only begin to imagine the vastness of this process. As Helena Blavatsky states in her masterpiece *The Secret Doctrine*:

> Our "Universe" is only one of an infinite number of Universes, . . . each one standing in the relation of an effect as regards its predecessor, and being a cause as regards its successor . . . and this stupendous development has neither conceivable beginning nor imaginable end.

To help give order to this "stupendous development," metaphysics recognizes that God manifests in three basic ways. In traditional Christian theology, this relationship is interpreted as the Father, Son, and Holy Ghost. Hindu theology speaks of the Trimurti: God as creator, preserver, and destroyer—Brahma, Vishnu, Shiva. The Taoists speak of the Three Pure Ones. These are all beautiful ways to describe different aspects of the divine process.

In our metaphysical work, the threefold aspect of God is recognized as the following:

God the Father/Holy Mother

God Almighty

God the Absolute—Absolutely All There Is

When humanity first tried to understand the divine, we looked to the sun and said that it was God. We looked to the sky and stars and said that this was heaven. Through the ages, we have developed a greater understanding of the physical universe we live in. Today, we have come to realize that what seemed like a fairly simple system of physical life is, in fact, far vaster than we could possibly have imagined. One of the biggest challenges is how to reconcile our modern understanding of the vastness of life with our comprehension of the intimate nature of God. Understanding the hierarchal nature of God can help reconcile these ideas. The Rosicrucian Max Heindel expressed this challenge in understanding the dynamics of God in his seminal work *The Rosicrucian Cosmo-Conception*:

When the name "God" is used it is always uncertain whether the Absolute, The One Existent is meant; or The

Supreme Being, Who is Great Architect of the Universe; or
God who is the Architect of our Solar System.

Let us first turn to God the Father/Holy Mother. God the Father and Holy Mother are our spiritual parents. God the Father is the dynamic principle and God the Holy Mother[6] is the magnetic principle. These two polarities represent the dual aspect of all manifested life under the ONE power. It is the union of these two aspects of divinity that gave birth to our souls and all material form. The great goal of our spiritual evolution is to return Home to the kingdom of God our Father/Holy Mother.

Perhaps the closest thing humanity could imagine as a personal God would be the Creator as our celestial Father and Mother. When Moses asked the divine what name to call God on behalf of the people of Israel, he was given the name *Ehyeh* ("I am"): "Tell them Ehyeh hath sent you."[7] And here we find the mysterious and mystical reference to the Heavenly Father/Holy Mother of us all. This biblical proclamation is an esoteric reference that not only Israel but all humanity shares the same divine parents.

It is God the Father/Mother who tenderly ushers us on the spiritual path and gives us the power to reach our spiritual potential. Our celestial parents, in coordination with the hierarchy, helped us in our first spiritual steps of spiritual awakening. Our divine parents are the ones who awaken us in our immortal identity when we are ready, who usher us through the door of enlightenment. And it will be God the Father/

---

[6] Please note that the usage of *Holy Mother* does not infer a specific person such as Mother Mary. This is in reference to the celestial mother from whose womb each of us was born in our pilgrimage as a human soul.

[7] Exodus 3:14.

Mother who will joyfully greet us when it is time to enter our celestial Home after our long pilgrimage, where we will become co-creative beings with God and the spiritual hierarchy.

Then we move to God Almighty. God Almighty is responsible for the entire design of the evolutionary plan. It is by the grace of God Almighty that there is a path of Divine Light to walk upon. You might say God Almighty works *behind* the scenes, guiding and steering the unfolding process of life, not just for us but for all other levels of creation as well. God Almighty is the grand architect of the universe. It is the Almighty who gives us the know-how and power to fulfill our life's purpose. Each of us has a purpose in life, and that purpose is an essential part of the overall divine plan. Yet we must remember that our purpose is not just about us. You and I are part of a grand cosmic plan that everyone is a part of and contributing to. And even the entire spiritual hierarchy is contributing to that plan. This stupendous plan is composed and orchestrated by God Almighty. You could say the very planets are in their orbit and the stars in their glory shine by the majesty of God Almighty.

Then we come to God Absolute. God Absolute is the ultimate. He is absolutely *all there is*. He is the ultimate expression of the unknown root of all existence. He incorporates the highest aspect of our spiritual nature and encompasses all aspects of creation in all its various levels. He is the ONE. The Hindus speak of God Absolute as the imperishable *Brahman*, which is different from Brahma, who is part of the Triune. The Kabbalists use the term *Ain Soph* (without end, infinite) in speaking of God Absolute.

It was God Absolute who initiated the first holy out-breath of creation into the "great void" before there was anything we would call active existence. Before there was a universe, there was God Absolute. The first Primordial Light that was to become the multifaceted energy rays we incorporate into our auras came from God Absolute. All aspects of God the Father/Mother and God the Almighty are incorporated in God Absolute. In terms of our spiritual evolution, it is God Absolute who gives us our very consciousness. There would be no way to climb the spiritual ladder, no way to express the creativity of life and realize the divine plan, if there were no wellspring of life that is God Absolute. God Absolute is the celestial divine spirit from which everything in life is powered.

What makes God Absolute even more awe-inspiring is that as vast and staggering as the infinity of God Absolute is, this celestial holiness is at the very heart of the most intimate and minute aspects of life as well. He is truly closer to you than hands and feet.

All these aspects of God work in perfect harmony with each other. The amazing thing is that we are an integral part of this incredible process. We may be tiny next to God, but that does not make us unimportant. It is said by the hierarchy that if one soul were missing, creation would not be complete. We are all precious in God's eyes because we are part of God the Father/Mother, God Almighty, and God Absolute— right here, right now.

YOUR ONLY OBLIGATION IS TO GOD

How can you comprehend the infinite nature of God? Start by recognizing that you are part of that infinite nature too. It is by getting to know your divine nature that you can know God. Start with a sincere heart and an ardent desire to commune with the divine.

There are so many distractions in life, so many possible ways to digress and divert your attention that it is easy to forget what is most important. God truly is your only obligation in life. Make room for God in your daily affairs. Make room to pray, reflect, and meditate, and watch how your life unfolds in divine rhythm and power.

Certainly you have duties and responsibilities. These are part of your learning and growing experience, but remember to whom you are ultimately answerable. We live with each other. We love, work, and play with each other. Yet in the end, it is God to whom we have to answer.

I would like to conclude this chapter with a meditative prayer.

MEDITATIVE PRAYER TO FEEL CLOSER TO GOD

Heavenly Father/Holy Mother God, I ask that You down-ray the pure white light to bring forth Thy divine essence so that I may feel closer to Thee in my heart, mind, and soul. I thank God the Father/Mother, God Almighty, and God Absolute, and the great celestial beings of eternal life for granting me Thy divine power so that I may serve Thee in Eternal Light and love, so be it.

CHAPTER 3

THE TWELVE KINGDOMS OF NATURE

The acceptance of spiritual hierarchy ensures that those
of greatest experience and understanding
are able to guide and inspire.
—SUBHUTI, *Buddhism for Today*

How is the spiritual hierarchy organized? When I first became aware of the varying levels of spiritual beings, it was an amazing experience. It revealed that there is a great order in the universe. Life is not happenstance or a random occurrence, as some believe. Look at the incredible balance of nature and how well-ordered your own physical body is. It staggers the imagination to conceive of the divine intelligence it took to create such order. Yet at the same time, we have free will and are participants in this creative order of life.

We face several challenges in clearly understanding the order of the Holy Ones. First, available material is often conflicting and contradictory. Compounding this is the fact that specific groups may be following a belief system that places special emphasis on one aspect of the divine rather than other aspects. The Christians emphasize the Holy Trinity and the nine choirs of angels. The Kabbalists teach of the attending divine beings connected to the Ten Sephiroth. The Hindus teach the Trimurti, out of which flow the genealogies of avatars and generations of divine beings and devas. The Neo-Platonists along with the Sufis teach of divine emanations. The Buddhists speak of devas of the Five Suddhavasa Worlds. The list goes on and on. So we have quite a job to put order to this whole system! My goal is to share with you my own clairvoyant experiences and find the unifying thread that runs through all genuine spiritual systems.

Another challenge in understanding the spiritual hierarchy is that there is more than one hierarchal order! The universe and our earth are *teeming* with life. There is a grand hierarchy connected to entire solar systems, groups of solar systems, and beyond. Then there is a hierarchy that is connected to our planet as a whole. On the other end of the spectrum, there is a hierarchy connected to microbial life, helping to develop the most simple (but not unimportant) life-forms on earth. This includes all types of algae, cells, bacteria, fungi, parasites, and viruses—all the way up to the insect kingdom. The first physical expressions of life on earth were generated from this kingdom, billions of years ago, and serve as a foundation for the other kingdoms.

Then there is the hierarchal order that you and I are part of. This hierarchy is known as *the Twelve Kingdoms of Nature*. What is so amazing about this hierarchy is that it not only includes aspects of nature such as plants, animals, and humans, but it includes the Holy Ones we are focusing on in this book—the angels, the archangels, and other celestial beings. In other words, the divine beings who guide our evolution are part of the same hierarchal order of life that you and I are in!

THE LADDER OF LIFE

Organizing life has been one of the most profound studies, whether in science, religion, or metaphysics. Modern science classifies organic life according to physical similarities. Aristotle was the first to systematically classify organisms. He arranged life in a ladder with inanimate matter at the bottom and humans at the top. This was known as the *scale of nature*. Many centuries later, in the 1700s, the botanist Carl Linnaeus laid the foundation for the modern scientific study of taxonomy. Today science has devised an intricate system of organizing life according to physical traits.

Metaphysics and religion have had their own systems of ordering or classifying life. One of the most famous of these systems from the ancient world was an expansion on the scale of nature to include *everything* from the mineral kingdom all the way to the angels and God. This classification became known as *the Great Chain of Being*. It was enormously influential. As time went on, it unfortunately became distorted and used as a political tool for ordering society. Yet despite its imperfections, it was an attempt to unite all creation from matter to spirit under one grand plan. It may seem strange to classify celestial beings in this way, but in fact this is the best way to objectively understand the nature of the Holy Ones as part of a natural order of life.

There are three principles to consider when studying the order of the Holy Ones:

1. Life is organized according to levels of consciousness.
2. Life is inherently dynamic and unfolding toward great perfection.
3. Life works from the top down, not the bottom up.

Metaphysics teaches us that life is organized according to levels of *consciousness*. Spiritually speaking, form is an expression of consciousness. This brings us back to the idea that we are not our body. We are a soul inhabiting a body. Our body is a tool of expression for our soul. This form can take many shapes and is not restricted to being physical. Celestial beings are in a glorified ethereal form of their own.

The second principle is that life is inherently dynamic and creative, not static. The soul is most definitely going through a process of evolution toward greater perfection and expression. To accommodate this developing perfection, form adapts to accommodate this gradual perfection, and this is the reason for the physical changes we see. This means that even celestial beings are going through a process of evolution.

The third principle of metaphysics teaches us that life works from the top down. This means that the simplest expression of life has within it the pattern or design of the most developed and is striving to realize what is already inherently within it. An analogy would be that if the highest stage in the Twelve Kingdoms of Nature were a rose, then the first stage would be the seed. All the potential for becoming a rose is already in the seed, yet it must grow through all the stages of life before it can become the beautiful rose. This means that as the soul evolves through one kingdom of nature, it is then born into a new kingdom to start a new phase in its spiritual journey.

TWELVE STAGES OF UNFOLDING CONSCIOUSNESS

What is presented here is the metaphysical system of the Twelve Kingdoms of Nature as taught by the Kingdom of Light Teachings. This system uses nomenclature such as *angels* and *archangels*. Please note that this terminology is meant nondenominationally. Other mystical schools use differing terminology but still refer to the same system, as there is one unifying spiritual hierarchy for all humanity. Once the cultural elements of differing schools are taken into consideration, there is a remarkable unity.

The Twelve Kingdoms of Nature represents twelve stages of developing consciousness in the overall arc of one grand design. The categories are as follows (from most developed to least):

1. The Unnamed Sacred Twelfth Kingdom
2. The Unnamed Sacred Eleventh Kingdom
3. The Archangelic Kingdom
4. The Angelic Kingdom
5. The Human Kingdom
6. The Animal Kingdom
7. The Fish Kingdom
8. The Unnamed Nonphysical Kingdom
9. The Plant Kingdom
10. The Elemental Kingdom
11. The Mineral Kingdom
12. The Structure Kingdom

In the early stages of development—such as the plant, fish, and animal kingdoms—there is great diversity of form, hence many species. In the human and angelic kingdoms and beyond, there is less variety but much more powerful and expressive forms. As we shall see, the human kingdom is the pivotal kingdom where the evolving soul becomes consciously aware of its divine potential and can participate with self-awareness in the creative process. One day, when we finish with our evolution through the twelve kingdoms, we will go on to even more glorious evolutionary plans.

In terms of developing consciousness, these twelve kingdoms can be divided in the following way:

Full Expression of Divine Consciousness
Unnamed Sacred Twelfth Kingdom
Unnamed Sacred Eleventh Kingdom
Archangelic Kingdom
Angelic Kingdom

Awakening of Divine Consciousness
Human Kingdom

Expression of Consciousness through Form
Animal Kingdom
Fish Kingdom
Unnamed Nonphysical Kingdom
Plant Kingdom

Awakening of Consciousness
Elemental Kingdom
Mineral Kingdom
Structure Kingdom

Let us now explore these kingdoms one by one. Although our focus is on the divine beings who are more developed than we are, to understand our place in the divine plan, we need to have a big picture of how we fit in the structure of the twelve kingdoms. We'll proceed from the bottom up.

The Structure Kingdom

The first stage in our ascent through the twelve kingdoms is a non-physical experience yet still very much part of our planet earth. Infant souls in this kingdom have a primitive etheric form that is round and about five to six inches in diameter. They have beautiful auras with many colors. These spiritual beings are playful and can be clairvoyantly seen floating in the atmosphere. They are very much attracted to spiritual energy and in fact serve the function of helping to channel Divine Light. Without the help of the structure kingdom, we could not effectively receive spiritual energy, as they act as a conduit for the light. They play an important part in our life and the life of the twelve kingdoms.

The structure kingdom evolves by becoming more and more in tune with the higher flows of spiritual energy. They learn to absorb the qualities of the various spiritual energy rays.

The Mineral Kingdom

Once an embryonic soul has learned all it can in the structure kingdom, it progresses to the mineral kingdom. The evolutionary experience moves from the air to the earth. Like a seed planted in the earth, the souls of the mineral kingdom are immersed in the dense matter of physical life. They, too, have a primitive etheric form, of varying sizes yet again spherical in shape.

Souls starting out in this kingdom begin with an incubation period to acclimate the vibration of dense physical matter. There is a lot of spiritual power connected to the earth, and the mineral spirits learn to embody and harness this power. They have the ability to move around to a certain degree. Of course there is much more confinement and resistance in the mineral kingdom. Yet through this resistance these souls build strength, as it takes more power to spiritually develop in the mineral kingdom than it does in the structure kingdom.

The mineral kingdom helps in sending light to the depths of the earth, as there is life in the earth and the planet itself is in a process of evolution. The mineral kingdom helps with the growth of plants as well as insects and animals that live in the ground. They also help with the release of negative black and gray atoms that are sent to the mineral kingdom to be reconstituted in the light. They assist in the creation of oil and coal and even play a part in the geology of the earth.

Like the structure kingdom, their goal is to become more conscious of the light. It is a more difficult process while immersed in physical matter, yet the rewards are greater as they develop an even deeper awareness of the Divine Light. An interesting quality of the mineral spirits is that as they evolve, they move closer to the core of the earth.

The Elemental Kingdom

The elemental kingdom is not to be confused with the famous elemental spirits that are part of the early human kingdom we will look at in chapter 9. Like souls in the structure and mineral kingdoms, these souls are encased in spherelike etheric forms. They can move through any of the elements of the earth: air, water, fire, and earth. They, too, work to help channel Divine Light to the other kingdoms. They are a guiding force for the mineral and structure kingdoms.

Their goal is to fully mature in their attunement to the Divine Light and fully awaken their own sense of consciousness. This kingdom represents the culminating of awakening consciousness of the first three kingdoms.

The Plant Kingdom

Once souls develop to the plant kingdom, a whole new phase of development presents itself. Now we are dealing with a life spirit that inhabits individualized physical form. So much can be said about the inner life of plants. Plant spirits learn how to harness consciousness through organic form. They are concerned with the struggle for physical expression. Yet what we think of as merely a survival instinct is really a mechanism for experience and spiritual growth. As the plant soul learns to harness physical life, it builds spiritual power and consciousness. Plants work under an archetypal consciousness connected to their individual species and to the plant kingdom as a whole.

Plants possess new powers, such as the ability of assimilation and elimination. As we know, they draw in sunlight for nutrition through the process of photosynthesis. They also draw in water and carbon dioxide and, in exchange, give out oxygen. Without the plant kingdom, organic life on earth could not exist. They go through the process of propagation, which opens a new door to creative expression. It also means they go through the process of birth, life, and death. Spiritually, plant souls have new challenges and opportunity for creative expression.

Although plants do not have sense organs or a nervous system, they are highly sensitive to vibrations. In addition to a physical form, plants possess an etheric counterpart as well as a primitive astral form. This astral form gives them a nature of primitive desire in that they experience attraction and repulsion. So while they do not have independent motion to move around in their environment, they most definitely react to their environment. They express likes and dislikes. They do not experience pain and pleasure the way we do, but again they are sensitive to stimuli.

Plants are extremely responsive to the Divine Light. They absorb the Divine Light as they do sunlight, air, and water. They evolved by embodying spiritual energy in all levels of their structure and being. This is why you can send light to plants to help them grow and why it is so inspiring to have plants and flowers around you.

The Unnamed Nonphysical Kingdom

Little knowledge of the unnamed physical kingdom is given. I am told by the Holy Ones that this kingdom is similar to the plant kingdom, although the souls are only in their astral/etheric forms. These plants are animated. Although they are still rooted in the ground, they can move of their own volition. There have been legends of carnivorous plants. Even in the physical realm, we see plants that echo this quality of motion, such as the Venus flytrap.

Souls in this kingdom evolve by embodying the Divine Light even more strongly than souls in the plant kingdom can. They possess a primitive type of central nervous system, which means they have the beginnings of a mental body, which is used primarily for sense perception and independent motion.

The Fish Kingdom

As we move to the fish kingdom, we are now working with individualized physical form. Although one would think fish are part of the animal kingdom, from the point of view of consciousness, they are definitely in a different level of evolution.

The fish soul must learn to express consciousness through a free and mobile material body. Several things have happened in this new development. First, the fish has come under the collective consciousness of the species the fish is a part of. Some metaphysical schools have misunderstood this to mean that fish and animals have no individual souls—that they are part of a collective soul—but this is not true. A fish most definitely has an individual soul. The group consciousness means that it draws a great deal of its behavior and ability to relate to others from a single group *consciousness*. Call it the herd mentality. We see this even in the human kingdom when a group of people react as one unit at, say, a sports event or while watching a theatrical performance.

The fish has developed a primitive mental body, which is why it has a central nervous system and sensory mechanisms. It also has motor abilities, which give it more expression of free will. These are all tools of physical and spiritual evolution.

Of course, the unique feature of fish is that they live in water! And this brings up the spiritual attribute of water and its part in the process of evolution. As we know, water is essential to all organic life. We cannot live without water. Water is an excellent medium for molecular activity. From the spiritual perspective, water is an animating force for physical life. There is a spiritual vitality found in water that the body and soul need for their development.

Some ancient schools call water the primordial mirror, reflecting the divine image into physical life. And we can see that all physical life develops in a medium of water or fluid. You could say that water is the lifeblood of nature.

Another important aspect of the fish kingdom is that they are cold-blooded. This means that their body temperature varies according to their surroundings, so they do not need the same level of food intake to maintain body temperature as warm-blooded animals do. This tells us that although fish have to fight for their survival, the physical demands are not at the same level as in the animal kingdom. It also means that they are more dependent on their environment to sustain themselves.

As fish evolve, the soul develops the ability to see the Divine Light. In a sense, they live in a world of spiritual light through the playful interactions in the water. They absorb and embody the Divine Light and serve the divine plan by giving power to the spiritual vitality that is in water. Truly there is a world of activity in the waterways and oceans of our planet.

The Animal Kingdom

As we move to the animal kingdom, we have reached another pinnacle in the ascent through the twelve kingdoms. Animal souls have developed a high sense of conscious awareness through form. Notice that I used the term *conscious awareness*, not *self*-conscious awareness. All the higher kingdoms use form for expression, but self-awareness is very different from awareness. Animals are aware, but not *self*-aware, which means they have not yet developed the power of abstract objective thought and have not yet reached the place of being able to directly connect with the Higher mind for guidance and direction. They do work through the group consciousness and have evolved this group consciousness to its highest peak.

Animals are most definitively aware of the Divine Light. But now they can develop the added awareness of spirits and the Holy Ones. They can see into the spiritual realm as part of their instinctual nature. Animals can even reach a place of tuning into their own higher nature. In this way, they go through their own type of enlightenment and take on qualities we would start to identify as human. In many ways, they are more in tune with the spiritual realms than humans are, until the human has learned to awaken its spiritual nature.

The animal serves the divine plan in so many ways, but mainly by the giving of itself. Humans gain strength from the animals. Animals possess a developed astral and etheric form. As there are many species, there are many experiences the animal soul will go through. With warm-blooded animals, the demands for survival are the greatest, but also the spiritual gains are greatest. They develop their instinctual nature to its zenith. Domestic animals will start to take on human qualities. This helps in the evolution of the animal spirit, which is why it's so important to treat animals well, as they are striving to reach the human level. As they reach the high advanced stages of evolution, they start the process of more individualized consciousness, which prepares them for the human kingdom.

The Human Kingdom

The human kingdom is a pivotal kingdom between the lower and higher kingdoms. Modern science tries to classify humans in the same category as animals, but spiritually this is not accurate. While we share many similar physical characteristics with animals, the human is most definitely not animal. I can tell you from the aura—the human aura has a completely different structure than the animal aura.

The human kingdom is the bridge between consciousness and self-consciousness. The Kabbalists call this human world, especially in its unenlightened state, the *Assiah*—the elemental world of substance. As we bridge the divine part of our nature, we can then train to become part of the spiritual hierarchy ourselves.

In the early stages of the human kingdom, there is a revisiting of the instinctual nature. At this stage, we do have animal-like qualities, but from the beginning, it is not the same as the animal. At a certain point in development, the human soul is given the gift of mind and self-awareness. This opens the door to the intellectual levels of development, and from there the divine levels of awareness.

In the human kingdom, we develop awareness of Divine Light and our higher nature. We learn to perceive and interact with the higher and nonphysical realms. But most of all, it is in the human kingdom that we are given our first direct experience of God while in physical form. For the first time in the journey through the twelve kingdoms, the evolving soul has reached the level of God perception. This is the great goal of human evolution, the enlightenment we all seek.

In working our way through the human condition, we have this strange mix of good and bad, sinner and saint, awake and asleep. This is all part of being in this pivotal kingdom. There is a dual nature in the human kingdom that, when undeveloped, can become an endless source of frustration and confusion. Yet when we make the effort to develop the divinity within us, the human duality resolves itself and merges into the unity of the divine life. This opens the door to higher, divine glories.

Humans are no longer under the group spirit consciousness. Diversity of form merges into a single more powerful and expressive form. Humans are invested in the Higher mind faculties and, with that mind, self-awareness. Through this connection to the Higher mind, which must be developed, we express the right of free will and greater creative expression. We can build complex civilizations, arts, and sciences. We can contemplate and aspire to the divine awareness.

Once in the enlightened levels, the human soul becomes part of the spiritual hierarchy and starts to consciously participate in the divine plan. The culmination of human experience is to work our way back to the celestial kingdom from where we were born. It is this direct union with God that crowns all the efforts in the human kingdom.

The Angelic Kingdom

Many people feel that being human is as good as it gets. On a physical level, this is true. The human physical form is the most developed there is on earth at this point. But our evolution does not stop here. We continue our spiritual development. The next realm above the human is the angelic kingdom. The angels are our elder brothers and sisters in light.

The Kabbalists call this realm of angels *Yetzirah*, the hierarchal world of formations. The closest Hindu term referring to angels would be the *suras*, which is often used interchangeably with the term *devas*. The defining feature of souls who have evolved to the angelic kingdom is that they are endowed with divine self-awareness of God by birthright. We in the human kingdom spend our evolution learning to fully awaken divine self-conscious awareness. It has to be built. Those in the angelic kingdom are born with this divine awareness and spend their entire evolution learning to fully express that awareness. This gives the angels tremendous God power and abilities. They are the very embodiment of light that all the lower kingdoms, including the human, have been learning to experience and harness.

As we shall see in Part 2, angels have humanlike features, or we should more properly say humans reflect features of the angelic realm. They are taller than humans and have extraordinary auras. There are no wings, but their energy can flow in such a way to give the impression of winglike forms. And the fact that they can move through the air as easily as they walk on the ground adds to the lore that angels have wings.

At this stage, the angels are in nonphysical form, yet paradoxically they are still very much part of our physical world.

The Archangelic Kingdom

Once angels have assimilated all they can in the angelic kingdom, they move to the archangelic kingdom. The Theosophists sometimes used the term *Dhyani Chohan*, "Lords of Light," in reference to these celestial giants. The Kabbalists call this archangelic realm the world of *Briah*. The Hindus sometimes use the term *raja-deva* in reference to archangels.

Spirits in the archangelic kingdom have evolved to the point that they are now beginning to express omniscience—a type of God awareness on a collective level. This is not group consciousness in which you share a similar awareness. This omniscience is the ability to direct your attention to more than one place at the same time, yet maintain your individual awareness. The consciousness of the archangels is so developed that they can embrace whole groups of angels and humans in their consciousness.

They appear in a form that resembles human in that they have faces, hands, and feet, yet their features are so exquisite that it makes one realize how much potential there is in form. They are very tall—giants really. Their auras are absolutely radiant and expansive. They immediately impress you with their complete command of the energies and powers they embody.

They possess a consciousness of inner knowing of God that the angels have not yet reached, and they possess extraordinary talents and skills. The truth is, when we are dealing with archangels, even though they are part of the same hierarchal order we are in, we are dealing with a consciousness that is difficult for us to understand from our human perspective.

They guide the evolution of the masses of humanity. With their elevated consciousness, they can put their attention on the evolution of the group as a whole, yet they are able to concentrate on individual souls and their needs. They can assist in the evolution of any aspect of the kingdoms below them and play an instrumental part in humanity's development.

The Unnamed Sacred Eleventh Kingdom

As we enter the eleventh kingdom, we cross a bridge to a consciousness so God-like that the mystics of many spiritual schools have defined the spiritual beings who are part of this kingdom as aspects of God. The name of this kingdom as well as the twelfth kingdom is too sacred to share in a book designed for the general public. The full understanding of these top two kingdoms is reserved for the awakened initiate who have made the direct contact with the Holy Ones.

The keynote of the eleventh kingdom is "creative consciousness." These spiritual beings are part of the direct co-creative process of life. They contain an awareness of God that surpasses the angels and archangels. All life is inherently creative, but here we are speaking of a direct participation in the creative work of God of a very high order. Although it was God who designed our physical form, it was the celestial beings of this kingdom who built and initiated the evolution of form and are responsible for their maintenance. Members of this kingdom are the progenitors of the human race as well as all organic forms on earth. All biological evolution is under their care.

The Hindus speak of these holy beings in many ways, including the *manus* and *pitris* expressing their divine procreative quality. Yet this creative impulse translates into many other aspects of life as well. Our creative impulse is many times inspired by the beings in this kingdom.

Kabbalists have dedicated one of their highest spiritual domains to this realm, *Atziluth*—the Boundless World of Divine Names. This is one of the reasons that Jewish mysticism gives many names for God, as a reflection for the creative power of these God-inspired beings. Christian mystics made this kingdom, and one of its greatest representatives, part of the Trinity of God by acknowledging it as "the Holy Spirit."

As these beings are part of the twelve kingdoms, they too have recognizable form. They dearly love us and work tirelessly to uplift and guide humanity. The angels and archangels look up lovingly to these sacred beings. In addition to their creative powers, divine guidance is a big part of their job, as they are responsible for the objectification or execution of the divine plan. They possess a level of omniscience that is even more encompassing than that of the archangels.

The Unnamed Sacred Twelfth Kingdom

Now we move to the top of the spiritual ladder in terms of the entire evolutionary plan of the Twelve Kingdoms of Nature. This kingdom too is so sacred that it must remain unnamed. The keynote of this kingdom is "divine consciousness." The entire conscious awareness that we build through the twelve kingdoms is all filtered through the divine con-

sciousness embodied in this kingdom. Every stage of the twelve kingdoms is in essence a degree of this divine awareness.

Since this kingdom represents the completeness of the potential within
all the kingdoms, some mystical schools speak of this kingdom in broad
general terms, such as "the Cosmic Man." This is the Adam Kadmon of
the Kabbalists, the Purusha of the Hindus that animates Prakrati—the
primordial substance of material life. The praises of the animating life of
Purusha generated the Vedic chants, which are the foundation for the
entire Hindu faith. These celestial beings have also been known as the
avatars of Vishnu, including Rama and Krishna. The Native Americans
called the divine spirit of this kingdom who watches over their people
"the Great White Spirit." The Zoroastrians' Ahura Mazda is a celestial
being of this kingdom. Christian mystics acknowledged this kingdom
and its holy leader as the second aspect of the Trinity—the Christ.

Once you get to the twelfth kingdom, you *are* the divine consciousness you seek. You have embodied the highest level of awareness and
understanding of God that you can. The glorified souls of this kingdom
can step into the inner sanctuary of God that the other kingdoms cannot. They guide all the other kingdoms and are the leaders of the spiritual hierarchy.

Like the Sacred Eleventh Kingdom, the Sacred Twelfth Kingdom is
so glorious that many traditions have spoken of it in the highest superlatives. And I can tell you from my own experience that to interact with
members of this kingdom is a life-changing event. They are so endowed
with the God presence that to behold them is to make you feel like God
is right in the next room. Yet what is so amazing is that not only are we
connected to and work with these beings, it is our destiny to one day
evolve into this kingdom. This kingdom represents the highest level of

consciousness, the most developed aura, and the most developed celestial form. It is the culmination of a long spiritual journey that started humbly in the structure kingdom.

All twelve kingdoms are interlocked in the grand plan of life. Although some kingdoms are more developed than others, all are working together. The lower kingdoms support the higher kingdoms, and in turn the higher kingdoms uplift their younger brothers and sisters. This means that not only do we receive from the Holy Ones, but the Holy Ones receive something from us too!

This gives you a master key in working with the Holy Ones—harmony. Every part of life is essential to the divine plan. It is not the job of the Holy Ones to lord over us, simply "telling us what to do." They are there to help us fulfill our destiny and spiritual potential because that best serves life as a whole. In the same way, by cooperating with the Holy Ones, we help them fulfill their mission. It's a two-way relationship. We come back to the unifying principle of life—the Oneness. We are all part of this Oneness.

WHY AREN'T ALL
THE KINGDOMS PHYSICAL?

In looking at this order you many wonder, if we are all part of the same order of life, why aren't all the kingdoms physical? Why aren't the angels and archangels in a physical form if they are part of the same evolutionary order we are in?

What must be understood is that there are many forms of expression, not just the physical. Our physical earth is enveloped in several interpenetrating nonphysical forms. Although you inhabit your physical body, your physical form has nonphysical counterparts, such as your astral and etheric bodies/templates, which together support the physical you. It is the combination of these forms that gives the soul its expression.

In the kingdoms above the human, the angels and other Holy Ones use ethereal forms that are still part of the earth expression. These non-physical forms are too rarefied to be confined to a physical body. Perhaps one day, when the earth itself is more evolved, the physical vibrations will be such that it could contain the angelic vibration and greater.

This tells us that when we behold a celestial being, we are connecting with the ethereal counterpart in us. This is a great key to having direct clairvoyant experiences with the Holy Ones, which we will explore in Part 4. Connecting with our own etheric counterpart within us helps to awaken our divine consciousness.

CHAPTER 4

A HISTORICAL PERSPECTIVE

YSTICS THROUGH THE ages have always had knowledge of the spiritual hierarchy, as it is this connection that gave them their spiritual power. Every culture has had its own understanding of the divine and described this spiritual order in its own way. In this chapter, we will look at some of these cultural influences and their relationship to the collective understanding of the divine ones.

The term *hierarchy* first came into prominence in the early Christian era. At the time, there was an organizing of spiritual material from the Hebrew tradition. This organization included a more comprehensive understanding of angels. An unnamed Christian mystic who used the name Dionysius wrote several highly influential works, including *The Celestial Hierarchy* in the fourth or fifth century CE, which carefully illustrated the ascending order of angels. Dionysius did not take credit for new inspiration. Rather, he organized a long history of understanding on the topic. Although not everyone adopted this system, it reflected the developing understanding of the spiritual hierarchy.

Centuries later, Saint Thomas Aquinas was so influenced by the works of Dionysius that he built his system of the angelic order on Dionysius's model, which became the most widely accepted interpretation of angels to this day. As Rufus Jones states in his book *Studies in Mystical Religion*:

> . . . even the Summa Theologiae of Thomas Aquinas the angelic doctor is but "a hive in whose varied cells he duly stored the honey which he gathered" from the writings of Dionysius, and he became, as we have said, the bee-bread on which all the great mystics fed.

In the late nineteenth century, awareness of the spiritual hierarchy resurfaced with the advent of theosophy and the writers who were influenced by the theosophical works. They described great hosts of divine beings that guide and steer the evolutionary process. There was also an influx of Indian mystics who brought to world consciousness their insights into the ancient study of the Holy Ones.

From the beginning, genuine teachings of the hierarchy have been delegated to the sacred mystery schools and ashrams and were reserved for initiates who were ready for such knowledge. Early attempts to disseminate some of this knowledge to a wider audience were many times suppressed or misunderstood. Adding to this is the fact that the subject of the Holy Ones is not a simple topic. It is one of the most intricate aspects of spiritual study but also one of the most rewarding.

Perhaps most important of all, there is an unfolding revelation by the Holy Ones themselves. Through the centuries, humanity is meant to add to its knowledge of the spiritual principles of life. There are eternal truths, but these truths are given in stages so that humanity has time to assimilate and use such wisdom. Religious and metaphysical studies were never meant to be a fixed thing. New inspiration is constantly being given and we must remain open to that new inspiration.

The good news is that today we are looking for ways we are alike in our spiritual approach rather than how we are different. We are uncovering things from our ancient past that we didn't know were there, or thought were lost forever. More than ever, we are being given the needed mystical keys to commune with the Holy Ones.

THE JEWISH TRADITION

Spiritual beings have been part of the Hebrew tradition from the first book of Genesis. We can trace back our modern understanding of angels to the Hebrew tradition.

As we all know, the Jewish faith is largely responsible for helping humanity understand that we are all children of the same God. We call this belief monotheism. At the time, this was a revolutionary concept, as people believed in a multiplicity of gods or a polytheistic view of the divine. As the religious concepts of monotheism developed, the Jewish faith downplayed the role of angels and the spiritual hierarchy to emphasize the unity of God. The exception to this trend was Jewish mysticism, which continued to place a strong emphasis on the importance of celestial beings in our life.

Jewish metaphysics started as far back as Abraham. Centuries later, there was a reincarnation of the metaphysical tradition, during the days of Ezekiel, which placed a strong emphasis on the spiritual hierarchy, although that specific term was not used. Then during the Second Temple period, there was a flowering of religious and metaphysical texts that would not make it into the formal biblical canon. These writings were known as the *apocrypha* and the *pseudepigrapha*. One of the most famous writings of this time is the Book of Enoch, which spoke a great deal about angels.

Later, there were Talmud mystics who more systematically wrote some of the metaphysical teachings down to preserve them. Two of these traditions became known as the *Ma'aseh Merkavah* ("Works of the Chariot") and the *Ma'aseh Bereshit* ("Works of Creation"). Both were genuine schools of metaphysics in their day. These schools focused on different aspects of Jewish mysticism. The Ma'aseh Merkavah followed the Ezekiel tradition with its realms of angels and the heaven worlds. The Ma'aseh Bereshit focused on the esoteric aspects of Genesis, the Hebrew alphabet, and numbers. These differences were not reconciled until centuries later with the development of the Kabbalah. With the Kabbalah, a more comprehensive understanding of the Holy Ones developed as part of the Sephiroth Tree or the Tree of Life.

THE CHRISTIAN TRADITION

With the advent of Christianity, the spiritual hierarchy was accepted and embraced. An essential new aspect of the divine was emphasized—the Holy Trinity—which included the part that the Christ plays in the life of humanity. As generally practiced today, Christianity sees Christ as an aspect of God and the savior of humanity. Yet metaphysics sees the role of Christ in a somewhat different way—as the crown of the spiritual hierarchy and a door to the direct experience of the divine. (We will delve more deeply into the mystical understanding of the Christ in chapter 8.)

From its beginnings, there was a mystical as well as religious aspect to the Christian movement. Christian mystics emphasized the idea of *direct knowing*. They taught that one could have a direct personal experience of the divine and the celestial ones without the intervention of a centralized church or ecclesiastical organization. They emphasized that the days of the prophets were not numbered, delegated to a select few—or only conscribed to a particular religious group—but were potentially open to those who took the time to gain the knowledge it took to awaken such an inner knowing. We have come to label this mystical aspect of early Christianity as Gnosticism.

The early Christian mystical movement was complex, as it was not one unified group. They welcomed and studied non-Christian mystical traditions. For example, there was the Neo-Platonic movement, which attempted to reconcile the Greek philosophical system with the blossoming Christian movement. Later this philosophy would exert great influence on Christian thinking of the Middle Ages. Dionysus's book on the spiritual hierarchy was influenced by Neo-Platonic thought.

As the number of people who joined the faith grew, the need for structure became necessary. The leaders of the religious aspect of Christianity emphasized order, ritual, and the role of the Church in the spiritual life of the individual. Unfortunately, many of the priests and bishops of the blossoming Christian Church saw the idea of direct knowing without the need of a church as heresy. As they grew in power and influence, they successfully suppressed the mystical roots of Christianity. The mystics went underground and quietly continued their work behind the scenes. This was a great loss, as both the religious and mystical were meant to work side by side. This created an imbalance that has contributed to misunderstandings regarding Christian teachings.

THE MUSLIM/SUFI TRADITION

Islam includes the spiritual hierarchy as part of its theology. It includes angels as one of its six articles of faith (not to be confused with the five pillars of Islam). Tradition teaches that it was the Archangel Gabriel, known as Archangel Jibrael, who revealed the Qur'an to Muhammad. Angels are part of the three aspects of beings created by Allah: angels, humans, and jinn. Jinn are spirits that can be good or bad. The famous idea of the "genie in the bottle" comes from the folklore of the jinn. The Qur'an speaks of watchers, who are like guardian angels. For every soul there is a watcher who is "as close as our jugular vein." Angels are considered so integral to Islamic life that it is said that an angel comes down with every drop of rain.

Islam shares a common ancestry with Judaism and Christianity, as it acknowledges Abraham as its patriarch. Muslims believe that Islam offers a fuller, or final, revelation of truth presented by the primordial faiths from the prophets and sages of old. So rather than creating a new hierarchal order, Islam aims to clarify our understanding of the hierarchal order already established.

The great keynote of Islam is devotion and surrender to God. Of course all religions emphasize devotion, yet with Islam, devotion is particularly emphasized. Faithful Muslims build their life and daily activities around devotion to God. This brings up an essential point in understanding the spiritual hierarchy. As has already been said, the Holy Ones are there to help us reach our highest spiritual potential. Yet to fulfill this potential, we must learn to align ourselves with forces of life that are more developed than ourselves, and this requires a great deal of dedication and devotion.

The metaphysical or esoteric aspect of Islam is the Sufi tradition. The

Sufis emphasize the potential for direct knowing of God as an essential human need. They have a hierarchy of enlightened humans who act as spiritual leaders guiding aspirants to this place of spiritual knowing. They call the leader of their esoteric order the Qutb. The Qutb is said to have a direct connection to the divine. He is part of an unbroken chain of spiritual leaders going back to Muhammad and reveals himself only to a select group of mystics. Students in the Sufi tradition spend many years working with their mystic teachers to reach this place of divine knowing.

It is a great regret that extreme factions of Islam have clouded a clear understanding of the esoteric tradition of this faith. For centuries, even before Muhammad, the Arab world was influenced by Greeks, Romans, Jews, and Christians. In the Middle Ages, when religious intolerance grew in Europe, the light of knowledge shone brightly in the Islamic world, which at that time was still open-minded and advanced in learning. Baghdad, in those days, attracted some of the greatest minds in the world. It had a sophisticated academy and library known as the House of Wisdom.

THE HINDU TRADITION

When we turn to the Hindu tradition, we find a seemingly endless wealth of knowledge and information on celestial beings. The terms *hierarchy* and *angels* are absent from the Indian cosmology. Yet in the Indian terminology there is a strong emphasis on spiritual lineages and dynasties, which is another way of saying a "spiritual order." Part of the reason for this great variety of spiritual beings is the age of this religion and its tolerance for varying beliefs. This tolerance and variety has proven inviting to the Western mind, which for centuries was fixed on one spiritual interpretation of life.

Although there is much diversity in the Indian system of deities, there is in fact an underlying unity. All aspects of divinity in the Hindu faith are emanations from the ultimate being or Absolute God known as Brahman. Out of the Supreme comes forth Brahma/Vishnu/Shiva and all the devas, kumaras, dynasties, manus, progenitors, avatars, and divine incarnations that bless and uplift humanity on earth. The Hindu faith gives a vision of the vastness of the Holy Ones—the many levels of hierarchies that are all a manifestation of the One Supreme Absolute.

At first glance, it can appear that this hierarchal order has little to do with the angels and archangels of Western culture, yet throughout this book we emphasize that there is an underlying unity. Although different names and terminology may be used, there is a unifying hierarchal order for all humanity.

The foundation of the religious and esoteric traditions aspects of the Hindu faith is the Vedas—especially the Rig Veda. The Rig Veda is a collection of hymns dedicated to the divine. Hindus used these hymns in their ritual practices and, at first glance, they may appear to be almost a form of nature worship with such deities as Agni (fire), Surya (sun), and Vayu (wind) or Indra (sky). Yet these ancient seers or rishis who composed the Rig Veda were mystics in the best sense of the word and embedded in these hymns metaphysical truths that, with time, would surface and develop in later works such as the Upanishads, the Mahabharata, the Bhagavad Gita, The Book of Manu, and the later Puranas. Through these and other works, the full Hindu cosmology, with its dazzling display of Holy Ones, emerged.

The metaphysical aspect of the Hindu faith we know as yoga. There are several branches of yoga. Mystical yoga is much more than the Hatha yoga that has become so popular as a form of exercise and physical well-being. Yoga such as Raja yoga is the practice of training the soul to unite with the divine. The yogic tradition emphasized the relationship of the spiritual teacher *(guru)* who taught the student *(chela)* how to build the direct connection to the Holy Ones and become enlightened. The guru was part of a lineage of gurus who maintained the divine connection.

The Hindu faith is undergoing a revival and reevaluation, not only in places like the United States but also in its homeland of India. Indians went through a crisis of faith with the Muslim influence in the 1700s, and especially with the British influence in the nineteenth and twentieth centuries. Many Indians saw their own heritage as old superstitions. With Indian independence after World War II, there has been a resurgence and pride in its ancient history, and a much more systematic attempt to organize the diverse ancient teachings. With the migration of genuine Indian spiritual teachers, the Hindu tradition has been felt all over the world. And of course we cannot ignore the influence Western culture is having on India. This exchange of ideas and cultures is paving the way for a greater spiritual understanding that is unfolding.

THE KINGDOM OF LIGHT TEACHINGS

As has been mentioned, the metaphysical knowledge imparted in this book is part of a tradition known as the Kingdom of Light Teachings. This tradition follows a four-thousand-year history and finds its root with the original Hebrew mystics. The teachings went through a fuller blossoming with the origins of mystical Christianity and complement the most ancient of all metaphysical arts—the Hermetic sciences. My mentor, Inez Hurd, called these teachings Christos Wisdom, as they are a metaphysical interpretation of the Universal Christ Teachings. They are nondenominational in that they are not designed for any single group of people or culture but are open to any aspiring soul willing to walk the metaphysical path. They are designed to accommodate the blossoming in human consciousness and to honor every genuine mystical tradition. This tradition has worked quietly for many centuries yet has influenced many groups, such as the Gnostics and the Rosicrucians. These teachings are making a strong resurgence today, as metaphysical study is truly going global.

A unique feature of this tradition is its emphasis on working with Divine Light. The Kingdom of Light Teachings offers one of the most comprehensive studies in working with spiritual energy. From my work with the aura, I can tell you that spiritual energy is the key to making lasting changes in your life. And this will be a strong emphasis in this book—how to work with the Holy Ones in your life, to strengthen your spiritual power and auric field, thereby enhancing every aspect of your being.

THE MYSTERY SCHOOL TRADITION

Throughout the ancient world, especially in places like Greece and Egypt, there were esoteric training centers known as mystery schools. These schools flourished in the beginning of the Middle Ages. Mystery schools were secluded learning centers where the aspiring soul was initiated into the mysteries of life. You could join these groups only if you were invited. Once you were part of the school, you would spend years in the school—if not your entire life—learning many aspects of metaphysics. The goal of the mystery school was to help the initiate reach enlightenment and build his or her direct connection to the divine.

These schools had an extensive understanding of the Holy Ones and the spiritual hierarchy. In the days of old, the only way you could receive accurate information about the hierarchy was if you belonged to one of these groups. Along with the ashrams of the East, these schools laid the foundation for the metaphysical understanding we have today. My first education in metaphysics was in the mystery school tradition. It is fascinating to note that today we are being given the opportunity to gain some of the esoteric knowledge of the mystery school tradition without being part of these schools. The demand for quality spiritual education is so great that the divine is opening doors that were kept sealed for ages except to the initiate.

The challenge we face today is that while the information of the divine is being given to many, the path to reaching the spiritual pinnacle remains the same as it has been for ages. This means that instead of building our connection to the divine while in the seclusion of a mystery school or ashram, we have to accomplish this task while in the midst of our active lives, while we are pursuing our careers, having a family, or being caught up in the many pursuits of the twenty-first century. This creates greater challenges but also greater rewards.

OTHER GLOBAL TRADITIONS

All genuine mystical traditions in every culture—from China and Japan to the Incas, Aztecs, African tribes, and Native Americans—play a part in the understanding of the spiritual hierarchy. From the early archaeological finds in Mesopotamia and Egypt, it is clear that spirituality played a part in the life of humanity and, with it, knowledge of celestial beings. Sculptures found in the ancient Indus Valley city show mystics in the meditative lotus position, indicating metaphysical practices dating back three thousand years. And now perhaps the oldest archaeological site yet found, at Gobekli Tepe in modern-day Turkey, offers evidence of spiritual practices going back twelve thousand years. We can only imagine what other archaeological finds yet await humanity.

Even Buddhism has its traditions of divine ones. Buddha was very much a reformer and tried to correct many misunderstandings in his native India. He tried to end the caste system, which doomed millions to a life of servitude. His focus was on enlightened behavior and taking personal responsibility. His eightfold path is a handbook on how to live a true life and attain the ultimate goal of enlightenment, or become awakened. It is true that Buddha downplayed the role of celestial ones. This is because many were caught in superstitious beliefs and idol worship, and he was trying to break that ignorance. It does not mean, however, that the Buddha negated the Holy Ones. There is a developed Buddhist cosmology that includes devas and brahmas. One of these Buddhist traditions is known as *Sattha Devamanussanam*, or "the Teacher of Gods and Humans." In this teaching, the Buddha is honored by devas. They support him and learn from him.

The Buddhists also emphasized the Arhat. Arhats are awakened souls who have reached enlightenment and help others attain the same goal. Once again, we find an emphasis on enlightened souls helping others reach that place of enlightenment and spiritual awareness.

WHAT'S IN A NAME?

In rounding out the historical perspective of the spiritual hierarchy, I would like to bring up one more essential point—the names of the Holy Ones. When using terms such as *angels* and *archangels*, immediately the Western tradition from which these names originated comes to mind. When one uses the terms *devas* and *avatars*, immediately the Eastern tradition comes to mind, and so on. Using certain words and language can create a feeling of partiality and favoritism. Although this feeling is unavoidable to some extent, it is my hope to see through the mask that language can create. Despite the nomenclature of various cultures, it's the same hierarchy for all humanity. Although specific Holy Ones may work in different parts of the world, the hierarchal order is unified.

In taking this synergetic approach, I hope to reconcile apparent contrary belief systems of the spiritual hierarchy. Sometimes, these contrary beliefs cannot be fully reconciled. Yet even in these cases I will try to demonstrate the underlying unifying spiritual principle. The terminology emphasized in this book uses the nomenclature of the Kingdom of Light Teachings, which takes on the quality of the Judaic/Christian background out of which it was born, but these terms are used metaphysically and nondenominationally.

Most important, all names of celestial beings we use on this physical earth, including our word for God, are human-made creations. These are human words that the divine has sanctified and made holy. In the celestial realms, the Holy Ones do not go by these names. There are heavenly languages spoken in the divine realms, and the Holy Ones use names appropriate to these celestial languages, which they do not generally share with us.

As a matter of course, I will use terms such as *the Higher, the Holy Ones*, or *celestial beings* interchangeably as generic terms for the hierarchy. When specific aspects of the Higher are mentioned, I will attempt to draw parallel terms from various cultures. I am not an expert in comparative religious study and am not attempting to oversimplify or trivialize various belief systems. My goal is to encourage those of every faith to work more closely with the divine, and to see that we are children of the same God, and brothers and sisters of the same spiritual hierarchy.

Who's Who

in the

Spiritual Realms

THE GLORIES OF THE ANGELIC KINGDOM

B Y THE TIME I was in my thirties, I had developed a strong rapport with the spiritual hierarchy. As part of my work with them, I was taken to the inner worlds for instruction. One time, the divine signaled that they were going to take me to an extraordinary place the mystics call Spiritual Etheria. Words cannot describe this realm. It is a place of extraordinary power and light. I was excited yet curious as to why I was going there. I knew the Holy Ones did not do things without a purpose. They took me to a place in this heavenly realm where there was a group of people gathered on a hill. It was a serene, pastoral setting with trees and flowers. Below was a gorgeous purple-blue lake. Everything was so very peaceful. There was a lot of white light radiating everywhere.

On top of the hill were three of the most radiant angelic beings I had ever seen. I was thrilled to be there, yet wondered what was going on. Who were these angels and what were these people doing here? I walked closer to the group of about fifty people. They appeared to be citizens of Spiritual Etheria and were told not to leave until I had arrived. They were intently listening, as the angels had been teaching them something.

There had just been a ceremony and these people had received a blessing from the angels.

As I moved closer, the angels sent the thought to come forward to them. I walked through the group to the top of the hill. The area around the angelic beings had been roped off. I stopped at the demarcation, but they urged me forward, so I crossed over the roped area.

There was so much love coming from these angels. They were tall, maybe twelve feet, and wearing white robes. Their auras were glowing, and so expansive that they practically encircled the people they were blessing. The central figure was the leader, but all three were representatives of the highest order of angels.

The leader came closer, and I thought he had a message, but instead he congratulated me, saying, "We want to let you know how happy we are with the work you are doing. We are with you and supporting you." They then thanked me for someone I had helped. I was amazed at how aware they were of things. The group could hear what was going on, and for some reason the angels wanted them to be aware of what I was doing.

The experience didn't last long, but it made a strong impact. It deepened my understanding that, by being of service to the Holy Ones, I was part of their ministry. Being recognized by these celestial beings gave me confidence. It made me more aware of how cognizant they are of the things we do on earth and how every good deed does not go unrecognized—even if we are not patted on the back for it by others. The divine is aware.

In this section, we will look at the various orders of divine beings. There are many aspects to the spiritual hierarchy, and it can be easy to get lost in the vastness of the Holy Ones. So while we will look at the big picture of things, we will target specific celestial beings as the ones to start working with. Let's start our journey by exploring the angelic host.

Angels are extraordinary. Every aspect of the spiritual hierarchy is essential, but on a day-to-day basis, we work with the angels the most. They are the governing agents of God and carry out the duties of the divine plan. As we saw in chapter 3, they are part of the Twelve Kingdoms of Nature and are the next step up from the human in spiritual evolution. What makes them so wonderful is that they are endowed by birthright with divine awareness of God. They do not have to awaken and build that awareness as we do in the human kingdom. Regardless of the dimension of life they are working on, they can maintain that divine awareness. This gives them tremendous spiritual powers and talents. They can harness the Divine Light in extraordinary ways.

The word *angel* comes from the Greek *angelos*, which means "messenger." The Hebrews use the term *mal'akh*, which is very similar to the Arabic word *malak*, which again means "messenger" or "courier." Knowledge of angels can be traced back to the ancient religion of Zoroastrianism. The Hebrews carried the torch and further developed the understanding of these divine ones. In the Second Temple period in Israel, there was an explosion of interest in angels, as many were exposed to the tradition during the Babylonian captivity. Eventually the Christian faith further solidified and systematized the angelic order. It was followed through in the Islamic faith as well. In this age of reason and science, angels have been relegated to myth, but this could not be further from the truth. They are more alive than ever, and they play an intimate and active role in our lives.

The term *angel* can be used to indicate any spiritual being in the celestial order, or it can refer to a specific class of spiritual beings, which is the way we will use this word. Although the term appears to be specific to Judaism, Christianity, and Islam, angels are for everyone, not just for one segment of the population. For example, Hindu cosmology has no exact corresponding term for *angel*, but recognizes beings known as *suras*. These suras are the maintainers of the realms ordained by the Trimurti (Brahma/Vishnu/Shiva) much in the same way that the angels are the administrators of God.

SEVEN CYCLES OF ANGELIC EVOLUTION

There are seven evolving cycles of angelic life, so there is great variety of angelic expression. They are developing just as we are, and they go through definite stages of development. Through each stage, their goal is to draw closer to God and serve the divine plan.

These seven stages are as follows:

1. Cherubs
2. Joy guides
3. Divine Energy angels
4. Guardian angels
5. Teaching angels
6. Choir angels
7. Great Divine Brotherhood angels

Cherubs

The cherubs are the babies of the angelic world! They are not to be confused with the cherubim, which are a much more developed class of angelic beings.

The cherubs are the first cycle in the spiritual development of angels. They appear about two feet tall and look a lot like a human baby, but their head is not as disproportionately large as with human infants. Cherubs have full awareness of their divinity and are very alert and aware of what is going on around them. They are pure joy and fully enjoy their newly earned divinity, as they have an inborn awareness of God. They uplift humanity by their very presence. They come around those who are depressed or unhappy. They don't come alone but come with other angels (although you may not see these other angels). They have, in essence, angelic parents, those of the guardian angelic order, who watch over them and help to nurture their gifts. The cherubs have these celestial parents through their whole cycle of evolution in the cherub state. They can communicate with each other but do not have responsibilities as more mature angels do.

They have beautiful auras and share key essential auric components common to all angels, such as the auric shell and up-rush of energy, but of course they have not fully developed their potential, so the breadth of energy is not nearly as strong as that of more mature angels. White light is a strong energy seen with the cherubs.

MEDITATIVE PRAYER TO WORK WITH THE CHERUBS

Heavenly Father/Holy Mother God, I ask for a blessing from the delightful angelic cherubs that I may receive their wonder and hope. I ask to be quickened with the radiance of new beginnings.

Joy Guides

The joy guides are the children of the angelic world. The ones I have seen appear like ten-year-olds, but taller, and, as the name implies, they are full of life and joy. They have more freedom of expression than the cherubs and are beginning their independent service to the divine plan. They too have angelic parents, which are the angels of the teacher class. Each soul on earth has two joy guides assigned to him or her. As the name implies, their job is to lift our spirits. Though angels do not give their names, joy guides give us their nicknames, as they want us to call on them. These names are for our convenience and are not their inner esoteric names. Joy guides encourage us to do fun things, and they love to travel. They are a reminder to take time for play and fun.

MEDITATIVE PRAYER TO WORK WITH THE JOY GUIDES

Heavenly Father/Holy Mother God, I ask for a blessing from the angelic joy guides to receive their joy and vitalizing exuberance encouraging me to keep a smile on my face and a song in my heart. Help me to enhance my loving expression of joy and fun.

Divine Energy Angels

You could say that the Divine Energy angels are the teenagers of the angelic world. They are young and vital. These angels are really coming into their own glory and power. They are thrilled at the prospect of participating more directly in the divine plan.

It is at this stage that angels learn to become administers of Divine Light and other spiritual powers. All angels are channels of light and energy, but these angels will take on specific attributes of the light and act as the embodiment of that light. One may be an angel of love, while another may be an angel of balance. The spiritual currents of light that flow through these beings are truly magnificent. For example, an angel of peace has violet and purple energies that are dominant colors in their auras, along with white and gold rushes of light, radiating brilliantly, showing the purity and inner power that accompany this intense peace. No wonder the Indians call these beings "shining ones." An angel of peace might work with war-torn countries to restore peace to tormented souls. Or they may send peace to a grieving wife or husband. Wherever there is strife, the angel of peace will be there. As you work with the Divine Light and other spiritual powers, you attract these great beings. We will be working a great deal with these angels in the meditative exercises offered in this book.

**MEDITATIVE PRAYER TO WORK WITH
THE DIVINE ENERGY ANGELS**[1]

*Heavenly Father/Holy Mother God, I ask for a blessing from the
Divine Energy angels to receive the Divine Light and power
I need in all levels of my consciousness. I ask to fill my
aura and consciousness with whatever spiritual power
I need and to the degree of my need.*

Guardian Angels

A great deal has been written about these tutelary angelic beings. As Saint Jerome states, "How great the dignity of the soul, since each one has from his birth an angel commissioned to guard it." The presence of

---

[1] Please see chapter 15 for a detailed list of Divine Light angels to call on.

guardian angels can be traced throughout all antiquity, as many monuments depict protective angelic beings. The Zoroastrians call their guardian angel a *fravashi*. They believed that the guardian angel sends the soul into physical experience and that one day, after passing on from physical life, the soul will return with the *fravashi* and assimilate the experiences of the material world.

Each of us entering physical life is assigned two guardian angels to watch over us—a dynamic angel and a magnetic angel. This guardianship will be maintained throughout our life. They have an enormous job to do in helping humanity. They are particularly close to us when we are young because our consciousness and auras are still developing, so we need that added support.

Many have interpreted the guardian angel as a sort of bodyguard. Although they serve this function, their job is much more encompassing. They are guardians in the sense that it is their job to maintain the divine connections of the people they are helping. When a soul incarnates into physical life, many spiritual connections support it through its physical experience. The guardian angel is responsible for making sure those connections are maintained.

Guardian angels work with Divine Energy angels to make sure we receive the light properly. They are responsible for making the connections with all aspects of the spiritual hierarchy, as they act as a link to all levels of the spiritual hierarchy. They make sure the inspiration and guidance is accurately transmitted. Even if we are not aware of their presence, they are lovingly helping us. It's incredible, all that they do. The first time I saw a guardian angel I was nine years old and it was an exhilarating experience.

Some have wondered that, if everyone has guardian angels, why do bad things happen? Wouldn't the guardian angel prevent accidents and other calamities? Many times they do just that. They protect us in so many ways that we don't recognize. But remember, it is the job of the Holy Ones to help us in our spiritual journey, not to interfere in the affairs of free will. Many times, the angels have to patiently stand by as we make our mistakes, sometimes big mistakes. Otherwise we could not learn and grow. There are also karmic conditions to consider. The spiritual hierarchy will administer, but cannot interfere with, our karma challenges. If they did, we would never learn from our mistakes. Having said this, of course there are many acts of grace that the Holy Ones do for us. Make no mistake. They have tremendous compassion, and love us dearly.

MEDITATIVE PRAYER TO WORK WITH THE GUARDIAN ANGELS

Heavenly Father/Holy Mother God, I ask for a blessing from my two
guardian angels. I thank You for all You do to keep me protected and
to maintain my spiritual connections to the celestial hierarchy.
Thank you for being like a parent to my soul. I ask to
strengthen my connection to the guardian angels.

Teaching Angels

Of all the celestial beings who work with us, without question, the most essential ones to connect with on a day-to-day basis are the teaching angels. For all they do for us, it is ironic that there is not more known about these celestial beings. Teaching angels are just that—angels who teach us the ways of the divine life. They are magnificent to see. Their auras are highly developed and extend quite far. If you are fortunate enough to see one, there is no question in your mind that you are dealing with a sacred being.

Teaching angels are assigned to us. They know us better than we know ourselves. They know our strengths and weaknesses, what we are to accomplish in our life, our karmic credits and debts. Every day they are helping us to reach our highest potential. Some teaching angels stay with us for a long time. Others change, depending on what we're going through. The reason we have more than one teaching angel is that they have specialties. One may be an expert with healing, and another helps us with our spiritual growth. Still another helps us with our creative flow. There are teaching angels who are experts in matters of business and finance, and others who are experts in science and technology.

As we evolve up the spiritual ladder, we attract more teaching angels. Generally, most people will have two or three teaching angels assigned to them. They are not with you every minute of every day, but it is amazing how often they tune in to help. This shows that you are *never* alone during your sojourn on earth.

For those who are not ready for this celestial support, teachers are assigned to them from the human kingdom. These teachers are souls, like you and me, who have lived on earth and gone through the same evolutionary process we are now going through. The difference is that they have graduated to the heaven worlds. Teachers from the human kingdom have been in the heaven worlds for some time. They have been specially trained to be teachers of Divine Light. These teachers are ideally suited to help us in our evolution because they understand what we are going through, having gone through it themselves.

I'd like to say here that even though you may not see the teaching angels does not mean you cannot intimately work with them. They want to connect with you. They want you to see them. They love you and are doing everything in their power to help you come up into your true spiritual self where you *can* commune with them. Please see chapter 14 for exercises to connect with the angelic teachers.

MEDITATIVE PRAYER TO WORK WITH THE TEACHING ANGELS

Heavenly Father/Holy Mother God, I ask for a blessing from my
assigned teaching angels. I thank you for all you do to guide
me on the spiritual path and help me to fulfill my Tapestry
of Life. Inspire me with Thy guidance, healing, and
inspiration. Thank you for connecting me to
the entire spiritual hierarchy.

Choir Angels

The choir angels are perhaps the best known and celebrated of the entire angelic host. This is because they offer extraordinary help, and also because their order is mentioned by name in the Bible. The Hebrew mystics based an entire level of the sephirothic tree—the Tree of Life—on this angelic order. The Kabbalah calls this level the *Yetzirah*, the hierarchal world of formations. When Dionysus wrote his seminal book, *The Celestial Hierarchy*, which became a template for angelic understanding for the next 1,500 years, he based his work on the hierarchal order of the choir angels.

Many teachings today interpret the ascending order of choir angels as the order of the entire spiritual hierarchy. It's easy to understand why this is so. It was recognized and supported by both the Judaic and Christian faiths. While these beings play an essential part in the divine plan, choir angels represent only one aspect of a much broader hierarchal order.

Another reason for the confusion is the terminology. Angels and archangels are mentioned by name as the first two degrees in this choir order, yet at the same time *all* beings in the angelic kingdom are called angels, not just the first order in the choir hierarchy. Then there are archangels listed as the second choir of angels, but this is different from the kingdom of the archangels. Perhaps the best way to explain this is to recognize that these names are titles of office. For example, a president is a president, whether of a corporation or of a country. In the same way, *angel* could refer to the whole kingdom of angels or to a specific order of the choir angels. *Archangel* could refer to the entire kingdom of archangels or a specific order of choir angels.

The primary job of the choir angels is to help you reach your true spiritual self. It is the choir angels who awaken you on the spiritual path and help you conquer your lower nature so you can resurrect into your Higher Self, which eventually leads to enlightenment.

The reason choir angels are so celebrated is that they work intimately with the various religions to aid in their spiritual work. They bless congregations during church, synagogue, mosque, or temple worship. They help us strengthen our faith in God and live by that faith. They are there in those moments of sacrifice and surrender when the lower nature is letting go and permitting the higher nature to shine. These angels are very involved in the teacher/student relationship, giving gurus and teachers the power necessary to help their students. They are the angels who take us to the inner worlds for guidance and direction. These angels are not assigned to us the way the teaching angels are, yet they play an intimate part in our evolving lives.

There are nine orders of choir angels: angels, archangels, principalities, powers, virtues, dominions, thrones, cherubim, and seraphim. All have been given a designation according to their level of development and represents the service they perform in helping humanity fully awaken into their higher consciousness.

MEDITATIVE PRAYER TO WORK WITH THE CHOIR ANGELS

Heavenly Father/Holy Mother God, I ask for a blessing from the choir
angels to help me release the negative energies of my lower nature
and grant me the spiritual power to ascend to my immortal self.
Help me to live to my highest potential in every facet of my life.

Great Divine Brotherhood Angels

The angels of this order are the most developed and advanced of all in the angelic kingdom. They are the administrators of the other angelic orders and are a guiding force in humanity's development. This group of angels also goes by the name "Great White Brotherhood," indicating the extraordinary purity these beings possess. Theosophy popularized the term, although they used it in reference to a hierarchy of advanced human souls.

The Great Divine Brotherhood angels are the elite of the angelic world. They have gone as far in the angelic world as you can go. Angels from this level evolve into the kingdom of the archangels. The job of these great angels is to help us reach enlightenment and get into our full God consciousness. Once there, they work with illuminated souls to help them reach even higher levels of awareness and to more fully express the divine gifts they have worked so hard to earn.

MEDITATIVE PRAYER TO WORK WITH THE
GREAT DIVINE BROTHERHOOD ANGELS

Heavenly Father/Holy Mother God, I ask for a blessing from the Great
Divine Brotherhood angels. I ask to receive the power to grow in
the light and to help awaken me in Thy divine consciousness,
leading me to my enlightenment.

ANGELS AT WORK AND PLAY

How do angels work with us? Some think that angels have no free will, that they are compelled to obey the will of God. But this is not true. Angels, and all Holy Ones, most definitely have free will. They participate in the divine plan out of their own joy and desire to do so. Otherwise the hierarchy would be nothing more than a network of automatons. There would be no creative spirit. And the Holy Ones are the very embodiment of originality and creative power.

There are three basic ways the angels work with us. First, they can objectify themselves to wherever we are. These types of experiences are called visitations. While these are without question the most dramatic and exciting, it is not the most common way they work with us. A second way is by working with our higher nature. All of us have a Higher Self, whether we are aware of that Higher Self or not. The Holy Ones identify with that higher nature, and it is easy for them to connect with that part of us and send Divine Light or inspiration that we may need. Of course it's up to us to accept that guiding hand. Sometimes we do, and other times we do not.

A third way is that they can work from their celestial realm and tune into us, projecting the energy or power we need from there. This is the most common way the angels and all Holy Ones reach us. They can still touch any aspect of our consciousness that they wish. The divine power can be transmitted quickly and very efficiently.

I have had experiences working with the divine ones in all of these ways, but the most dramatic is when they choose to pay us a visit. There are many examples of angels at work and play. One time, when I was very young, I was sitting in church at a Sunday service. Being the daughter of a Greek Orthodox priest, I never missed a Sunday service! This one Sunday, my attention was drawn to a woman who seemed to be in deep and reverent prayer. To my surprise, I saw a very dynamic-looking angel come very close to her, almost looking at her face-to-face. She couldn't see him, but I could. He seemed drawn to her vibration. A moment later, he was in prayer with her and the combined prayer energy was elevating her consciousness. I could tell by the way that her aura was brightening that she was in a state of exaltation. He was adding a lot of power to her prayers. This was not only deepening her sincere efforts but building a rapport with the angels.

I have seen angels interacting with each other many times. The keynote is always love. So much love comes from and through them. One time in meditation, two angels objectified themselves in the room I was in. One was a very dynamic angel, and the other a magnetic angel. One sent light to the other, which made that one's aura glow even brighter, and then that angel returned the favor by sending energy back, raising the vibration of the other angel. This back-and-forth went on for a little while, and the entire exchange was thrilling to observe. There is also a lot of mental-to-mental exchange of ideas and consciousness, which again creates this feeling of euphoria. I have not observed this but have been told by the Holy Ones that sometimes angels can become intimate with each other by merging into each other's angelic form. They can actually merge momentarily, which creates a feeling of spiritual ecstasy.

It is not uncommon to see groups of angelic beings working together. I have seen them in meditation, prayer, singing (they love to sing, and they have wonderful voices!), chanting, and reciting, as well as sending light and love to each other and to us. They give spiritual gifts to each other. Then there is a whole different type of exchange, in which angels interact with celestial beings more developed than they are, such as with the archangels. Angels interacting with archangels is extraordinary. There is such reverence and joy. You can see how thrilled they are to be in the presence of the archangels, and how much they look up to them for guidance and direction. The archangels in turn love to work with the angels and rely on them a great deal in carrying out divine directives.

There are times when conclaves of celestial beings at every level join together in great gatherings. There is so much light and power that it's absolutely dazzling. To be part of such a gathering is a great honor. You are overjoyed to bear witness to such spiritual splendor and truly feel you are part of the grand plan of life.

ILLUSTRATION OF AN ANGEL

What do angels look like? There have been numerous depictions through the ages, some of them accurate, some of them more imaginative. Many times they are portrayed symbolically, depicting their attribute or act of service. For example, an angel may be represented as a lion or ox, depending on whether courage or strength is being depicted.

A challenge in depicting angels is that they sometimes take on different forms and qualities depending on how they are working with us. So they can appear differently and sometimes take on a semblance that looks remarkably human. And I am sure they possess spiritual traits they simply do not share with us. In Figure 5.1A, I depict a Great Divine Brotherhood angel.[2] This represents an angel in its most developed form. As

---

[2] In all the color illustrations in this book, it is my goal to be as accurate as possible in depicting these beings as I have actually seen them. In this way, the illustrations are diagrammatic. Yet, in depicting angels and other celestial beings, it is very difficult to physically illustrate the essence of these divine beings on a two-dimensional canvas. So we have chosen to take a more artistic approach to convey the feeling and emotional impact of these great beings. While the artist, Howard David Johnson, has done a wonderful job of conveying the majesty and auric details of the Holy Ones, some artistic license has been taken for dramatic impact.

always, I will be as accurate as I can, knowing we cannot possibly understand all that there is to an angel until we ourselves becomes angels.

There are three things to consider in observing angels: their form, their aura, and the radiations of power that flow through them. Often the latter is so powerful that it can become difficult to clairvoyantly observe the other aspects. The aura and appearance of angels differ depending on whether they are in their angelic infancy or are of the Great Divine Brotherhood, as depicted here.

Let's start with form. Do angels have a body? Yes, they do. But let's

FIGURE 5.1A. *A Great Divine Brotherhood Angel*
(See inside front cover for full-color figure 5.1.)

understand what is meant by "a body." A body is a vehicle of expression. It allows the soul that is in that body to express itself. Regardless of the spiritual plane of life you are on or the evolutionary level of advancement you are at, you need a body to express yourself.

In its most developed state, the angelic form is about twelve feet tall and elongated. This form is humanlike, or, I should say, our human form is a reflection of the divine forms of the higher kingdoms. The higher we go in the twelve kingdoms, the more refined this form becomes. The angels possess a celestial form that allows them to express their divinity. They have a face, hands, and feet, but, contrary to many depictions, they do not have wings. They most often wear ethereal robes of light, but again they can appear differently depending on what they are doing. Their bodies are so luminous that sometimes it's hard to make out their form because of their brilliance.

The angelic form is full of white light and radiates an aura of various colors about a foot in all directions. It looks like the body is shimmering. They have facial features, lovely yet strong. They are very expressive but, because of the great power that flows through them, their expressions can sometimes be mistaken for sternness. They are loving but no-nonsense. This is because they are the reflection of truth divine. So any imperfection in us stands out in the presence of such perfection. This is one reason why it takes time to develop the ability to directly see angels. We must be mentally and emotionally prepared to stand in the presence of such perfection.

In terms of their aura, I will start by describing the energies that flow in and out of them. One of the most dominant qualities to their aura is an up-rush of energy that starts from below them and flows around them and dovetails gracefully above their heads. This flow can give the impression of wings and undoubtedly is a reason for the traditional depiction of angels having wings. Of course they can move through the air very easily, which is another reason for the belief that they must have wings. On rare occasions they can appear with wings, for our benefit.

This upward rush appears when they are near the earth and performing their angelic ministry. It is a blessing from God, which gives them the spiritual earth power to do their work. It's an amazing sight to see and takes on different colors depending on the work they do. A surge of vitality is associated with this power, showing the tremendous currents of divine power they are capable of harnessing.

There is also an upward surge of white light moving from the head area, depicting the elevated flows of divine mind they express. From the body itself, from the shoulders down, radiations of golden light extend in all directions beyond their auric shell, which indicates their power and command over their form. As with any body of expression, we learn to harness and develop control over the form we inhabit. These radiations indicate complete mastery of their celestial form.

The basic shape of the aura is slightly oval and extends beyond arm's reach, similar to the aura of a human. The aura has seven well-defined compartments, and it is beautiful to see in it various bands. The magnificent outer aura extends sixty feet or so. Its basic color is white, but it takes on energies depending on the work they are doing.

They have seven chakras, but three of those chakras are far above the head, so only four are within the body. They correspond to the mental, throat, heart, and solar plexus. They perpetually radiate beautiful flows of light. From the top down, their basic colors are white, blue, pink, and pink. Their foundation color is white.

Most important, the seat of the angelic soul resides in the mind center. In the human kingdom, the seat of the soul is in the heart center. This is where the soul gathers up the experiences of life, but the heart needs the mind to guide it. Yet the angels have reached that place where they are in self-aware divine consciousness, perpetually aware of God. So now their growth happens through that perpetual conscious awareness of the divine.

Above their auric shell, they do have halos! This represents their enlightened status. In the human kingdom we build our enlightenment through all the planes of consciousness leading to God. In the angelic kingdom, you live in a perpetual enlightened status and learn to experience enlightenment in even greater facets. The color ray of the halo is different depending on the primary power ray associated with that angel. And above that is a beautiful white pyramid, which represents their unique angelic status and is a sign of their spiritual accomplishment and divine support.

The great angel in Figure 5.1A is blessing the Higher Self nature of a man who is aware of this celestial being. Such a blessing is not uncommon and demonstrates the extraordinary support we receive from the angels. The artist has done a masterful job of depicting this angelic being. The light-upon-light effect of the angel's aura as well as the balance between form and spiritual power are beautifully captured and emphasizes the holy grandeur of the angels.

CHAPTER 6

THE GREAT ARCHANGELS

WHEN I WAS seventeen years old, I was in New York City about to go to college at Columbia to study journalism. After an initial delay, I was very much looking forward to beginning, when I received word that my mother had become ill and needed my help. I returned to Los Angeles but had hopes of returning to New York to continue my studies. Yet somehow I knew this was not going to happen. Back home, I had taken an office job to help with the bills, but I was at a standstill as to what to do with my life. My mother was grateful that I was there and I was happy to help, but I had become despondent. It was a spiritually quiet time. At this point, I was trying to live a "normal life" and not pursue metaphysics. I was seeing auras and having other experiences, but the intense spiritual work that was to come had not yet started.

One afternoon, I was in my living room reading a book and feeling sad. I knew I had gifts, but I was feeling rather lost as to what to do with them. Suddenly I had a visitation with a celestial being I had never seen before from the other side. I had been honored with many angelic visitations, but this was very different. As magnificent as the angels are, this was a being of a completely different order. He was absolutely magnificent. He was extremely tall, had golden robes, and wore a gold cross.[1] His aura was dazzling. It extended well beyond the walls of the room and had dominant gold and white light. The vibration made me feel like I had been taken to heaven right then and there. I was almost frightened, although I knew it was a great privilege to have such a high spiritual being come so close.

He had a strong face—but not stern—radiant hair, and strikingly colorful eyes. He was the picture of wisdom and strength, not young- or old-looking, but timeless. For a few moments, I sat there stunned, just trying to take this all in and understand what was happening.

He then smiled and communicated to me mentally, "I'm happy we're here together. I'm Archangel Michael."

I had no idea what to say and blurted out, "Ohhh! I'm so glad you're here."

I was then drawn to his extraordinary heart chakra. It was unbelievably brilliant. He started projecting a great deal of light from his heart chakra to mine. I went into spiritual ecstasy. Any feeling of despondency or sadness was completely gone. I felt a tremendous upliftment and sense of purpose. A few moments later, he left as mysteriously as he had appeared.

I was speechless. Words cannot describe the majesty of what happened and what it's like to be in the presence of a Holy One such as this. I was not really aware of the archangels up to that point, other than what the Greek Orthodox Church taught about them. He did not present himself as traditionally depicted—with wings, armor, and a sword—but

---

[1] I have often seen Holy Ones wearing crosses, but this is not meant as a religious symbol. It is a high esoteric symbol used in the inner worlds.

there was no question that I was dealing with one of the primal forces of life. The mark of God was so strong with him, it made me truly realize that there were not only angels but a definite spiritual hierarchy beyond my wildest imaginings. It was my job to get in alignment with these divine ones.

The experience was, up to that point, the greatest moment in my life. And even to this day, when I have the privilege to work with Archangel Michael, it remains awe-inspiring. I did not know what this experience meant, but now I felt a strong sense of purpose and a greater appreciation of my gifts. I realized more clearly that there were bigger things in life going on than my own personal concerns.

This experience started a sequence of visitations with other archangels and holy beings of unimaginable beauty and splendor. In the coming days, I was to begin a most beautiful phase of my life, training with these Holy Ones, and especially Archangel Michael. Ironically, I was to face many personal challenges during this time, but even when it appeared that things were dark, the spiritual hierarchy was always there, as it is to this very day.

The celestial beings of the archangelic kingdom are tremendous beings of Divine Light. Not to be confused with the rank of choir angels who bear the same name, the archangels are in a kingdom all their own. They have been on the divine path for eons and have auras that are vast and encompassing. God has awarded whole segments of the heaven worlds to these celestial beings to guide over. They have a tremendous job to do.

The word *archangel* comes from the Greek *arkhangelos*, meaning "chief, or first, angel." Even though archangels play prominently in Christian faith, the term itself is used only twice in the New Testament. Yet the concept of divine support of this stature is common to many spiritual traditions. *Dhyani Chohan*, or "Lords of Light," is a Sanskrit term the Theosophists used for divine beings of the archangelic order, who supervise the activities of creation. The Indian term *deva-raja*, or "king of the gods," has been used in reference to the archangels. The Kabbalists have dedicated an entire dimension of the sephirothic Tree of Life called *Briah* to the archangelic world of creations. In Zoroastrian tradition, the first of Ahura Mazda's creative acts was to emanate six divine beings called the Amesha Spenta, or "Bountiful Immortals," which came to be personified as archangels, each of which is responsible for an aspect of creation they helped to manifest.

Like the angels, the archangels are full of the divine presence and maintain a direct awareness of God, regardless of the spiritual plane they are on. Yet they possess far greater powers and deeper awareness of God than do the angels. This gives them the ability to work on a *collective* level, which is why they are leaders in the spiritual realms.

Because of their developed status, they have begun a new phase of spiritual unfoldment through the Twelve Kingdoms of Nature. This new phase is the beginning of *omniscience*. The word means "having total knowledge." In spiritual terms, omniscience is a state of awareness in which you have the ability to put your attention on the collective whole, yet at the same time zoom in and pay attention to the smallest detail. Omniscience is a term we use for God's ability to be aware of everything as a whole, yet give attention to each aspect of creation. Of course the archangels do not have this same breadth of omniscience. Yet in their own sphere of activity, they are building this state of awareness, and this is what makes them so spectacular.

With the archangels we have names. Angelic beings do not give their names even though they want you to call on them. Yet with the archangels specific names are given. This is because with the archangels, you are not just dealing with spiritual beings, you are also dealing with a spiritual office. It's a little like naming the governor of a state or province. Yes, it's a person, but the person also represents an office. In the same way, when you call on the archangels for help, you are calling on an entire stream of spiritual evolution and hierarchal support. If you do so sincerely and with humility, you tap that energy flow and receive the benefits. And although you may think the archangels are so far above that you cannot relate to them, the archangels work with you intimately in their own way, and they want you to work with them.

This brings up an important point about invoking celestial beings. There is power in holy names when spoken with reverence. In this book, we offer several meditative prayers to call on the archangels for help. This does not mean that by doing this, you will automatically receive a visitation of that celestial being. What it does mean is that you will invoke the office and divine power associated with that archangel.

Invoking the help of the archangels is particularly relevant to the process of working with spiritual energy because it is the archangels who are ultimately responsible for making sure the Divine Light is down-rayed to all humanity. They have legions of angels helping them in this task, but the archangels are the custodians of tremendous reservoirs of Divine Light. Without this downpouring of light, humanity could not function and grow.

There are vast numbers of archangelic beings of varying degrees of development. Yet there are twelve primary archangels who are the leaders for humanity. These twelve hold a special place in the divine plan. Many other archangels have been named as well. Some of these names are accurate, while others are not. Sometimes, several names are given for what appears to be the same archangel. Unfortunately, traditional descriptions and duties of these archangels are at times confusing and contradictory in character and quality. I will try to reconcile differing beliefs, but my approach is to present the archangels as I have experienced and worked with them over many years.

Out of these twelve, four archangels hold a special place in the spiritual hierarchy, and we will emphasize these four archangels. These are the four who are best known, and for good reason. They want us to call on them and are an essential part of our work with the spiritual hierarchy. They are the following:

Archangel Michael
Archangel Gabriel
Archangel Raphael
Archangel Uriel

In addition to these famous four, there are eight other archangels who are leaders among the archangels and angels as well. They work in more specific areas of the divine plan and take their lead from the celestial four. We will look at them more carefully in chapter 7. These eight archangels are the following:

Archangel Zadkiel
Archangel Samuel
Archangel Sariel
Archangel Lucifer (celestial)
Archangel Haniel
Archangel Raziel
Archangel Jophiel
Archangel Sandalphon

These twelve archangels work beautifully together in tireless service to God. I don't know where we would be without them. They are the embodiment of compassion and intelligence. They possess every positive attribute you can name and more. They are the forerunners who keep creation going. They have earned the right to be where they are through long effort and tireless service. It's an evolutionary climb on every level. We never stop growing.

ARCHANGEL MICHAEL

Archangel Michael is the senior archangel. In almost all traditions, he is ranked as the highest of the archangels. He is mentioned by name in both the Tanakh (Old Testament) and the New Testament. He is considered the guardian angel over the Hebrew nation. In Revelation, it is Archangel Michael and his angelic army who successfully battle the satanic forces.

The name Michael is Hebrew for "who is as God." The Hebrew name is Chaldean in origin. And here I must interject a note regarding the names of the archangels, as there is some confusion in this area. Many of the names we use for the archangels are derived from Hebrew words that were established during the Second Temple period in Israel after the Babylonian exile. Although the foundation of angelic knowledge was part of the Jewish religions from the days of Abraham, there was an exchange of ideas with Chaldean mystics during the exile period. These Chaldean mystics were connected to the Zoroastrian mystical tradition, and angelic beings were prominent in their esoteric schools. Many of the Hebrew names for divine beings were influenced by the Chaldeans. We see this influence in the books of Ezekiel and Daniel, in the latter of which Archangel Michael is mentioned by name. This is also part of the reason why there was an explosion of pseudepigraphal writings during that time that elaborated on the angelic order.

Sometimes, as we shall see with some of the other archangelic names, however, there were inconsistencies in the translation and adaptation of these words into Hebrew. Some of these inconsistencies have been perpetuated to maintain the tradition yet are not entirely accurate in reflecting the duties and jobs of these celestial ones. What's more, these names are respectful titles but are ultimately of human creation. The archangels have blessed these names so that we can call them by those titles, but within their own realm they have other esoteric names that they do not share with us.

Archangel Michael works under the *dynamic* aspects of God. He is the senior archangel in the sense that the other archangels look up to him. He is a leader among the archangels. He inspires human leaders in all areas of life, including politics, religion, and education. He works with Archangel Raphael in the business, scientific, and financial arenas. He assists Archangel Gabriel in helping to inspire leaders in the medical and artistic worlds. He works with Archangel Uriel in helping to inspire parents of families. On a personal level, he's a tremendous power for purification, protection, and wisdom. He helps to build self-confidence and self-esteem. He's the embodiment of divine will and illumination.

Archangel Michael is the archangel of protection. He works with the military and is the archangel who deals with the lower negative energies and forces. He goes to spiritual battle to cut loose negative influences. This is perhaps why he is traditionally depicted with sword and armor, even though that is not his real appearance. He's also the senior metaphysical teaching archangel and is responsible for directing the various esoteric schools in the world. Many key lessons I have received over the years have come from Archangel Michael.

Legions of wonderful spiritual beings are under Archangel Michael. These include members of all seven levels of angels. There are angels of protection who protect your aura and keep your spiritual connections intact. They help protect you from malefic forces and other people's negative emanations. Spiritual bodyguards are also under Archangel Michael. These are divine beings who alert you to dangers that may be coming up and help protect you from accidents and other mishaps. They are especially with you when you travel.

Angels of purification work under Archangel Michael. Their job is to dissolve black and gray atoms, negative energies, and blocks in our auras. The great angels of wisdom light, who bring forth all the dynamic attributes of the golden light, are under Archangel Michael, as well as the angels of energy. Other divine beings who work under Archangel Michael include angels of faith, angels of dynamic power, angels of patience, angels of tolerance, angels of divine power, and angels of understanding.

MEDITATIVE PRAYER TO WORK WITH ARCHANGEL MICHAEL

*Heavenly Father/Holy Mother God, I ask for a blessing from
Archangel Michael. I ask to receive his ray of inner strength
and dynamic power so that I may be illumined by
God's light of wisdom and understanding.*

ARCHANGEL GABRIEL

One of the first times I encountered Archangel Gabriel in his full splendor, I was in the desert in Southern California near a town called

Twentynine Palms. I was with my best friend, Kathy. My friend Leah had given me the keys to her desert home to stay for a week. It was a desolate place, but I was looking forward to a time of rest, prayer work, and meditation. Kathy was seriously ill at the time and we were planning to do some concentrated healing work for her.

On our way there, my car had broken down in a particularly remote part of the desert, and we were stranded in the middle of nowhere. It was a hot day and no one was around. This was before cell phones, so I didn't know what I was going to do, as there was no help in sight. After sitting by the roadside for a while, I looked up at the sky and saw this magnificent presence. There was so much light that I could not see a discernible form at first. The being was enormous and had an aura that extended a hundred feet, with prominent blue and white energies. I picked up that this was the great Archangel Gabriel. I had worked with Gabriel before but had never seen him in such full power. He did not stay long or communicate, but his very presence told me things were going to be okay. In my mind's eye, I saw that he was overshadowing a man driving a truck, and before long a rather bewildered man did drive by in a truck and helped us. He told us that he had somehow gotten lost but then saw us stranded on the road. He was an able mechanic and fixed the problem with our car.

That very night, we had settled in the desert home and were doing a meditation for Kathy's health. She had been diagnosed with a brain tumor and the prognosis was not good. After a while in meditation, to my amazement, the room lit up with golden light and Archangel Gabriel appeared again. This time, he came right into the room and stayed a while, communicating many ideas of healing. You may ask how an archangel so expansive could fit in a room in a house. It must be said that celestial beings can adapt their form according to the situation. His previous visitation was in part to show his full power and strength. But now, so we could withstand his presence, he came in this more approachable form. Of course even in this form, he was very tall and impressive.

With Archangel Gabriel so close, I could see his aura in more detail. There was a rush of gold light radiating from the heart center and an electrifying pink coming from the solar plexus center. Above his head was a magnificent crown of golden light. What was perhaps even just as amazing was that Kathy actually saw him as well! She didn't see his aura but saw his celestial form. She asked me who this being was, and I told her it was Archangel Gabriel. We were both awestruck. Fortunately she did feel more secure with herself. Needless to say, my friend was greatly helped and I was elated for days after this visitation. For a while things looked more hopeful, but in the end, she did succumb to the cancer and died at age forty. She related that this experience was immensely helpful in dealing with her situation.

Archangel Gabriel works under both the dynamic and magnetic aspects of God.

His name is Hebrew for "God is my strength." Gabriel appears in both the Tanakh, in the book of Daniel bringing prophetic visions, and the New Testament, where he is famous as the announcer of the births of John the Baptist and Jesus of Nazareth. According to Islamic tradition, he was the archangel who dictated the Qur'an to Muhammad.

Archangel Gabriel has a diverse range of spiritual duties. One of his most essential roles is as *the healer archangel*. I know that that title is generally designated to Archangel Raphael, and of course all the archangels heal, but the master healer is Gabriel. As mentioned, perhaps there were some discrepancies in the adaption of the names from the Chaldean to the Hebrew, which may account for differing interpretations. Yet I can tell you from personal experience that the archangel who is responsible for the healing energies is Archangel Gabriel. If you're sick and need help, call on Archangel Gabriel. You feel a lot of compassion with Archangel Gabriel. There is also levity and an adventurous quality with Gabriel. He's upbeat and loves people and interacting with humanity, and of course he loves to heal.

In addition to his healing skills, Archangel Gabriel is the Master Artist. The creative energy rays are under his direction. This means that Archangel Gabriel and his legion of spiritual beings inspire painters, sculptors, musicians, writers, and other artists in their craft. There is tremendous artistic activity in the spiritual worlds. Painting, drama, and even movies (in a little different form than we have here) all exist in the spirit worlds. The angels and archangels have wonderful singing voices, and there are angelic choirs of extraordinary beauty and power. Art is an expression of creativity, which is the wellspring of life itself. It brings us into God's beauty, rhythm, and harmony. Art inspires and uplifts us. It also educates us to the mysteries of life. Mystery exists at every level of life. And of course art is entertaining and fun! It brings amusement and joy. This creative nature can come out in other ways, such as helping people build their spiritual character. I remember one time Archangel Gabriel taught me that I was too impatient and gave me some advice to be more patient. This creative power is also essential for creating new inventions that will benefit humanity.

Along with healing and creativity, Archangel Gabriel is the prosperity archangel. He helps to show humanity that they are part of the infinite wealth of God. He can bring you up out of poverty consciousness and possessiveness and embody the divine attributes of wealth in all of its expression: material wealth, wealth of ideas, friendship, health, vitality, and so on. He also helps to get you up out of greed and the selfish attributes that restrict the God flow of abundance in which all on earth are meant to partake. In terms of management of wealth, Gabriel works a great deal with Archangel Raphael.

Under Archangel Gabriel is an army of celestial beings working with him. These are the magnificent healing angels. These angels help to cure disease and distress in all forms. If the situation is beyond cure, they help to prepare the soul to make its transition to the other side. There are also healing angels known as body chemists who have specific skills in helping with alleviating physical distress. They work with the angels of healing and are adept at working the physical form. I have seen these body chemists overshadow surgeons during surgery to make sure they do a good job.

Under Archangel Gabriel are prosperity angels. They help cut you loose from poverty consciousness and limitations in your thinking and steer you toward ways of increasing your prosperity. Angels of inspiration, spiritual artists, and musicians all fall under Gabriel's direction. Other angelic help includes angels of balance and harmony, angels of spiritual growth, and angels of determination.

MEDITATIVE PRAYER TO WORK WITH ARCHANGEL GABRIEL

Heavenly Father/Holy Mother God, I ask for a blessing from Archangel Gabriel. I ask to receive his power ray of healing and new life force so that I may be refreshed by the bounty and creative power of God.

ARCHANGEL RAPHAEL

My first experience with Archangel Raphael was many years ago. At the time, I was living at home and there were a lot of people in the house, so it was difficult to find a quiet moment. There were times that I would go into the closet to meditate. One night I was in my room getting ready to go to sleep and Archangel Raphael appeared unexpectedly. The room lit up in white light. He looked at me intently and wanted me to know that despite the chaos around me, I was doing good work spiritually. He was serious, but I found out that he had a good sense of humor. He used his wit to make me feel at ease. He was very handsome and had a younger-looking face. His aura was extraordinary and sparkled with lightning flashes of power. There was a striking, deep, royal blue energy in his aura, indicating his divine loyalty and devotion to God. As I have found out through the years, he is extremely knowledgeable on a variety of topics. He was very sincere and approachable, if that is the right word. There was something personal about him that made me feel a friendship with him. He is eloquent and has an embracing way of saying things.

The name Raphael comes from a Hebrew word that means "God who heals." Raphael is mentioned only once in the Bible, in the apocryphal book of Tobit, although he appears in other ancient writings such as the Book of Enoch. He is traditionally depicted as the healing archangel because of the name given to him. As mentioned in the discussion of the other archangels, however, the Hebrews adopted many of these names from the Chaldeans, and sometimes these names do not fully reflect the actual duties of the archangels. In the case of Archangel Raphael, certainly he has the power to heal, but the primary duty he embodies is divine intelligence.

Archangel Raphael has his own splendor. He has a lot to do with having a keen perception and awareness of things. Like Archangel Michael, he is very dynamic. He's a no-nonsense archangel. Archangel Raphael has a big job to do—to bring in divine intelligence and perception to keep humanity going in the right direction. In other words, it is Archangel Raphael and his legion of angels who quicken the awareness of humanity so that we may become more cognizant of life in all its facets. Without his help, we would remain asleep spiritually and would not be able to respond to the divine impulse very well. He assists in the flow of business and commerce, as well as banking and finance, and he works to inspire scientist and inventors. He's also the archangel connected to education in general and is the communications expert.

Under Archangel Raphael are many wonderful spiritual beings. These include the angels of rightful direction and divine guidance. Along with the angels of intelligence, they help you make decisions, be more perceptive, and have a clear vision of things. If you have a question or are in a quandary, you can call on Archangel Raphael and these wonderful angels for help. The angels of business, such as described in chapter 1, are also under Raphael. Archangel Raphael, along with other Holy Ones, also works strongly in the scientific arenas. The modern scientist may think that science is apart from spirituality, but this is the furthest thing from the truth. There is not one great idea or invention that has benefited humanity that was not inspired from the divine. And the divine beings under Archangel Raphael have exerted a great influence in this area.

Along with Archangel Gabriel, Raphael has been working to inspire those in the financial world to help manage the wealth of the world. This means that bankers and investment brokers are all receiving support from Archangel Raphael and his angelic legions. As humanity awakens even more to the divine potential of money, the world's wealth will flow in a much more diverse and equitable way.

MEDITATIVE PRAYER TO WORK WITH ARCHANGEL RAPHAEL

Heavenly Father/Holy Mother God, I ask for a blessing from Archangel Raphael. I ask to receive his power ray of intelligence, that I may be quickened by the radiance of God's eternal mind.

ARCHANGEL URIEL

I first encountered Archangel Uriel while I was in meditation. This was during the same period when the other archangels were making themselves known. What was first so striking about Archangel Uriel was her magnetic presence. The archangels I had encountered up to that point were all very dynamic and masculine-looking. Archangel Uriel was powerful, yet feminine and strikingly beautiful. She had the features of an angelic woman.

When she appeared, I did not know who it was at first, but she soon announced herself as Archangel Uriel. I was a little overwhelmed by her power, but she radiated an aqua blue light, which had a wonderful, soothing effect, to make contact with me. Her aura had a lot of pink in it, indicating the loving power she had at her command.

Archangel Uriel is very beautiful and her beauty has a radiant, uplifting quality. She looked to be in the fullness of life, not old or young, and very exuberant. She had shimmering, radiant hair that looked full of light; dazzling eyes; and a clear, soft, round face. She was wearing powder blue robes and had a happy demeanor, even though she could be serious when she needed to be. In this visitation, she did not say much but simply wanted me to get to know her and tune in to her vibration. Later, she would return and teach me a great deal about love and about being one with God. She also taught me to be brave and to accept my imperfections.

The name Uriel is from the Hebrew word that means "fire of God." Even though it is a masculine name, Uriel is most definitely a magnetic archangel. It must be remembered that in the ancient days, the masculine was used not only in the male sense but also as a generic term, as in the word *mankind*. Uriel does not appear by name in the Bible but figures prominently in noncanonical lore, and she is generally recognized as one of the four most prominent of all the archangels.

Archangel Uriel is under the *magnetic* flows of God the celestial Holy Mother. It must be remembered that while the soul is androgynous, during the cycle of manifested life, there is always an inherent polarity of dynamic and magnetic. It's part of what life's about. On earth, we recognize that polarity as male/female. In the heaven worlds, this polarity continues in more beautiful and ethereal ways. So the Holy Ones throughout all kingdoms express this dynamic/magnetic polarity.

Archangel Uriel brings in Divine Love and compassion. She is magnificent. There is a radiance about her that is indescribable. She is the embodiment of love. Naturally, she has the responsibility of keeping our love flow going and opening hearts that have been hardened. She works with God the Holy Mother to bring compassion to earth. She is the great teacher of true love. She's extraordinarily beautiful and helps to bring out the beauty in all of us. She helps us to recognize who we really are as spiritual beings and the sacredness of our own souls.

Archangel Uriel directs many wonderful divine beings in her ministry. The angels of love, peace, and compassion are all under Archangel Uriel. There is a beautiful group of angelic workers under Uriel called Sisters in Light. These divine beings work with the children of the world, from birth to around ten years old. They are an integral part of a child's development. The Sisters in Light help all children during their early formative years, especially children who are going through illnesses or accidents. They help abused children and orphans too. They also attend to the needs of tiny tots who have gone over to the astral worlds via abortion or disease.

MEDITATIVE PRAYER TO WORK WITH ARCHANGEL URIEL

Heavenly Father/Holy Mother God, I ask for a blessing from Archangel Uriel. I ask to receive her power ray of love and peace, that I may be enfolded in the magnetic glory of God.

ILLUSTRATION OF AN ARCHANGEL

In Figure 6.1A, I have chosen Michael as an example of an archangel in its advanced state of development. The archangel evolution is a continu-

FIGURE 6.1A. *Archangel Michael*
(See inside front cover for full-color figure 6.1.)

ation from the angelic realm, so there are similarities in auric design to the angels, but on a grander scale and much more pronounced. One major difference is that the archangels do not have the up-rush of energy that angels do when working with humanity, because it is not needed.

The body of the archangel is absolutely magnificent. They can easily be eighteen feet tall, yet they can appear almost human-size if they wish to present themselves that way. There is an auric shell that is completely full of gold light, as there are no compartments as with the angels. The out-rush of energy from the body is a white-silver light and illustrates the incredible power of the form itself. There is also the up-rush of light from the mental area, indicating the complete connection with the divine mind. There are four chakras within the body concurrent to the mental, throat, heart, and solar plexus areas. In the case of Archangel Michael, there is a beautiful pink energy within these centers, indicating that, as dynamic as Archangel Michael is, love is his motivating impulse. Above Archangel Michael's head is a penetrating silver star indicating his level of mastery. Archangel Michael is often seen with golden-blue robes, as depicted here.

Archangels have an outer aura that can expand to one hundred feet. It's incredible to see. Archangel Michael's outer aura is a radiant gold. Above the head of advanced archangels is a configuration of seven flamelike diamond energies, representing areas of responsibilities and dominion. These archangels have legions of holy beings working under them. There is also the halo above the auric shell, indicating the conscious connection to God.

A most striking feature of the archangelic aura is the connection to their Higher Self. The higher nature of the archangels is where their collective power resides. There are five large sphere chakras above the head of Archangel Michael, and they radiate incredible light rays. This incredibly developed Higher Self also represents inner awareness of God's omnipotence. From these points, archangels can send light to more than one place at a time. These higher points also act as receiving stations for blessings from realms of life even beyond the archangels. We all have a higher nature, but with the archangels one has full *conscious* control of the higher points and can send collective energy from these points. They can send light from the lower chakras, but they generally do so when working one-on-one with someone. In their leadership work, they generally send light from these higher points. In this illustration, the higher nature of the archangel is depicted a little smaller than it actually is so that the grandeur of the figure can be more clearly seen. In actuality, the higher nature of Archangel Michael is higher up and considerably larger.

With the archangels you also get the sense that, even when they choose to reveal themselves to you, you are still not seeing the full picture. There are colors in the spiritual realms that we simply cannot perceive while on earth. They also possess celestial bodies of even greater splendor than depicted here. With all the Holy Ones, there is always a mystery about them, as we in the human kingdom can understand them only to a certain degree. What perhaps always keeps the harmony flowing is the great love they share and the loving exchanges that go on as we express our love to them too.

WORKING WITH THE ARCHANGELS

How do they do it? How do the archangels work with so many people and still give individual attention? Once again, these are incredible beings of light capable of more than we can understand. They possess omniscience as earlier described. The other thing to remember is they do not work alone. The archangels look up to celestial beings even more developed than themselves for guidance and assistance. As we have seen, the archangels have amazing abilities to work on a collective level. They have extraordinary power, but in general they work mainly through their angelic legions and will come in for specific things as the need arises. There are also other unnamed archangels who work with them. So when you speak of archangels, you truly are referring to whole segments of the celestial realms.

A question often asked regarding the archangels is: Can they be in more than one place at a time? With so many people to tend to, not to mention the celestial beings under their command, how could they have time to do all that they do? In truth, an archangel is like you and me in that there is an indwelling soul that is the essence of that archangel. This soul is individualized, so an archangel can be in only one place at a time. Because of their developed state of consciousness, however, they are able to project living forms to many places at the same time and endow those forms with their powers and intelligence. So in this sense, they can be in more than one place at a time. Yet even here they do not work alone. As the archangels we are speaking of are spiritual offices, there are many unnamed regional archangels working in harmony with the archangelic leaders.

They can project power and light to more than one place at a time and can multitask in incredible ways. In fact, the organization of an archangelic office is quite complex. What we need to do in starting our relationship with the archangels is to start including them in our prayers and meditations, as we open up to a wonderful world of divine support.

CHAPTER 7

THE CELESTIAL EIGHT
ARCHANGELS

IN ADDITION TO the celestial four archangels, the eight other archangelic leaders work in specialized areas of life. They take their
lead from the celestial four yet are very much leaders in their
own right. Together they comprise the twelve archangels guiding humanity. There are many other archangels in addition to these
twelve, some known and many unknown. The Jewish Encyclopedia[1]
indicates that more than a thousand angels and archangels are mentioned by name in various religious and mystical Jewish sources. Many
of these names represent real divine beings but not ones we regularly
interact with.

In working with the archangels, I strongly recommend *first* becoming
familiar with the famous four explored in chapters 6 and 14. Once you
have gotten in the vibration of these magnificent beings and are familiar
with how to work with them, then I encourage you to follow through
with these eight glorious archangels in your meditations.

To understand how to work with these other eight archangels, I must

---

[1] JewishEncyclopedia.com.

introduce another facet of the spiritual life. The archangels, and all Holy Ones, are part of a hierarchy of Divine Light. Each of these celestial beings embodies a Divine Light ray, and this is what gives them their power. Yet in addition to the Divine Light, there are other holy powers that are part of the creative process of life. All twelve archangels work with these other divine powers, yet the administration of these other powers is delegated to these eight archangels. So the emphasis will be on the mystical powers they embody.

ARCHANGEL ZADKIEL

Zadkiel means "righteousness of God." He is a magnificent archangel with many mystical duties. He is a commanding presence, and the powder blue ray is strong in his aura. His name fits him well, as Archangel Zadkiel is the archangel of karma. Karma is the law of cause and effect. This means that Zadkiel is the chief administrator to help souls navigate through their karmic actions—both good and bad. Working with him is a magnificent team of other archangels known as the Lords of Karma. The Lords of Karma manage the Book of Life for humanity. Everything we do on this earth is recorded in this celestial book. When you cross over to the other side through the door we call death, you meet the Lords of Karma, where they review your life by opening this celestial book to your page.

Next to the famous four archangels, I have probably worked with Zadkiel the most. When I take on a new student, the Holy Ones often show me a portion of the karmic chart related to this person. In this way, I can be more helpful in guiding the person on their spiritual path and helping them work out their karmic debts and credits. This is all under the guiding hand of Archangel Zadkiel. Under Zadkiel are legions of angels of karma who help people work through their karma challenges as well as manage their karmic credits. If you feel you are going through heavy karmic challenges, or know you have done something that may have generated karma, these angels can be of great help.

Archangel Zadkiel deals with divine justice and is the one to call on when dealing with legal issues. His angelic administrators work in every courtroom in the world to help inspire judges, lawyers, and juries to make the right decisions in every case that is before a court. Zadkiel works a great deal with Archangel Michael and others in this important work.

The Holy Ones teach us that there is always justice, even in what too often appears to be an unjust world. Free will must play out, and the divine does not want to interfere in that freedom for the most part. Eventually, the law of karma will balance all our actions out. So even when people do not live up to their potential or do not always do what is right, divine justice eventually prevails. There are spiritual laws, just as there are physical laws. If we break natural physical laws, we suffer. In the same way, when we break spiritual laws, we suffer as well until we get on the right track.

To help in the management of karma and divine law, Archangel Zadkiel works with a special power ray known as the Primordial Light (see chapter 15). All the archangels work with the Primordial Light, but Zadkiel works with this ray as it pertains to divine law. The Primordial Light is the first ray to emanate from God Absolute. Within this power are all the inherent attributes of the spiritual and natural laws of life. Creation has order. And this order can be maintained only by spiritual laws. The entire spiritual hierarchy embodies and lives by these laws. We do too and, through the divine, we are learning how to work in better harmony with these holy principles.

MEDITATIVE PRAYER TO WORK WITH ARCHANGEL ZADKIEL

Heavenly Father/Holy Mother God, I ask to receive the Primordial Light
of God Absolute under the direction of Archangel Zadkiel and the
angels of the Primordial Light. May this power bless all levels of
my consciousness to help me work in better harmony with the
law of cause and effect. I ask that this energy help to
balance my karma and inspire me to live my
life in better harmony with Divine Law.

ARCHANGEL SAMUEL

Samuel is a very handsome and forceful archangel. He has a pronounced purple in his aura. While he is a dynamic archangel, he has a wonderful balance of dynamic and magnetic energies at his command.

Not to be confused with the fallen Archangel Samiel, Archangel Samuel is responsible for handling the process of reincarnation. I was very fortunate to meet this archangel early on while I was being taught how karma and reincarnation work. Reincarnation is the process through which a soul returns to physical form in a new physical body to continue in its spiritual journey. Metaphysically speaking, earth is a schoolhouse. Our soul comes to learn the many lessons of life. Each lifetime is like a grade in school. The soul reincarnates on earth to learn more life lessons and to correct mistakes from past lives. It's a miraculous process each of us has gone through many times, although we may not remember these past lives.

The process of preparing the soul for reincarnation is an intricate one. It involves many stages, and Archangel Samuel and his many angels are responsible for making sure this process goes smoothly. He works strongly with Archangel Uriel and the Sisters in Light to help in the spiritual preparation for new incarnating souls. This means, along with Uriel, he's strongly involved in the conception process and pregnancy period. As there is so much to reincarnation, many other spiritual beings get involved. For example, Archangel Raphael and his angels help in the transition process when souls are moving from the earth plane to the other side. Archangel Samuel works closely with Zadkiel, as karma and reincarnation are intimately linked. Karma is the law and reincarnation is the means through which that law is administered.

Archangel Samuel works a great deal with the royal blue light of truth. If you are seeking honesty and truthfulness, Archangel Samuel and his angels can be of great assistance. There may be a situation when you need to see the truth in something that is happening, or maybe you are half deceiving yourself for whatever reason. In either case, the royal blue light under Samuel is most helpful.

MEDITATIVE PRAYER TO WORK WITH ARCHANGEL SAMUEL

Heavenly Father/Holy Mother God, down-ray to me under the direction of Archangel Samuel the royal blue ray of truth. May this light bless all levels of my consciousness so that I live my life in an honest way to see the truth in people and situations around me.

ARCHANGEL SARIEL

Archangel Sariel is a dynamic archangel. He is incredibly intelligent, and in this way he shares similar traits with Raphael. His primary energy is emerald green, which brings in a balance of the dynamic and magnetic energies.

Archangel Sariel works a lot in the world of psychology. He's very involved with maintaining mental and emotional stability. He and his angels help to guide and direct psychologists and psychiatrists, as well as those in other disciplines that involve psychological techniques.

Sariel works with a mystical power known as the *spirit light*. This power is part of the hierarchy of light but is in its own category. This spirit light brings in a specific attribute—divine desire. Metaphysics has a specific definition of desire. It is defined as "the ever-expanding creative activity of God." Spiritually speaking, desire is the natural urge to grow and develop yourself. It is the creative spark in you. This is distinguished from false desires or appetites, which are a form of sense gratification. Desire and appetite are two completely different things.

As you have the Divine Light, you also have the spirit light in you to a certain degree. It's what fans the flame to turn your desire for the spiritual path into a burning desire where nothing can stop you from pursuing your spiritual goals. The biblical teaching sums up very well the essence of this power: "Where your treasure is, there will your heart be also."

Your desires are a reflection of how effectively you are using the spirit light. This spirit light can be used for the purpose it was intended: to fuel your creativity and spiritual evolution. Yet like any spiritual energy, once in your consciousness, it can be directed along other less productive lines of endeavor.

Be careful when using spirit light, as this power is impartial. It is a fuel that feeds the higher, nobler part of you, but it can also unintentionally feed the lower desires. If you are filled with appetites and lusts, the spirit light can have the effect of unintentionally increasing such lower desires. Of course, if this were to happen, your ability to receive this power would lessen as a safeguard against misuse. Still, work with this power carefully. Make sure you are in a steady place in your consciousness before doing this exercise. If you feel out of alignment, first work with the Divine Light ray meditations offered in chapter 15 to clear out old energies and build up the aura, then later work with the spirit light.

Take time to reflect on the things that matter most to you. What are the things that you take deepest in your heart? A useful tool in helping to clear out any unintentional misuse of this energy is to first place the desires of your heart on the divine altar. Put it all in God's hands and ask the divine to help you separate the false desires from the true desires. Archangel Sariel does a loving, magnificent job of helping you to navigate through this glorious power. He helps to transmute the lower desires and fan the flames of celestial desire. He is excellent to call on when you are in the process of overcoming addictions, along with Archangel Michael and Archangel Gabriel.

MEDITATIVE PRAYER TO WORK WITH ARCHANGEL SARIEL

Heavenly Father/Holy Mother God, I ask to receive according to the divine law and love the magnificent spirit light under Archangel Sariel and the angels of this holy power. I ask that it awaken me to my truest desire of the heart and to increase my spiritual desire to reach my highest good. I ask to be released from the false desires and appetites of the lower nature.

THE CELESTIAL ARCHANGEL LUCIFER

There is much to say about this archangel. He is not to be confused with the fallen Lucifer, who became Satan, which we will explore in chapter 11. The celestial Archangel Lucifer is a powerful, dynamic archangel and one of the most developed among all of the eight archangels. The golden ray of wisdom is strong in his aura.

The celestial Archangel Lucifer is very important in the maintenance of the physical form. He works closely with Archangel Gabriel and members of the eleventh sacred kingdom in this area. He administers a potent spiritual power known as *spirit-substance*. Spirit-substance is the fabric of life. It is the cosmic material out of which everything in the universe is made. Spirit-substance is the building block of every atom, every physical particle in the universe. This material has been called by many names, including *akasha* and *prana*—although prana is a particular form of spirit-substance received through the air we breathe. Many holy beings are involved with this divine material, yet among the archangels, the celestial Archangel Lucifer is particularly important in this area.

As explored in my book *The Healing Power of Your Aura*, spirit-substance is an essential component in healing, as this divine material helps to maintain the integrity of the atomic structure of the body. This material is especially important when healing and repairing the body. Celestial Lucifer helps to make sure you receive a renewing flow of spirit-substance in your body to maintain health and well-being.

In addition, the celestial Archangel Lucifer works with this spirit-substance to help rarefy the physical form. The importance of this cannot be overestimated. Right now, as you are evolving, your physical body is changing. It is become spiritually stronger and more resilient. Remember that all the spiritual power you build in your aura is ultimately expressed through your physical form. There must be mind/body/soul harmony. The celestial Archangel Lucifer helps to uplift the physical form so it can contain and express more spiritual power.

In calling on this archangel, I urge you to call him "the celestial Archangel Lucifer," so as not to be confused with the fallen archangel. If you feel uncomfortable using the word *Lucifer*, even in its celestial context, you can ask for this power under Archangel Gabriel. This spiritual essence cannot be down-rayed on its own. It needs the Divine Light to work with it, in order to direct this power where it needs to go.

**MEDITATIVE PRAYER TO WORK
WITH THE CELESTIAL ARCHANGEL LUCIFER**

Heavenly Father/Holy Mother God, I ask to receive the divine spirit-substance infused with the white light under the direction of the celestial Archangel Lucifer and Divine Energy angels. I ask this light to infuse me with spirit-substance, helping to rarefy the physical form to contain as much spiritual power as possible. I ask this light and power to raise the vibration of the physical body to its highest level. Inspire me to take better care of my body and to do things that bring mind/body/soul harmony.

ARCHANGEL HANIEL

Haniel is Hebrew for "glory or grace of God." She is a magnetic archangel, beautiful and very energetic. The deep rose-pink ray of spiritual love is very strong in her aura.

Archangel Haniel works closely with what is known as the *cosmic light*. This celestial power is part of the hierarchy of light (see chapter 15). The cosmic light is a special energy of the devas. The various attributes of these powers are often known as the ascension rays. The cosmic light is an evolutionary light and is given when the soul is getting ready to ascend from one spiritual plane of consciousness to the next level up.

We are all in a process of spiritual evolution. Part of what evolution means is that we are all growing through the various spiritual dimensions. While you are in physical form, your soul and consciousness are vibrating at a certain level of consciousness. This level is determined by how much Divine Light you have earned through every good word, thought, act, and deed. As you build up more spiritual power, you are enlightening your aura and growing through the various spiritual dimensions. The cosmic rays help to sustain you through whatever spiritual level you are presently at and give you power when you are ready to cross over to the next spiritual plane. This energy is especially strong during periods of initiations that the Holy Ones usher you through.

This is not a power you can call upon at will, as it is not up to you when the divine feels you are ready for the next step in your spiritual growth. You can, however, work with Archangel Haniel and her angels to help strengthen you in your spiritual ascent and prepare you so that you are more ready for that next step in your spiritual growth. It is interesting to note that Archangel Haniel is particularly busy in our era of humanity, as more people than ever are getting ready for leaps in their spiritual ascent. This is partly what is fueling the spiritual renaissance that is going on.

MEDITATIVE PRAYER TO WORK WITH THE ARCHANGEL HANIEL

Heavenly Father/Holy Mother God, if it be Thy will I ask to receive the white light under Archangel Haniel and the Divine Energy angels. I ask to steady my spiritual ascent and the cosmic light flowing in me. May Thy angels strengthen my current level of spiritual development and help prepare me for my next stage of divine unfoldment.

ARCHANGEL RAZIEL

Raziel means "secret of God," and he is traditionally depicted as an archangel of the spiritual mysteries. There is a bit of irony here, as in my experiences with Archangel Raziel he is a very direct and straightforward archangel. Of course all the archangels are this way, but there is something about Raziel that tells it like it is. One has to be ready for such frankness. In this way he is a little like Archangel Samuel. The pale pearl-luster green is strong in Raziel's aura.

The mystique around Archangel Raziel may have to do with the spiritual power he is assigned to. Raziel has the sacred duty of being the administrator of the Holy Breath of God. All the celestial leaders are involved in the Holy Breath, yet it is Raziel who is intimately involved in administering the divine breath to humanity.

What is the Holy Breath? As we know, the body breathes. When we breathe, we draw in oxygen to be used by the cells of the body through the process of cell respiration. When we exhale, we release carbon dioxide, the waste of this cell respiration. If there were no breath, the body would not be alive.

In the same way, your soul breathes. Your soul is life itself, and this life is active. It is going through a process of *soul* respiration, where it draws in more of the eternal life essence. The Holy Breath brings in this life essence. This breath can appear as white light, but this is only because white light works with it. You take in some of the life essence every time you draw physical breath. You also draw in some of this Holy Breath every time you call on Divine Light. The Holy Breath of God is how we receive God's Divine Light. With every in-breath of God, Divine Light flows to all creation to receive spiritual nourishment, and with every out-breath, negative black and gray atoms are drawn back to God to be reconstituted in the light.

You are part of this Holy Breath every day of your life. As you learn to raise your consciousness, this has a direct connection to the amount of Holy Breath you are receiving. As you keep expanding your light rays, you can take in more light and can take more power of the Holy Breath. You can also call on the Holy Breath directly to amplify the receiving of this divine essence. It refreshes the soul in its spiritual journey.

Calling on this Holy Breath is excellent when you feel soul-weary. If life seems to have gotten the better of you and it's difficult to move forward, call on Archangel Raziel and his angels of Divine Light to grant you this power. I remember that one time, when many things were coming at me at the same time and it felt like it was more than I could handle, I received a wonderful blessing from Archangel Raziel, refreshing my soul with the Holy Breath. My sense of burden lifted and I was reinvigorated.

Before doing this meditative prayer, take a few deep breaths and visualize the pure white light flowing in. As you take each breath, sense the pure white light flowing directly into your lungs and physical heart and dispersing that light from this point into all your physical cells. With each breath, think, "I am breathing in the Holy Breath," sensing the white light coming in and releasing all energies of distress.

MEDITATIVE PRAYER TO WORK WITH THE ARCHANGEL RAZIEL

Heavenly Father/Holy Mother God, I ask to receive under Archangel Raziel and the Divine Energy angels the white light and with that light to down-breathe the Holy Breath of God. I ask to breathe this eternal life force in my soul, body, and mind to refresh me in all levels of my consciousness. I ask to be released of any discouragement or distress and feel in rhythm with the breath of life.

ARCHANGEL JOPHIEL

Jophiel or Iophiel means "beauty of God." She is a magnificent magnetic archangel. Her name is appropriate, as she is a strikingly beautiful archangel. The fuchsia pink ray is very strong with her and there is a won-derful joyful and uplifting quality about her. She has similar qualities to Archangel Uriel, and the two work closely together.

Archangel Jophiel brings in the divine qualities of beauty. We some-times forget that beauty is a divine attribute. We cannot help but admire beauty in all forms. Beauty brings in harmony, desire, motivation, and mystery. As our soul is part of life, we are all inherently beautiful. Yet like all aspects of spiritual growth, we have to develop this beauty in us. We have to learn how to bring it out and let it shine.

In addition to the attributes of beauty, Archangel Jophiel is responsi-ble for the magnificent pearl-luster pink ray of celestial love. This is a lighter shade of pink than the deep rose-pink ray. This power brings in the high selfless love of God. If you are trying to release an attachment to someone or something, this energy can be very helpful. Selfless love means you are giving and expressing love for the joy of its expression, and not for what you might receive in return. Too many times we con-dition love. We love what we're *getting* from someone or something. While this is not necessarily wrong, it doesn't build our connection to the divine source. We have to learn to love the way the divine loves us: without condition.

MEDITATIVE PRAYER TO WORK WITH THE ARCHANGEL JOPHIEL

Heavenly Father/Holy Mother God, I ask to receive the pearl-luster
pink ray of selfless love under Archangel Jophiel and the angels
of love. Help me to release attachments and realize that
all love comes from God. Inspire me to love for the
joy of loving without thought of return.

ARCHANGEL SANDALPHON

The Archangel Sandalphon is considered one of the oldest archangelic figures in Jewish mysticism and is connected to the Merkaba metaphysical tradition. He's described as unusually tall. Having worked with Archangel Sandalphon, I find this to be true. He's very tall and regal in appearance. The gold ray is strong with him.

Archangel Sandalphon has the honor of being responsible for administering spiritual tone. Spiritual tone is the power that is in the words you speak. When you speak, it's not just words—there is spiritual power behind those words. Your words are going to go out in one of two ways: spiritual tone or harsh sound. Harsh sound is void of spiritual power, while spiritual tone brings in divine vitality. As you issue forth spiritual tone, this vibration goes out in the ethers and begins the process of realization. You *create* with your words. So make sure you are saying the things that you want to see happen in your life.

This creative tone exists on all levels of creation. When God desired to set the universe into motion, He issued forth the creative word. So the Word of God is the *activator* of creation. That same activating power exists in you.

If you are careless with your words or feel you don't speak up for yourself the way you should, Archangel Sandalphon and his angels can inspire you with new spiritual power to use your verbal expression more creatively. The power of your words is one of the most important yet underestimated aspects to your consciousness. Your words count. Choose your words carefully and when you speak, speak with purpose and intention. This will help you enormously realizing your divine purpose.

MEDITATIVE PRAYER TO WORK WITH
THE ARCHANGEL SANDALPHON

Heavenly Father/Holy Mother God, I ask to receive the royal blue ray under Archangel Sandalphon and the angels of spiritual tone in my throat center (chakra) to strengthen my spiritual tone. Help me to say the right word at the right time. I ask You to help me be more courageous and careful in my speech pattern so that the spiritual tone may go out into the vibrated ethers into manifestation.

CHAPTER 8

THE LEADERS OF THE SPIRITUAL HIERARCHY

A S WE STEP into the leaders of the spiritual hierarchy, we are looking at aspects of life so developed that many spiritual traditions speak of them as if they were aspects of God. Certainly we are dealing with powers so potent, so God-filled, that to be in their holy presence can make you feel you are in the presence of God. Yet we must remember that the leaders of the spiritual hierarchy are still part of the Twelve Kingdoms of Nature. They are part of the same evolutionary ladder that you and I are on, yet they have advanced farther on the path. They are our elder brothers and sisters in light.

Remember why there is a hierarchy to begin with. The spiritual hierarchy is our connecting link to God. It is through the divinity of the celestial beings that God can be relatable to us until we can reach that point of making a direct connection ourselves. It is through the Holy Ones that we climb the various levels of creation until we can make our way back to the celestial kingdom of God.

The angels and archangels we have explored are filled with the God presence. That's what gives them their power. Yet when we cross beyond the archangel kingdom, we cross a spiritual bridge that takes us to a new understanding of the divine. The celestial members of the top two kingdoms in the Twelve Kingdoms of Nature are in charge of all other aspects of the hierarchy and the entire spiritual evolution for humanity. They represent the culmination of development through the twelve kingdoms, where all aspects of life come together in one grand whole. They are the embodiment of all the spiritual powers we are exploring in this book. They are the pinnacle of spiritual achievement.

THE DIVINE ONES OF THE UNNAMED SACRED ELEVENTH KINGDOM

The holy beings of the eleventh kingdom have evolved to the point where now they become direct participants in the unfoldment of creation. As mentioned, this kingdom is so sacred that its name cannot be given until one has crossed that bridge to the inner worlds. So for now, we respectfully call this level the Unnamed Sacred Eleventh Kingdom.

Creative consciousness is the keynote of this kingdom. We are all potentially co-creative beings. The angels and archangels express these creative powers with great eloquence, yet the Holy Ones of the Unnamed Sacred Eleventh Kingdom are the living embodiment of God's creative impulse. Not only has God awarded great regions of the heavens for them to guide over, but He has delegated to them direct creative participation in a variety of areas. This includes participation in the formation of organic form, orchestrating the execution of the divine plan, providing guidance and direction for individuals in their journey, and helping to bring souls into the fullness of their divine potential.

These Holy Ones have developed an inner awareness and understanding of God that surpasses that of the angels and archangels. As with the archangels, they too have a developed level of omniscience, yet their omniscience allows them to perform spiritual duties that are truly miraculous. The angels and archangels receive their guidance from the members of the eleventh kingdom, where the creative impulse is administered.

These divine beings work closely with the archangels in the various administrative duties of guiding humanity. They have been instrumental in establishing nations, religions, and major movements in society. They have been the inspiration behind scientific discoveries and have inspired new movements in art and philosophy. They are very involved in souls who are coming into the fullness of their spiritual potential and reaching enlightenment.

In conjunction with other celestial ones, these holy beings build the auric framework that our soul inhabits. Our aura has an anatomy just as our physical body does. These Holy Ones put the various facets of the auric field together. This includes the chakras, the auric shell, and divisions of the aura. As part of this work, these celestial beings put together our mental and emotional chakras, connecting us to Divine Mind. The Theosophists call these beings the *Lords of Mind*. The truth is, so much goes on within this dimension that many of the jobs that these Holy Ones do are simply not shared with us, yet we deeply benefit from their extraordinary love and devotion.

THE HOLY SPIRIT OF GOD

Many Holy Ones are part of the eleventh kingdom. Yet one spiritual being holds a particularly special place in the divine plan. I would like to focus on this being, as it is an essential key to a fuller understanding of the spiritual hierarchy. I am speaking of the Holy Spirit.

The Judaic tradition first introduced the term *Holy Spirit* (Ruah ha-Kodesh). Although the exact term is mentioned only a few times in the Tanakh, the presence and reference to the Spirit of God or the Holy Spirit is pervasive throughout the Jewish Bible. Understanding the Holy Spirit was further developed in the Talmud and Midrash.

The Hebrew mystics saw this Spirit of God or the Spirit of YHWH as a primal, creative, life-giving force. It is often described as a kind of breath or wind. Breath was the ancient interpretation for the incorporeal essence that gives life to creation. Esoterically, a basic tenet of the Tanakh is a greater understanding of God's creative Holy Spirit. From the beginning of Genesis, this spirit hovered over the void and gave the breath of life to archetypal Adam and Eve.

This spirit endows humanity with reason and understanding, which gives rise to divinely inspired actions. So the Holy Spirit also refers to the aspect of wisdom and prophecy. According to the Jewish conception, it was the Holy Spirit that gave the inspiration for the books of the Bible. It was the Holy Spirit that gave authority and voice to the prophets. There are numerous references that the Holy Spirit of God "rests upon man" and "surrounds him like a garment."

The Kabbalists gave great importance to the Holy Spirit. The ten names of God described in the sephirothic realm called Atziluth are aspects of the divine but also are connected to the Holy Spirit and the glories of the Unnamed Sacred Eleventh Kingdom. In his book *Meditation and Kabbalah*, Aryeh Kaplan teaches that the Holy Spirit is another way of saying *enlightenment*. To quote Kaplan:

> Meditation is primarily a means of attaining spiritual liberation. Its various methods are designed to loosen the bond of the physical, allowing the individual to ascend to a transcendental, spiritual realm. One who accomplishes this

successfully is said to have attained *Ruach HaKodesh*, the "Holy Spirit," which is the general Hebraic term for enlightenment.

The Holy Spirit became a key principle in Christian theology. Christian mystics taught that the Holy Spirit was revealed to the ancient Israelites as the mysterious and unpronounceable name YHWH. The Holy Spirit became the third aspect of the Holy Trinity of God.

It was the procreative power of the Holy Spirit who impregnated Jesus' mother, Mary, thereby initiating the Christ mission. It was the Holy Spirit who came to Jesus in the form of a dove at His baptism, giving the divine power to conduct His mission with authority. And it was the Holy Spirit who came as a comforter to the bewildered disciples shortly after Jesus' death and resurrection, giving them the power to conduct their apostolic work, which inaugurated the beginning of the Christian movement. The Book of Acts records the blessing of the Holy Spirit in this way:

> And suddenly there came from the sky a noise like a strong driving wind, and it filled the entire house in which they were. Then there appeared to them tongues as of fire, which parted and came to rest on each one of them. And they were all filled with the Holy Spirit and began to speak in different tongues, as the Spirit enabled them to proclaim.
> (Acts 2:2–4)

There is so much to say about the Holy Spirit. From the metaphysical perspective, if we follow the concept that God works *through* the spiritual hierarchy to reach us, then the God qualities attributed to the Holy

Spirit could be thought of as actual celestial beings who become the emissaries of these creative attributes. Metaphysics then makes a distinction between qualities of the Holy Spirit and the actual celestial being who is called the Holy Spirit.

Esoterically, the Holy Spirit is a definite spiritual being who resides in the celestial realms. This celestial being is a leader among the many "Holy Spirits" of the Unnamed Sacred Eleventh Kingdom. All work in beautiful cooperation with each other. As metaphysics teaches, this celestial Holy Spirit is not limited to any single religious or metaphysical system. This being is nondenominational and is universal to all humanity.

A unique quality of this divine being of the Holy Spirit is a *magnetic* presence, in the same way Archangel Uriel is a magnetic archangel. This idea of spirit having a feminine quality is not new. The actual Semitic word for *spirit* can be feminine in gender as well as masculine. *The Gospel of the Hebrews*, a lost noncanonical gospel quoted by its opponents, speaks of the Holy Spirit as feminine.

This divine presence has an actual form of extraordinary ethereal beauty. She is extremely tall, almost twenty-four feet. I have had the honor of working with this divine being and, without question, the first thing that strikes you about Her is Her spiritual command and loving presence. Her love flow is bubbly and is the embodiment of joy. So much energy is in her that it's difficult, especially when first encountering her, to fully appreciate the depth of Her power and creativity. Her eyes are extraordinarily luminous. She embodies so much of the magnetic attributes of God. Some of the matronly attributes of Mother Mary of the Christian faith reflect the beauty and majesty of the Holy Spirit. In fact, the initiate Mary who gave birth to Jesus was very much under the direction of the Holy Spirit.

In terms of the Holy Spirit's aura, it is expansive and can reach for 150 feet or more (see Figure 8.1A). She has a very developed Higher Self and does a great deal of work from that higher nature. As with the archangels, She also has five spheres in the higher nature, but those spheres are even more powerful and encompassing. A unique feature of the Holy Spirit is the concentric bands of light of many colors in Her outer aura that exude Her dynamic, creative power. In Figure 8.1a, the artist has done a wonderful job conveying the grand scope of the Holy Spirit. He chose a somewhat Grecian goddess look to Her, which in fact is close to the way I have seen Her. The beauty and majesty of Her form is very

FIGURE 8.1A. *The Holy Spirit*
(See inside back cover for full-color figure 8.1.)

well conveyed. Here, too, some of the auric configurations had been modified to give prominence to the figure, but the overall auric effect is very well done.

The Holy Spirit is intimately involved in your life. She is a steady, guiding hand, working with the angels and archangels in your spiritual unfoldment. It is the Holy Spirit who is responsible for implementing the divine plan for humanity. In this way, She is known as the "objective expression of the divine life," indicating her ability to carry out the divine directives. In other words, once the divine plan is set, the actual manifestation of that design is directed by the Holy Spirit and the various members of the Unnamed Sacred Eleventh Kingdom.

She makes sure that humanity stays on course and that evolution is moving in the right direction. When the Holy Spirit is sending spiritual energy, it is often seen in the form of a dove. I have clairvoyantly seen this blessing, and it is an exciting moment. You never know when it's going to happen, but this is something we all receive at certain times in our life. On our road to enlightenment, it is the Holy Spirit who brings us into the fullness of our spiritual power and into our higher consciousness, so that each of us may have the God experience.

As part of Her stupendous job of guiding and steering manifested life, the Holy Spirit helps us overcome our lower nature. She is responsible for helping us overcome our instinctual, irrational selves. Of course the angels and archangels are intimately involved in the tempering and dropping away of our personality ego, but they take their direction from the Holy Spirit.

The Holy Spirit is also the guiding force over the human body. When God designed the physical human form, it became the job of the Holy Spirit to bring this glorious design into actual manifestation. So the power behind the development of our physical form is not simply blind forces and random chance, as biological science would have you believe. There is an entire kingdom of life assisting in the spiritual as well as physical development of all organic life on earth.

This procreative power of the Holy Spirit is more clearly recognizable in the Indian understanding of the manus. The word *manu* comes from the Sanskrit for "man." Manus are seen as a line of progenitors and rulers of humanity, and are in fact celestial members of the Unnamed Sacred Eleventh Kingdom. Manus change from time to time. Each age of a manu is called a *manvantara*, or "creative cycle of life." They are in turn connected to what are called *prajapatis* or "lord of creatures," which the Rig Veda applies to the deities Indra, Savitri, and others. The current manu known as Vaivaswata is the inspiration for the Law of Manu, which has formed the cultural foundation for India, despite some gross misrepresentations of this teaching.

To accomplish all of this, the Holy Spirit does not work alone. As mentioned, working with Her are many celestial beings in the eleventh kingdom. Yet there is a celestial counterpart to the Holy Spirit that is Her equal and shares in the many duties of Her holy office. This counterpart is known as the *Holy Ghost*! This distinction of the Holy Spirit/ Holy Ghost is often thought to be merely grammatical, but it is much more than that. The Holy Ghost is a *dynamic* celestial being, who is separate but a complement to the magnetic Holy Spirit. He is the *Elohim* of the Hebrew tradition. He is the righteous hand of God. He represents the dynamic aspect of the Holy Spirit. The Holy Ghost is truly one of the most mysterious aspects of the spiritual hierarchy because, as involved as He is in our life, until we reach our enlightenment we do not work with Him in the same way we work with the Holy Spirit. It has been said that the Holy Spirit brings grace and the Holy Ghost brings in divine law. The Holy Spirit and the Holy Ghost work together leading the many divine beings of the Unnamed Sacred Eleventh Kingdom.

A PERSONAL EXPERIENCE

When I was in my early twenties, after my experiences with the archangels, I was privileged to have a visitation like no other. At the time, I had just committed myself to the work of the Higher but did not yet know which way to go with it. It was during a transitional time in my life. I had organized and produced a successful local variety show in Los Angeles and was given the opportunity to take the show to Las Vegas. It was a lucrative contract and I had three hundred people working under me, even though I was so young. I was planning to take the offer when the Holy Ones came in and told me that this was not my destiny. I was meant to become a spiritual teacher instead. To the dismay of everyone involved, I turned down the Las Vegas offer.

I intuitively understood the wisdom of what the Holy Ones said, but this decision put me in a difficult position, both personally and financially. I soon began to feel apprehensive about my decision. I thought that perhaps I had made a mistake. For a brief time, I tried to restart the variety show, but this time things did not click and the show fell apart. I found myself in a bit of a depression.

One afternoon, I was alone in my living room reading when this being of extraordinary brilliance appeared. His light was so intense, I almost could not make him out. He was extremely tall and had lovely features. He had a sort of round, jovial face. There was a sense of mirth and joy about him. He was dressed in blue robes.

At first I thought he might be an archangel, yet as glorious as the archangels are, this being was like no archangel I had ever seen. His aura was intensely brilliant with concentric bands of various colored light rays. He was not an archangel but some other type of spiritual being. He did not identify who he was.

After I had spent a few moments tuning in to his vibration, He spoke, or I should say He sent the thought to me.

"I'm here to enlighten you."

"I'm so glad you're here," was my mental reply.

"I'd like to help you with your evolution."

"What do you mean?" I asked.

"To help you move upward."

And with that thought, I felt a tremendous up-rush of energy. I felt ecstatic. The next thing I knew, I was no longer in my body. I was in my celestial body. This body is not the same astral form we normally inhabit when we are taken to the other side. I had been taken to the inner planes before, but not like this.

Words fail me here for such a sacred experience. I found myself with this celestial being in the heaven worlds. We flew through the air, past scenery of indescribable beauty and majesty. Something stirred in me and I soon realized this spiritual being was giving me an experience of my celestial Home. I was in tears and overcome with joy. With this awareness I realized who I really was—my *real* self. Not the persona that occupied that body on earth, but the eternal celestial me.

As He took me past glorious scenes, this being of Divine Grace took me somewhere else that was even more brilliant in power and Divine Light. I picked up the thought from Him that he was showing me the place in consciousness I was capable of reaching. At that moment I understood what He meant by evolution. He was talking about my spiritual potential. It all seemed too incredible to believe, yet—at the same time, in this one experience—I seemed to have been blessed with the big picture of my life.

I wanted to stay here forever, but before I knew it, I found myself back in my physical body. I felt like I didn't want to be in this physical world. The divine being was still with me and gave a final blessing of light, and with that He was gone.

Later I was to see this being again and learned that He was, in fact, the Holy Ghost. Blessed was I to have such an experience. This is the first time I am sharing this experience, and I do this only because I have been impressed by the Higher to share it with you to let you know that such divine wisdom and love does exist. There is love and care of the highest order looking after you. Needless to say, this experience helped me to accept my destiny and opened a new door in my relationship with the spiritual hierarchy.

MEDITATIVE PRAYER TO CONNECT WITH
THE HOLY GHOST/HOLY SPIRIT

Heavenly Father/Holy Mother God, I ask for a blessing from the dynamic
Holy Ghost and magnetic Holy Spirit. I ask for Thy guidance and
direction to fulfill my highest purpose and serve in the divine plan.
I ask that the Holy Ghost and Holy Spirit strengthen my physical
body and the objective expression of my spiritual life, so
that I may bear the fruits of spirit. I ask this with
the utmost reverence and humility.

THE UNNAMED SACRED
TWELFTH KINGDOM

Now we move to the top of the spiritual ladder in terms of the entire evolutionary plan of the Twelve Kingdoms of Nature. In this kingdom, the soul has reached the culmination of a long evolution that started humbly in the structure kingdom. There is an evolution within this kingdom, but at this point you have fully developed your soul's potential. Your aura has reached its fullest power and the celestial form you inhabit has reached the zenith of expression. You have developed your full divine consciousness and fully implemented your divine purpose.

The keynote of this kingdom is *divine consciousness*. All the awareness that you build in your evolution is filtered through the divine consciousness embodied in this kingdom. We have come to know this as the *Christ consciousness*. This encompassing consciousness has gone by different names, such as the *Krishna consciousness*. The Indian mystic Paramahansa Yogananda used the Sanskrit term *Kutastha Chaitanya*, or "that which remains unchanged consciousness," in reference to this divine awareness. It is through the Christ consciousness that you awaken in the light and eventually become aware of God. Every stage of the twelve kingdoms is, in essence, a degree of this divine awareness.

Like the eleventh kingdom, the twelfth kingdom is so glorious that many traditions have spoken of it in the highest superlatives when they speak of it at all. In ancient times, with the exception of a few famous examples, the Holy Ones of this kingdom were often not spoken of openly, except to the advanced initiates. With the opening up of so much esoteric knowledge to world consciousness, this tradition is rapidly changing. This is creating new opportunities, but also some challenges to overcome old conditioning.

I can tell you from my own experience that to interact with members of this kingdom is a life-changing event. Esoteric traditions sometimes depict the completeness, the all-encompassing quality of this kingdom as the Primordial Man or the Cosmic Man. The Kabbalists elaborated on the principle of the Primordial Man, calling it the *Adam Kadmon*. This was the first creation of God, out of which the primordial hierarchy of light and divine values or attributes emerged. And from this creation came what Kabbalists called "the Breaking of the Vessels" in which the Cosmic Man broke into various parts, forming different aspects of creation. And here is an allusion to the various kingdoms being "parts" of the all-encompassing Unnamed Twelfth Sacred Kingdom.

The Hindu metaphysical system known as *Sankhya* also prominently features the Primordial Man, calling it the *Purusha*. The Purusha is the infinite consciousness that animates *Prakrati*—the primordial substance of material life.[1] As with the Kabbalists, the Purusha is also divided up into various aspects, once again a reflection how the twelve kingdoms are "parts" of the culminating twelfth kingdom. According to the Rig Veda, the praises of the animating life of Purusha generated the Vedic chants, which are the foundation for the entire Hindu faith.[2]

---

[1] *Purusha* can be thought of as the infinite consciousness, or the individual consciousness animating material life or *Prakrati*. Here we are referring to this principle as part of the Cosmic Man.

[2] To quote the famous verse in the Purusha Suktam of the Rig Veda:

> The Purusha has thousand heads,
>
> He has thousand eyes,
>
> He has thousand feet,
>
> He is spread all over the universe,
>
> And is beyond the count with ten fingers
>
> From this sacrifice called "all embracing"
>
> The chants of Rig Veda were born,
>
> His face became Brahmins
>
> His hands were made as kshatriyas

Various members of the twelfth kingdom have been known as the avatars of Vishnu, including Rama and Krishna. The Native Americans called the twelfth-kingdom spirit, who watches over their people, the Great White Spirit.

Once you evolve to the twelfth kingdom, you *are* the divine consciousness you seek. You have embodied the highest level of awareness and understanding of God. These sacred spirits possess an awareness so fully developed that they can step into the inner sanctuary of God where other members of the hierarchy cannot.

These holy beings are the leaders of the spiritual hierarchy in every sense of the word. They are given extraordinary powers and responsibilities. As mentioned, they fuel the divine consciousness for all the other kingdoms. They possess an extraordinary level of omniscience. These Holy Ones participate with God in the conception of the divine plan, then work with other aspects of the hierarchy to implement that plan.

There are individual twelfth-kingdom spirits guiding every facet of human life. These spirits guide each of the nations and cultures. There is even a kingly planetary spirit who presides over the affairs of civilization as a whole. This exalted one is given the honored title Lord of the World and goes by other names, including the Sanskrit term *Sanat*

His thighs became Vaisyas
And from his feet were born the Shudras

From his face was born Indra and Agni

I know that great Purusha,
Who shines like the sun,
And is beyond darkness,
And the one who knows him thus
Attains salvation even in this birth
And there is no other method of salvation.
(Hymn 10.90)

Kumara. The Zoroastrian Ahura Mazda is a reference to this Holy representative of God. In the celestial planes, He goes by the name *Hermes Trismegistus*—Hermes, the Thrice-Greatest.

Hermes, in turn, answers to yet another celestial being in the twelfth kingdom. This Holy One has been given superlative titles such as Lord of Lords, Lord of the Kingdoms, and Lord of Creation. He is the leader of the celestial realm that is the headquarters for the spiritual hierarchy. This divine spirit is the door to the God experience and is ultimately responsible for uplifting the consciousness of humanity to this place of divine recognition.

Eventually, He will take on the administrative duties and become Lord of the World when humanity is ready for this administrative change. When this event happens, it will be the glorious New Day that has been promised and echoed through metaphysical schools for centuries. In the spirit worlds, He is primarily known as the Lord of Wisdom Light. On earth, He is more known as the Celestial Lord Christ.

THE LORD OF WISDOM LIGHT

The subject of Lord Christ, or the Lord of Wisdom Light, is difficult to talk about without bias. Most people identify Christ only with the religion that is built around His name. For the devout, any deviation from the accepted understanding of Christ is sacrilegious. On the other hand, many genuine spiritual truth seekers either avoid the subject or consider it inappropriate for esoteric study. Yet the influence that the Celestial Lord Christ has had on world consciousness is irrefutable. This tells us that despite any misrepresentations or misunderstandings, there is an enduring principle that is essential to metaphysics.

Let's start by understanding the names of this celestial being, and why there are two terms. The title Lord of Wisdom Light refers to the celestial power ray that this divine being embodies and is the administrator of. Remember, there is a hierarchy of light, and each Holy One is stationed at one of these great power rays. This represents their official office that they hold in the spiritual plan. The Ray of Wisdom Light represents the power ray that all of humanity is under. This ray appears as white light, but it is in fact a color beyond the human ranges of perception.[3] So the name Lord of Wisdom Light means that this Holy One is responsible for the spiritual ray of all humanity.

Now, the term *Lord Christ*, which is the same being as the Lord of Wisdom Light, brings out another facet to the Holy Ones, and this is something we are particularly working through right now—the Christ consciousness. The word *Christ* comes from the Greek *Christos*, which means "anointed." It was derived from the Hebrew word *Ha-Mashiah*. It is a term used in the Hebrew Bible to describe priests and kings who were traditionally anointed with holy anointing oil. In the Second Temple period in Israel, it came to be used in reference to the future messianic figure and was adopted by the Christians to represent the fulfillment of the messianic hope.

We must remember that the spiritual hierarchy is like any organized group. There has to be someone at the top of the ladder who's in charge and oversees the whole operation. In the army, that would be the commanding general. In a monarchy, that would be the king. In a corporation, that would be the chairman of the board, and so on. In the spiritual

---

[3] This energy is not the same thing as the golden ray of wisdom light under Archangel Michael. (I know the terminology can sometimes get confusing!)

worlds, it means there has to be a celestial being who has evolved to a greater degree than the others and is in charge of the whole evolutionary process for humanity under the direction of God. In our evolutionary chain, that privileged position is reserved for the celestial Lord of Wisdom Light. There are other hierarchies with their own celestial leaders. Yet in terms of humanity's development, it's the Lord of Wisdom Light who's in charge. This doesn't make him God, but it makes him closer to God than the angels and the archangels. The entire spiritual hierarchy operates under Him in loving harmony and unparalleled cooperation.

Lord Christ is the link between you and God. It is this celestial leader who will one day present you to God. This is why He is often referred to as our elder brother. He is the mediator between God in His glory and you as an evolving soul on your spiritual pilgrimage. His level of divine awareness is unparalleled. He works with you through the spiritual hierarchy and also directly. The Lord of Wisdom Light gives illumination when you are lost, hope when you have given up, patience when you are headstrong, love when you are lonely, understanding when you are confused, and peace to still your consciousness.

He divinely loves you whether you are spiritually asleep or awake. When awakened in your spirit self, this celestial being plays an even more prominent part in your life. He is the great teacher of the divine truths. He inaugurates you into the various levels of consciousness and spiritual dimensions. And it is through the Lord of Wisdom Light that the spiritual hierarchy is revealed to you.

The celestial Lord Christ is not exclusive to any religion or creed. He is far beyond that. He is lord of us all—and that includes Muslims, Jews, Hindus, Christians, Buddhists, Taoists, Shintoists, atheists, and agnostics alike. Regardless of our awareness of this presence, we are all receiving His loving care and attention.

JESUS OF NAZARETH AND THE CHRIST

Confusion sets in when we try to relate the understanding of the Lord of Wisdom Light as Lord Christ with the man Jesus and the formalized Christian religion, which seems to make Christ exclusive to one religion. To clarify this confusion, I must make a distinction between the man Jesus and the celestial Lord Christ.

The man Jesus who came to earth two thousand years ago was certainly no myth. He was a very real, flesh-and-blood person who was a very high initiate in spiritual truths. Because of his advanced status, he was chosen by the spiritual hierarchy to be the representative of the Christ, but Jesus was not the celestial Lord Christ. This is a very important point to understand. *Jesus is not Lord Christ.* The Lord of Wisdom Light is far too encompassing to inhabit physical form. When the man Jesus began His ministry, the Christ *overshadowed* Jesus, and the mission began. This overshadowing was not in the mediumistic sense, but as a glorious mediator for the divine. At the point Jesus was overshadowed, He became Jesus the Christ because of the power that was given Him. Jesus was then able to teach with real authority.

This distinction between Jesus and Lord Christ is not a new idea. The Rosicrucians make this distinction. The Christian mystic Max Heindel spoke of the difference between Jesus and Christ. The Gnostics made a definite distinction between Jesus and Christ. They believed that Jesus was a holy man who was overshadowed by the Christ at the baptism and withdrew before the crucifixion. The Christ was a celestial being, or *aeon*, who had come down to earth from what they called the *Pleroma*, or heaven worlds, to reawaken humanity to its divine identity. Jesus was His chosen emissary.

Several clues to the relationship of Jesus and Lord Christ are found in the New Testament. The personal moments certainly reflect the humanness of Jesus. The trials were tests for Jesus, not Lord Christ. The temptation in the desert was a test to see if Jesus was ready to begin His mission. His agony in the Garden of Gethsemane was again a test to see if He was ready to make the supreme sacrifice. In fact, mystics recognize that the life of Jesus is an example of the process of initiation that all of us must go through to win the crown of life. This is most poignantly dramatized at the moment on the cross when Jesus cried out, "God, why have you forsaken me?" Here is an example of the supreme emptiness one feels just before the highest initiation, an initiation Jesus passed brilliantly.

When we consider the transcendent Jesus, Jesus as the Word of God, proclaiming the great "I am" affirmations such as "I am the Resurrection and the Life," however, these are all clearly references to Christ, or the Lord of Wisdom Light, mediating through Jesus. The many miracles Jesus performed could only have been done with the help of the Holy Ones and especially Lord Christ. Yet even here, the Lord of Wisdom Light proclaims His own humbleness in the presence of God with the immortal words, "I of myself am nothing, the Father within doeth the works." This again reminds us that as exalted as this divine being is, He is not God. Even He is looking up, as there is always a greater spiritual mountain to climb.

What made the mission of Jesus unique, and one of the reasons why Jesus and Christ seem to be so connected, was that it was the first time the Christ teachings were brought to the public in a direct way. It was one of the first times that the Lord of Wisdom Light spoke openly about Himself through one of His emissaries. Yet the mission of Jesus, and the many who worked with him, was not meant for any single group of people. The esoteric knowledge and illumination the spiritual hierarchy brought through was meant for the world. This is very important because the whole purpose of the Jesus mission was to prepare the way for a new phase in the unfoldment of humanity and in the celestial administration of the hierarchy.

The bottom line is this: *If you want to know God, get to know Lord Christ.* One of the most joyous of my clairvoyant experiences is having seen this celestial being. By building your pipeline to the Lord of Wisdom Light, you're building your pipeline to God.

MEETING LORD CHRIST

My first experience with this celestial being was in my later twenties. I was living with my family in Los Angeles and it was late at night. The others in the house were either out or sleeping. This was a quieter period in my life. I had a simple sales job but was happy. I had rekindled my spiritual powers and felt good, although my metaphysical career had not yet started. I was continuing to receive steady instruction with various Holy Ones, receiving wonderful inspiration that I was to use later in my teaching work.

I was reading in my room, as I often did at that time when I had a free moment, when this incredible spiritual being appeared. The sheer spiritual power was staggering. He was very regal, true royalty in the best sense of the word. The human pomp and circumstance of monarchies are pale caricatures of this celestial presence. He was very tall with features so clear and distinct. He had a warm, captivating, intent expression. I didn't know who He was, but without a doubt this was the most extraordinary spiritual being I had ever had the honor to experience. I could discern only a portion of His aura, as it was so expansive and bright, but I could already tell it was the most dazzling I had ever seen.

He appeared to be studying me. Then He gently communicated, "I came to see how you are doing and to let you know we are helping you on the other side."

After a few moments, He quietly left. I was completely elated yet bewildered. This experience felt more like a preparation for something.

Later in my inner-plane journeys, I was told I was going to meet the Lord of Wisdom Light. I was taken to His celestial temple in the inner worlds. He was there with a lot of angels and Holy Ones. Here in His glory He was enormous. His figure must have been thirty feet tall with an aura that expanded for hundreds of feet. When I saw his face, I realized that He was the same being who had presented Himself in my home, yet he was even more glorious and grand here. He blessed me along with others. I felt so humbled that He would take the time to personally see how I was doing.

There are many unique qualities to the aura of Lord Christ. First is His size and regality (see Figure 8.2A). His form is very elongated with indescribably exquisite features and must be thirty feet tall. He most often wears white and blue robes. There is a magnificent crown of light of various colors above his head, given by God, indicating His holy office. He is the only one the hierarchy calls master. There is a configuration of seven blazing gold stars above His head, depicting his advanced status in the twelfth kingdom. Just below that is a brilliant green sphere of light that is His Higher Self Point. He uses this for personal work to connect with divine levels even more advanced than Himself. Yet He does not use this to send light as other Holy Ones do. In fact, there is no elaborate Higher Self nature. In terms of transmitting Divine Light and wisdom, He has other means to accomplish this purpose. There also is no auric shell, as His form is so powerful that He does not need it. There

FIGURE 8.2A. *The Lord of Wisdom Light (Lord Christ)*
(See inside back cover for full-color figure 8.2.)

are four chakra points within the celestial body, and they possess tremendous abilities to receive and transmit energy.

His outer aura is resplendent with a dominant royal blue along with gold and pink energies that reach out for hundreds of feet. The striations of light gracefully overlap each other in a dazzling display. To add to this dramatic outer aura, a shaft of light emanates vertically through the central form to the breadth of the auric field. And another shaft of light emanates horizontally through the celestial body to the full breadth of the aura, creating an equidistant, crosslike form. The cross, not to be confused with the crucifix, is a high esoteric form in the heaven worlds. It represents the immersion of spirit into matter. The Lord of Wisdom Light is the embodiment of this mystical union. The color of the crosslike energy appears white but is in fact of a color that does not exist in the physical spectrum. What is most extraordinary is that from any point on this crosslike form, the Lord of Wisdom Light can send light and power wherever He wishes.

Without question, this is the most difficult subject to depict in an illustration as you are dealing with such an expansive and elevated presence. Once again, the artist has done an inspired job of conveying the feeling and regality of the Lord of Wisdom Light.

My experiences with this holy being are too sacred to put into more words than I have said here. He loves each of us, and sooner or later, each of us will behold Him. In our own way, we are all familiar with the Lord of Wisdom Light. It is because of this being that I have been able to fully awaken my spiritual gifts and was given the ability to do the work I do, without which I could not have written this book.

For those who question the Christ, doubt who He is or *if* He is, I can tell you there is no other like Him. He is more real than you can imagine, more powerful, more loving, and more intimately connected to you. Please do not let humanity's frequent misrepresentations of the Christ discourage you from making your personal connection with Him and appreciating His worth. He is far above humanity's mistakes and is always there for you, ready to work for God's glory. Throughout my life, He has been the guiding hand in my evolution and my various metaphysical experiences, along with the other great Holy Ones.

AWAKENING THE
CHRIST CONSCIOUSNESS

To conclude this chapter, I would like to add that in addition to the actual celestial being, there is the Christ consciousness. This consciousness is an awareness given to help you perceive the divine process of life. In the heaven worlds, each plane is dedicated to one degree of Christ consciousness. This consciousness helps you understand your divinity. It gives you the clear picture of the divine plan. It helps you connect with higher levels of awareness and contributes to making a better connection with the Holy Ones. Eventually, this Christ consciousness helps you reach your celestial Home so that you may perceive God directly.

Within each of us is a spark of this divine awareness. This spark is called the Indwelling Christ Spirit. It's located in your mental center or chakra. The Indwelling Christ Spirit is a gift of the Higher. It is not actually part of your spiritual makeup. When this consciousness is strong, this indwelling spirit is brilliant, active, and energetic. Unfortunately, at too many times, this point looks like a pilot light. It's weak, which means the person has not been developing the divine powers within. It is a sad fact that many people do not pay attention to the prompting of this spirit consciousness, for if they did, their lives would go so much better.

The Indwelling Christ Spirit is one of the most important levels of consciousness that you possess. You build this divine awareness gradually. As you *live* the principles of Divine Light, as you meditate and pray daily, as you learn to love unconditionally, then you gradually build the power of your Indwelling Christ Spirit. In your spiritual ascent, it is *through* this consciousness that you will have the mysteries of God revealed to you. Step by step, this spirit power is activated to greater degrees to increase your spiritual awareness.

MEDITATIVE PRAYER TO WORK WITH THE LORD OF WISDOM
LIGHT AND THE CHRIST CONSCIOUSNESS

Heavenly Father/Holy Mother God, I ask for a blessing from the Lord of

Wisdom Light. I thank You for being my elder brother and guiding

the spiritual hierarchy. I thank you for all that you do in my

evolution to guide me upward. If it be Divine Will, grant

unto me Thy power ray to awaken my own Christ

consciousness, my Indwelling Christ Spirit,

so that the glory of God may be

revealed to me.

CHAPTER 9

SPIRITUAL TEACHERS

When the student is ready, the teacher appears.
—ANONYMOUS

HEN I WAS eleven years old, I was having many spiritual visions and visitations by celestial beings, but I did not understand what it all meant. In those days, metaphysics was not a popular topic, and it was difficult for me to find available material or someone who could answer the many questions I had. All that changed when I met my first spiritual teacher—Dorothy La Moss.

At the time, I was living in Kansas City, Missouri. Our family had moved to Kansas City so that my father could start up a new church and build up a congregation. I was one of six children and had learned to keep quiet about my spiritual gifts, because others did not understand. I was constantly getting into trouble when I did share my clairvoyant experiences.

I loved the theater and, when I was eleven years old, I joined a local acting group headed by Dorothy La Moss. She was well-known in the Midwest for having one of the best theater stock companies, and I was enjoying working with her. Dorothy was a very outgoing and knowledgeable person. When I met her, she was in her fifties and heavyset.

Her husband had died, and she lived alone in a modest home. I was particularly impressed by her aura, although at the time I did not yet understand what the colors and configurations meant. All I knew was that I was happy to be with her, even though she could be tough at times.

One day, after a rehearsal for a play we were working on, she told me to come alone to her home on a Saturday, as she had something she wanted to talk to me about. I was a little apprehensive, as I thought maybe she was unhappy with my work and wanted to drop me from the group. When I showed up at her home, she didn't talk about theater at all. She asked me how I saw things. I said I see things fine, like everyone else. She kept pressing the point of how I saw things and I then realized what she was getting at.

Finally she said, "You can see the aura."

I blurted out, "Is that what it's called?" I didn't even have a name for what I was seeing.

It turned out Dorothy could see the aura too. She was a Hermetic scientist and had come from two generations of Hermetic scientists, so she was well versed in the metaphysical arts. She wanted me to come on Saturdays, and she would personally start to teach me about my spiritual gifts. This was my first training in metaphysics.

It was a magical time. She taught me to meditate with Divine Light. We would go into meditation, and I would see beautiful light rays. As I worked with her, I began to see the aura more clearly. After several weeks of this, she began teaching principles of the Hermetic sciences. She had old, handwritten books and started sharing knowledge from their sacred wisdom. Soon she was letting me read from these books. It was incredible. There were illustrations and sketches of various aspects of the aura. I learned about the composition of the aura and the meaning of the various color energies. With this knowledge, I was able to interpret the aura.

She taught me a lot about the aura, clairvoyance, and other aspects of metaphysics—including an introduction to the spiritual hierarchy. At that point, I was not thinking of being on a spiritual path or that this might be something I myself would teach later on. Yet this experience gave me a much greater confidence in my talents. I knew now that I wasn't the only one with this gift. Dorothy was like a spiritual mother figure. No one else, including my family, had any idea of what was going on, as I was still in the acting company and participating in plays.

This training went on for many months. It was a sad day when I learned our family was moving to California and I had to cut short my training with Dorothy. We were both fond of each other and there was so much more to learn. I was so grateful for all she did. She changed my life and I wished I could have studied more. She urged me to keep up my meditations and keep working with the light.

Unfortunately, I got a little lax after we moved to California and did not meditate as I should have at first. Somehow, I didn't think I could make it without Dorothy's help. I once again found myself in a situation where I had no one to speak to about my experiences. At this time, I decided not to pursue things metaphysical and was trying to "fit in" and be a normal person like everyone else. Of course, the divine had other plans. During this next phase, the Holy Ones themselves started making themselves more clearly known. Later, I met another teacher who helped me unfold my full spiritual powers and connection with the divine. She helped prepare me to become a teacher.

I share this story to show you the importance of having a spiritual teacher. A teacher is an indispensable partner in your relationship with the Holy Ones. The question as to whether we need a spiritual teacher in physical form is a contentious point for many. In today's world, there is a distrust of authority, as it seems to go against the independent spirit. As a result, many are trying to climb the spiritual ladder on their own. They draw knowledge from many different sources and try to forge their own spiritual path. While the gathering of knowledge is wonderful, it cannot replace the role of a teacher. The truth is, you need a spiritual teacher. I can't say it's impossible to do it on your own, as nothing is impossible with God, but let's say it's a slower and more difficult process.

What exactly is a spiritual teacher? Many people can share with you spiritual knowledge or clairvoyant experiences, but this does not make them spiritual teachers in the truest sense of the term. A teacher of Divine Light is someone who can help you reach your highest spiritual potential. They can do this because they have reached that place for themselves and have been trained to be a teacher for many years. A true teacher has built the bridge of being a direct conduit to the Holy Ones and can act as an emissary for the spiritual hierarchy until the student can reach that place of direct knowing for himself or herself. Because of this, a spiritual teacher can help you reach your full spiritual potential. A spiritual teacher acts as a link for the student to connect directly with the spiritual hierarchy. The teacher/student relationship is one of the most sacred relationships there is. A teacher cannot do the growing for the student, but can help steer him or her and give the student the power to climb the spiritual ladder.

The practice of spiritual instruction is a time-honored tradition in all the great metaphysical training centers throughout the ages. In the Western tradition, the leaders of the metaphysical training centers were known as *hierophants*. It was understood that the hierophant was an advanced soul who had a direct connection to the Higher and could teach others in the mystical ways. In the East, the Indian metaphysical schools had the guru. A guru was acknowledged as an advanced soul who could lead their *chela* to enlightenment.

Some schools, especially in the East, took this tradition almost to the point of worshipping their teachers. The idea was that through the teacher, you were really worshipping God. I do not adhere to this philosophy. The teacher, no matter how advanced, is still human. Of course, honor and respect the teacher. Acknowledge the work that the teacher is doing for you. Recognize the divine working through the teacher. But if you really want to honor the teacher, honor the teachings. Do the work that is laid out for you.

It is rewarding but difficult being a teacher. There is so much work involved. In my own life, I hesitated following through with this work at first. It was not because I didn't recognize its value or I didn't feel qualified, but because I knew the responsibility involved. A teacher is karmically bound if he or she misleads a student in any way. Because of this, I have been very careful to put into practice anything I teach, to know it really works. I do not take it upon myself to make any judgment or personal evaluation regarding the work. These teachings may be filtered through my own consciousness, but they are the teachings of the Holy Ones. I rely on them completely in all aspects of my teaching work.

A HIERARCHY OF PHYSICALLY BASED TEACHERS

There are many levels and degrees of human development, which means there are many levels of teachers. Just as there is a hierarchy of celestial beings, there is a hierarchy within the human kingdom. When the spiritual hierarchy was first reintroduced to humanity in the late 1800s, it was thought of as an order of advanced human souls. Helena Blavatsky spoke of her teachers as "mahatmas." She referred to them as "Masters of the Ancient Wisdom." These masters were in both physical form and spirit form. Alice Bailey used the term *Spiritual Hierarchy of the Earth* in reference to the network of advanced human souls helping to guide humanity. Almost every metaphysical school speaks of the human hierarchy in their esoteric training. In the 1930s, the term *ascended masters* was coined as an honorary title to these elevated ones. Alice Bailey beautifully quotes the human hierarchy in this way:

> The spiritual Hierarchy of the earth is the aggregate of those of humanity who have triumphed over matter, who have achieved the goal of self-mastery by the same path that individuals tread today. These spiritual Personalities have wrestled and fought for victory and mastery upon the physical plane, and struggled with the miasmas, fogs, and dangers, troubles and sorrows of everyday living. They have trodden every step of the way of suffering, have undergone every experience, have surmounted every difficulty, and have won through. Herein lies their right to serve, and the strength and reality of their relationship to a still struggling humanity. They know the quintessence of pain, and can exquisitely measure their methods to the need of the individual. They are characterized by a love which endures, which acts always for the good of the whole; by a knowledge gained through living; by experience based on the evolution of time; by a courage as a result of that experience; by a purpose which is enlightened and intelligent and

adjusted to the purpose of the planetary Logos, and a dynamic will that brooks no interference to the eventual carrying out of that divine Purpose.[1]

This human hierarchy is working in every area of endeavor. There are enlightened souls working in education, business, medical arts, the sciences, the creative arts, civics, and politics—as well as the religious and esoteric arenas. The terminology for the varying degrees of this hierarchy and their duties can be confusing, as not all metaphysical schools use the same language. In addition, there was some confusion among the teachings themselves, and some of the early material given to the public was not entirely accurate. There have also been later groups that have misrepresented this divine order, which has added to the confusion. The hierarchal order I will offer here is one that is used in the spirit worlds, but I must note that other nomenclature is used as well.

This hierarchy can be listed in the following way:

1. Chela
2. Neophyte
3. Initiate

4. Disciple
5. Adept
6. Saint

---

[1] From the Lucis Trust website: http://www.lucistrust.org/en/service_activities/world_goodwill /world_goodwill_literature_on_line/the_spiritual_hierarchy.

7. Avatar

8. Buddha

9. Mystic

10. Celestial spiritual teachers

Let's start with the *chela*. This comes from the Sanskrit term *ceta*, meaning "student." A chela is a soul who is ready to undergo the training to develop his or her spiritual power and eventually attain enlightenment. This is the soul who is under the tutelage of a genuine spiritual teacher and is starting on the mystical path in earnest.

The next step is the *neophyte*. *Neophyte* is a term used in the Western mystical tradition to indicate a candidate for the spiritual mysteries. It is often used synonymously for *chela*, yet esoterically a neophyte is a chela who has reached a higher level of development and is ready to undergo the trials of initiateship. A neophyte has reached a connection with the Higher that the chela has not yet reached.

Then there is the *initiate*. Initiates have reached their higher nature. They have resurrected themselves up out of the lower nature and claimed their immortal self. This is the first step of enlightenment. From here, the initiate goes through a marvelous unfoldment as, slowly, the spiritual powers that have been latent for so long gracefully awaken. The initiate gradually awakens spiritual gifts such as clairvoyance and eventually becomes enlightened. It is during this phase of development that the initiate can be ordained by the Higher and become a true spiritual teacher.

A famous example of a highly developed initiate is Paramahansa Yogananda. I was graced once to have had a vision of him. He had already passed on to the other side. I was touring his home in Encinitas, California, and was in his bedroom. Suddenly I saw him in the corner of the room! He was in meditation, almost in a deep trancelike state, and very occupied with the higher energies. He had a beautifully bright aura. There were others there from the other side as well meditating with him. He didn't address me specifically but acknowledged that I could perceive him. Ironically, as I tuned into his vibration, I picked up sadness. I wasn't clear why. Perhaps he was unhappy that he left the earth in the prime of his life, or maybe something was not going the way he wanted it to.

Once you reach initiateship, you have reached an extraordinary spiritual plateau, yet your evolution does not stop here. Now that you have awakened your spiritual powers, it is time to more fully expand and use those powers. The next step from being an initiate is becoming a *disciple*. The common understanding of discipleship is similar to being an apprentice. This may sound contrary to the advanced spiritual status a disciple has reached. However, we must remember that spiritual evolution is an eternal process. As Helena Blavatsky said, "You grow from perfection to perfection." So this is a *celestial* discipleship. You are still incarnating on earth, but now you are a disciple of the heaven worlds and the celestial mysteries. The more recent term *ascended masters* is an honorary title to those who have crossed over to the heavenly realms.

From this celestial discipleship, you progress through a series of extraordinary levels of development, including the stages of *adept* and *saint*. Through these stages, new levels of awareness and spiritual command open up to you. From here, you cross into the level of an *avatar*. There is a mistaken notion that avatars or divine incarnations do not have a personal need to come to earth other than to help others, but this is not true. An avatar is still learning and growing in the Divine Light, as well as being an ambassador for the spiritual hierarchy. At this stage, a door is opened to extraordinary spiritual powers and abilities.

Then there is the *Buddha* stage, which was gloriously demonstrated with the life and teachings of Siddhartha, who became the Buddha. From this elevated level, there is the stage of the full *mystic*. This is the level where you pull together all the experiences in physical life and bring those experiences to their culmination. You have gone as far as you can go spiritually and still inhabit physical form.

Through all these phases, you develop abilities and levels of awareness that truly seem superhuman. Many of the great prophets, sages, and spiritual leaders through the ages were at these stages of development. In addition, many souls from this level work behind the scenes and do not make themselves known. These are the forerunners of humanity. What is most wonderful is that these levels are not only for the select few. We are all destined to reach these plateaus in our journey back to God.

Once you reach the mystic level, you have gone as far as you can in physical form. You have truly learned every lesson that the earth has to teach you, unfolded every possible spiritual power in physical form, and demonstrated complete mastery over physical life.

CELESTIAL SPIRITUAL TEACHERS

Once you have completed the mystic phase of development, your physical life on earth is complete. You have become an extraordinary emissary for the spiritual hierarchy and have made indelible contributions to humanity. From here, you pass into a most beautiful part of your spiritual journey. You train to become part of the spiritual hierarchy itself and complete your spiritual pilgrimage Home.

There are many qualities and attributes of souls at this level of development. You work side by side with angels, archangels, and other holy beings. You continue in your spiritual journey, leading all the way to your celestial Home, which is the culmination through the long pilgrimage in the human kingdom. There are souls in this level of development who no longer involve themselves in earthly affairs. Yet there is a special class of these advanced souls who work very much with humanity, and these souls are known as the celestial human teachers.

You will recall that one of the levels of angelic evolution is the angelic teachers. These angelic teachers are directly assigned to you to guide your evolution. Yet in addition to the angelic teachers, there are the celestial human teachers. These human teachers are assigned to souls who are not quite ready to work with the angelic teachers. They are particularly helpful for those who have not yet awakened to their spiritual potential and are not yet ready for esoteric work.

The celestial human teachers are wonderful. Their auras are very developed and extend quite far. If you are fortunate to see one, there is no question in your mind that you are dealing with a sacred being. A person can have several teachers working with him or her. This is not all at the same time. They come and go as the need arises. These teachers have specialties. One teacher may be an expert with healing, another helps you with your spiritual growth, another helps with your creative flow, and so on. This shows that you are *never* alone during your sojourn on earth.

SPIRIT GUIDES

Of all the aspects of the human spiritual hierarchy, one of the most recognizable is the spirit guides. Many New Age schools commonly invoke spirit guides for help and support. The term became popularized with the spiritualistic groups that started in the 1800s. Most psychics and mediums talk about working with spirit guides. It was usually a reference to a disincarnate spirit that acts as a guide or protector to a living incarnated human being. The spiritualistic church placed a lot of emphasis on demonstrating that there was a life beyond this physical world. They would delve into psychic phenomena to illustrate their point. When mediums communicated with someone from the other side, they would call the entity they were communicating with a spirit guide.

As the term became more popular, it became a generic phase for almost any spiritual being making a connection from the other side, from family and relatives to angels and nature spirits. However, this generalization is not accurate. Spirit guides are not just any beings from the spirit worlds who wish to help. Certainly, if a favorite uncle or aunt has passed over, they can visit you to offer love and support, but this does not make them your spirit guide. I remember once I was about to cross a busy street when I suddenly heard my godmother, who was on the other side, say in Greek, "Step back!" I did, and a moment later a car came barreling around the turn; I had not seen it, and it surely would have hit me. My godmother saved my life that day. I loved her dearly, but it did not make her my spirit guide.

In terms of the spiritual hierarchy, spirit guides hold a definite position in the hierarchal order. Spirit guides are souls at the initiate level of development who are in the spirit worlds. Spirit guides are particularly helpful for those who have not yet found their true physical teacher. Without an earth-based teacher, it is difficult to make a direct connection to your celestial teachers. Spirit guides act as a link to the human celestial teachers or the angelic teachers until the aspirant can find his or her true teacher.

Spirit guides are especially important for those who haven't yet started on that path. The reason they are so popular with mediums and psychics is that they are closer to us in vibration than other aspects of the Higher, and it is possible to communicate with them through psychic channels, whereas the teachers and angelic beings are not effectively reached psychically.

Spirit guides are supportive in many areas of life. Since they are enlightened themselves, they offer teachings and can bring in knowledge. Spirit guides assist in carrying out duties of the teachers. They are closer to us than the teachers, and we can often relate to them more easily. You must remember, however, that the spirit guides answer to the teachers, as it is the teachers who are responsible for your spiritual evolution. So this is why metaphysics teaches us to honor and acknowledge the help of the spirit guide, but the ones we really want to be connecting with are the spiritual teachers. In chapter 14, we will focus on making a strong connection with your teachers.

I remember a wonderful experience I had with a spirit guide many years ago. When my oldest child, Vasilli (we called him by his English name then, Billy), was around ten years old, he was going through a difficult time. He was a great kid, loved to draw and ride his bike, and was a good student. His father had died some years ago, and I was living with my mother and raising him. There were a lot of dynamics in the house and I was gone a lot. Later, he became very outgoing, but back then he was a little on the shy side. He had friends, but I could tell he was lonely and hurting on the inside. I didn't know what to do for him.

I had recently finished some intense training with my mentor, Inez, and had learned how to call on the Holy Ones in a more systematic way. I thought it might help to call on a spirit guide for Vasilli. Generally, spirit guides come around adults. The guardian angels work well with children, but I also wanted a being who was very relatable to Vasilli. I made the request, and a day or two later, this extraordinary spiritual being appeared in my room. He looked very much like a Native American and showed himself in traditional dress. He was tall, very strong, and dynamic-looking. He was radiant in light. I understood at once that this was the spirit guide I had requested. There was a lot of powder blue light around him, which was an indication of creativity and inspiration. I was delighted with this, as Vasilli was very creative as well, and thought that this spirit guide might help to open his creative flow. The spirit guide didn't speak at first, but sent the thought that his name was Tall Pine and that he would help Vasilli.

He started coming around Vasilli, often when he was playing with others. I could see him transmitting energy and uplifting him. Without Vasilli's realizing it, he gave support to him and, through his energy, encouraged him. This went on for several months, and I noticed a difference in Vasilli's behavior. He was more confident, more outgoing. I don't think he knew what was going on, although he was very intuitive with a lot of spiritual potential. I was deeply grateful to Tall Pine for the help he was giving.

One day, Tall Pine came and said he had finished his work and was leaving. He told me not to worry about Vasilli and that everything should be fine. Vasilli's confidence remained and continued to develop. Of course this was his own character developing, but I was grateful for the positive influence Tall Pine had given him. Later I did a similar thing for my daughter, Ria. Her spirit guide was named Red Feather, and he was a great help to her.

MEDITATIVE PRAYER TO WORK WITH THE SPIRIT GUIDES

Heavenly Father/Holy Mother God, I ask for a blessing from the spirit guides. I thank these illumined souls for helping me to connect with the spiritual hierarchy and I am open to any guidance and direction needed at this time.

A PERSONAL STORY

I would like to relate to you a personal story of a spiritual teacher who played an instrumental part in my life and work, as a way to illustrate the importance of working with a genuine spiritual teacher. This is my training with Inez Hurd. I have mentioned her earlier and would like to talk more about her now. I met Inez when I was in my twenties. I was living in Los Angeles, California. It was a difficult time personally. I was raising two children on my own (my mother and sister were helping) and was working a simple day-to-day job at a cafeteria, trying to make ends meet.

Spiritually, I had just finished an extraordinary period of inner development with the spiritual hierarchy, yet something in my work felt incomplete. I was gathering up a lot of spiritual experiences and inner knowledge but was unclear as to exactly where this was all leading. I knew I was somehow meant to share this with others, but the teaching door had not yet opened.

One day, a man came to the cafeteria where I was working and started to talk about a spiritual teacher he was studying with. Her name was Inez Hurd. As he spoke about her, I could immediately feel a lot of light and power around her, and I picked up that this was someone very special. I asked him if I could come to her class. He said the classes were closed but that he would ask her. To my surprise, Inez herself called me the next day and said I could attend.

She lived in Glendale, California, and held the class in her home. As I turned the corner to her block, I could feel so much power that I knew right away which house was hers, even without looking at the numbers. When I saw her, there was an immediate connection. She had a striking aura and I liked her right away. She was teaching an advanced group of about twenty students but insisted I sit next to her. As she started her lecture, it was clear she had an enormous amount of knowledge and awareness. She was very dynamic, yet she could be very funny. There was a whole glow about her, and it was clear that everyone in the room was very committed to her and her teachings.

She started bringing through instructions from a celestial being who simply called himself Brother A. Inez was not a medium but had developed a tremendous rapport with the spiritual hierarchy. She worked with Brother A on some powerful lessons that were coming through. The students were galvanized by the instructions. Yet as Inez was teaching, she would constantly turn to me and say, "Isn't that so, Barbara?" as if I knew what she was talking about. The others were wondering who this stranger was who was so familiar with Inez. She spoke as if I were her equal. I could feel Brother A appealing to me through Inez.

After the lesson, Inez asked me to come back so she could speak with me privately. I did return and, again, we hit it off personally. We both liked each other very much. She told me she recognized the spiritual gifts I had and that I was very special. She wanted to work with me, as she felt that I was an advanced soul but needed some help to pull my gifts together. She reiterated what the Holy Ones had told me years ago—I was to become a spiritual teacher.

So I started training with her. She became my mentor, spiritual teacher, friend, and compatriot in the Divine Light. I had finally met someone with whom I could freely exchange my spiritual experiences and personal feelings.

As Dorothy had done for me years earlier, Inez started me with meditation. She taught meditation a little differently than Dorothy had, as she was following a different spiritual tradition. Her training was in what she called Christos Wisdom, which was part of a metaphysical tradition known as the Kingdom of Light Teachings.

She taught me many different principles and helped me pull together the many experiences I had already had. She filled in gaps in my spiritual knowledge and helped me to develop my clairvoyant skills to even greater heights. She was the most developed clairvoyant I had ever met and could see the aura with extraordinary detail.

Then, at one point, it came time to go through a special training to really help me reach a high spiritual plateau—enlightenment. This is a difficult concept to explain, but there are different degrees of enlightenment, and even before Inez, the Holy Ones themselves had helped me enormously. But this process I was about to go through would take all these experiences to their full apex.

It was the most difficult undertaking I had ever started. To do this, I moved in with Inez. That was not easy, as I had to spend time apart from my family and children. My mother was taking care of the children and, of course, I went back and forth—but my family didn't understand at all what was going on and why I was doing this, although they had met Inez and liked her. I could not go into detail as to what was happening, and this created a lot of confusion and friction. Even now, in writing these words, it is painful to remember those challenging days. It was a difficult time for all involved, but there was no other way. I share this with you so you can understand the sacrifices that are sometimes required in this work.

My other challenge was that I didn't have the luxury of being supported during this training period. So it was a struggle financially. Several people did help as they could, but it was still difficult. Inez herself did not have a lot of money, as she was supported by a wealthy student of hers.

Yet I marched forward and lived with Inez for three years. During this time, my connection with the spiritual hierarchy became even closer. Before training with Inez, I was more or less a passive player when it came to the Holy Ones. The divine would present themselves, and I would go along with whatever they wanted to do. But now, Inez had taught me to systematically connect with the Holy Ones, which greatly deepened my appreciation of and relationship with them. And now there was much more interaction.

Finally, the hard work and sacrifice paid off. I reached spiritual maturity. I can't begin to describe the joy and exultation. It was marvelous in every way and worth every sacrifice. Many of my concerns dropped away, and although my earthly challenges did not disappear, my perspective on things was quite different.

After this, I moved back into my own home, but I continued to work with Inez as there was still more training involved, just not with the same intensity as before. From my training with Inez, I had developed the skill and confidence to teach, and eventually the opportunities did open to start my metaphysical career.

CHAPTER 10

THE DEVA KINGDOM

ITHIN THE TWELVE Kingdoms of Nature, there are hierarchies that work with all aspects of life. There is a hierarchy that works with the microbial kingdom, another for the mineral kingdom, another for the plant kingdom, yet another for the animal kingdom, and so on. For every aspect of the evolving life on earth, there is a spiritual hierarchy guiding over that kingdom. In rounding out this section on Who's Who in the Spiritual Realms, I would like to look at a hierarchy that works *beyond* the twelve kingdoms. This magnificent kingdom is known as the *deva kingdom*.

The word *deva* comes from the Sanskrit for "shining one" and usually translates into English simply as a "god." The devas play a central position in Hindu religious and metaphysical thought. It is a term used broadly for a variety of celestial beings throughout Indian scriptures, including the Vedas and the Puranas. In Western culture, the word *deva* has been used interchangeably for angels and archangels. They have been depicted as part of the nature spirits working with the elements of the earth. While the term has been aptly used generically in these ways, the actual hierarchal order of devas is something else altogether.

The deva kingdom is the next level up in spiritual development in the twelve kingdoms we have been exploring (see Figure 10.1). Once you have finished your journey through the twelve kingdoms, you have reached a level of being that is truly glorious in every way and unfolded all your potential within the twelve kingdoms. Yet your evolution does not stop. You begin a new spiritual journey through the deva kingdom.

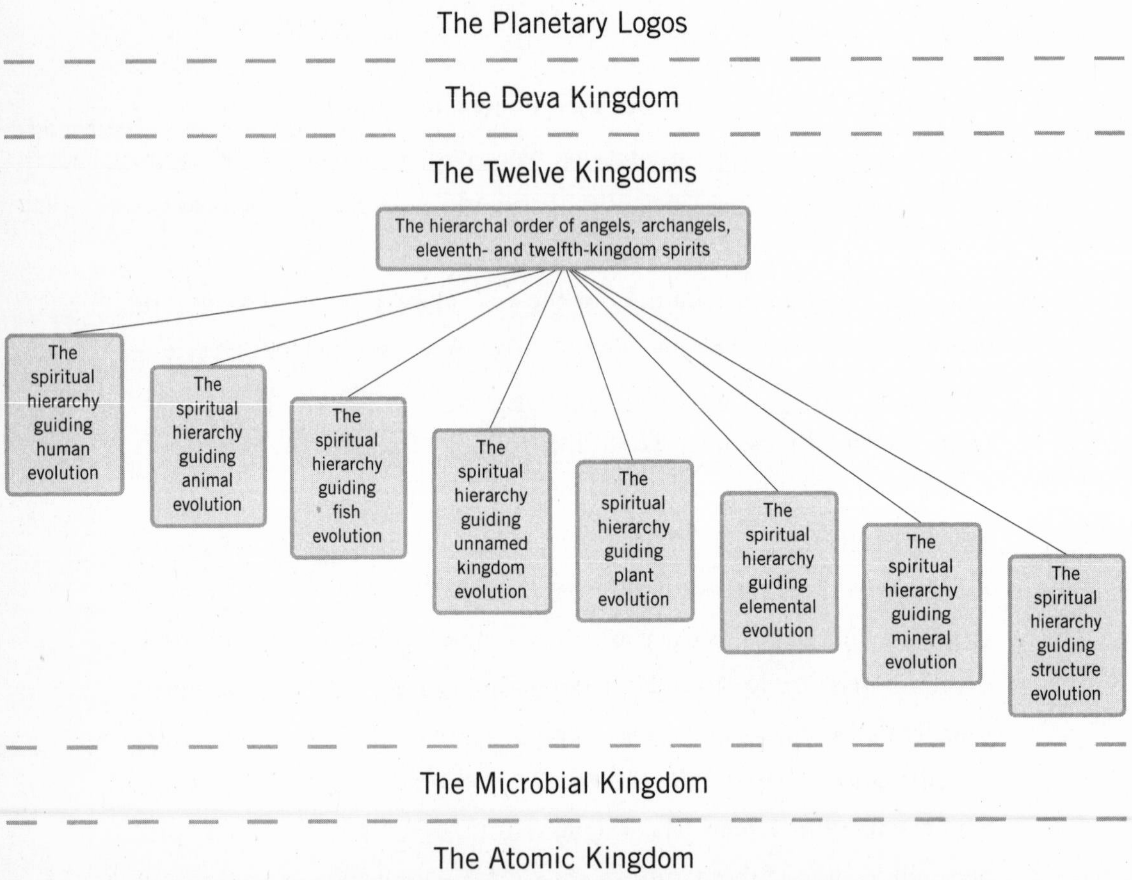

The Planetary Logos

The Deva Kingdom

The Twelve Kingdoms

The hierarchal order of angels, archangels, eleventh- and twelfth-kingdom spirits

The spiritual hierarchy guiding human evolution

The spiritual hierarchy guiding animal evolution

The spiritual hierarchy guiding fish evolution

The spiritual hierarchy guiding unnamed kingdom evolution

The spiritual hierarchy guiding plant evolution

The spiritual hierarchy guiding elemental evolution

The spiritual hierarchy guiding mineral evolution

The spiritual hierarchy guiding structure evolution

The Microbial Kingdom

The Atomic Kingdom

FIGURE 10.1 *The Hierarchies of the Earth*

This kingdom does many things. It coordinates all of the other hierarchies so that all are working together in the grand divine plan of earth. If the various hierarchies of the twelve kingdoms were like states in a country, the deva hierarchy would be the federal and even international governing body. The devas guide the Holy Ones who work with us.

These beings are colossal in stature and size. The best illustrations I have seen are the ones described by the Theosophist and author Geoffrey Hodson. His book *The Kingdom of the Gods* is a remarkable work, spanning many years of clairvoyant research and meticulous attention to detail. He describes various devas he was privileged to behold and does an excellent job illustrating the scale of these celestial beings.

The devas are truly like gods. They have a hierarchal order that leads all the way up to the great Planetary Logos of this earth. The Planetary Logos is a celestial being who is in charge of all evolutionary life on earth at every level. This being embraces the entire earth within the aura of this celestial presence. All the hierarchies and all life on earth receive their power and light from the Planetary Logos. This being is not God, but is extraordinarily God-like.

The devas are the guiding force for planetary-wide activities such as weather patterns and geological activities, including plate tectonics and volcanic activity. The devas have played an instrumental role in molding the earth to the place it is now, from its beginnings as a molten mass to the beautiful blue planet it is today. We must remember that all life is evolving and the earth itself is going through a process of evolution. Under the guiding hand of the Planetary Logos, the celestial devas are the divine administers of all this power.

The hierarchal order of devas, deva-rajas, and king and queen devas are strongly connected to astrological influences of the earth. There is spiritual energy pouring in from the various planets of our solar system, including the sun itself. The entire solar system is spiritually alive. The ancients esoterically acknowledged the living powers connected to the stars and planets. As spiritual power flows from the planetary systems to earth, the devas channel that power to the spiritual hierarchy and to us. It's an incredible process.

These great ones have rule over whole regions of the earth. For example, we think of a mythological god like Poseidon—the ancient Greek god of the sea—as a personification of natural phenomena. While Poseidon himself may have been mythical, the mystics who created this mythology well knew that there were actual devas of the seas who administered evolving life, and these devas answered to a planetary deva king of all the oceans of the world.

I have been honored to behold members of the deva kingdom. Once I was in the Angeles Crest Mountains near Los Angeles. I was with my co-author, Dimitri, and we were at a beautiful crest known as Charlton Flats. We had gone there to do some writing.

There were majestic Jeffrey pine trees of great height, which must have been very old. At one point I was looking up beyond the tree line and there appeared a family of devas in the sky! There were four devas: a king and queen deva, and two younger devas. They were staggering in size. The king deva was easily over one hundred feet tall. There was a semblance of form in the sense that these looked like figures with a head and torso. The light rays coming from them were so strong that if there was a more definite form, I could not make it out. Their auras stretched far beyond the mountain crest for miles in all directions. Many different energies were flowing in and out of them, and there was a series of outer concentric bands of light that seemed to amplify the radiance of their auras even more.

The devas did not communicate but wanted me to know they were there. I picked up the thought that they were the reigning devas of Southern California and this mountain forest was their headquarters. Often, the devas work away from very populated areas. From this mountain station, they were responsible for all the spiritual hierarchal activities in the area. With all the millions of people and activity going on in Southern California, you can imagine what a job that must be! It was interesting that this forest was the center of action, because it was a beautiful mountain range but not heavily visited. The forest was lush, as if the tall trees echoed the grandeur of these devas. Unfortunately, there was a major fire in the region, a natural part of the forest life, which devastated a large area of the forest. It is my understanding that these devas have moved their center of activity elsewhere.

For the most part, devas work through the hierarchy of angels, archangels, and celestial leaders to bless and inspire us. As we work more closely with the spiritual hierarchy, we receive the blessings of the devas. In my many years of working with the Holy Ones, it is rare to see a deva. When they do reveal themselves, they do it unexpectedly. This does not mean they do not show love and support. Behind the scenes, they are very involved in our lives. They will sometimes show themselves at key moments in a person's life.

MEDITATIVE PRAYER TO WORK WITH THE DEVAS

Heavenly Father/Holy Mother God, I ask for a blessing from the great devas so that I may feel part of the cosmic flow of all life and move in rhythm with the celestial drumbeat.

THE LITTLE PEOPLE

I have been asked if spirits such as fairies and gnomes are real and, if so, whether they play a part in the work of the spiritual hierarchy. There have been so many stories in metaphysical writings of nature spirits. Paracelsus believed that the four elements of the earth—earth, air, water, and fire—had nonphysical counterparts and that these counterparts were peopled with living spirits. As Manly P. Hall says in his encyclopedia book, *The Secret Teachings of All Ages*:

> The idea once held, that the invisible elements surrounding and interpenetrating the earth were peopled with living, intelligent beings, may seem ridiculous to the prosaic mind of today. This doctrine, however, has found favor with some of the greatest intellects of the world.

Literature through the ages has delighted us with stories of supernatural beings. While many of these creations may be fiction, the idea of invisible inhabitants with humanlike qualities is not fiction. Yes, I can tell you from personal experience that there are spirits such as fairies and gnomes. This earth is far more inhabited and diverse with life than we can possibly imagine. These spirits are part of evolving life that moves on nonphysical realms. There are many facets to these spirits, but the one I would like to focus on are the "Little People."

What are the Little People? They are souls who are part of the Twelve Kingdoms of Nature. As you will recall, when a soul finishes all its experiences in one kingdom, it moves on to the next kingdom. For example, when an animal soul has gone through all it can in the animal kingdom, it eventually graduates to the human kingdom. When the animal soul graduates to the human kingdom, however, it does not simply become like you and me. It first has to go through earlier stages of development in the human kingdom before it can graduate to the level of humanity that you are I are experiencing and enjoying.

This means that the Little People are, in fact, in the early nonphysical stages of human development. These are the salamanders, undines, gnomes, sylphs, brownies, elves, dryads, nereids, manikins, and fairies— all part of the varying degrees of development of the Little People. There is great variety within the Little People, and they have their own internal hierarchy. I have clairvoyantly seen fairies—everywhere from as little as a few inches high, to highly developed fairies almost two feet high. These delightful spirits go through the stages of experience, building up more spiritual power until they build up enough awareness to start their life as a physically incarnated human being.

The Little People are varied in character and temperament. There are Little People who work with the elements of the earth. The salamanders work and play with the elements of fire. The undines are beautiful spirits who live in the water. They are almost always seen as female in appearance but of course have their male counterpart. There are the sylphs who move delicately through the air, playing in the clouds and rain. Then there are the gnomes. These are spirits of the earth and have quite fascinating characteristics, from playful to grumpy to outright meanlooking. Separate from these Little People and the varieties associated with them are the fairies. This name does not quite do them justice, as there is great variety here as well. Some have the semblance of a Tinkerbell from J. M. Barrie's *Peter Pan*, but others, more developed, can be quite formidable.

Suffice it to say that the Little People play a part in the divine plan. Energetically, they form a foundation for the human kingdom itself. We could not enjoy the level of spiritual development we are at if it were not for the Little People. They are often thought of as nature spirits because they live in nature, but they are different from the actual spirits who watch over nature. I rarely see Little People in human-made environments such as cities with little greenery. They tend to live in gardens outside homes but rarely would actually inhabit that home. Even though they are a support system to the higher levels of human development, they generally stay away from people and like to keep to themselves.

In the spirit worlds, they are particularly expressive and prominent. On the other side are magnificent gardens around temple settings. During one visit, I remember sitting on a beach in one of these gardens and seeing three little fairy figures floating around the flowers. They were about six inches high and had auras that radiated about four inches in all directions with beautiful colors of pinks, greens, and blues. There were two female figures and one male. They were wearing light single-piece garments. They had power and were able to propel themselves through the air, although there were no wings. I watched them move from flower to flower, breathing in the fragrance. Each time they breathed in the essence of the flower, they got excited. They didn't interact with each other but clearly were a group of some sort. They would look at me, wanting me to know they were there. They had serene expressions, delicate and beautiful faces. I silently asked the Divine Light to go to them, which made them happy.

The Little People are extremely sensitive. If they like your vibration, they may appear to you. You have to approach them with a very pure heart. This is why they often appear to children. If they sense you are disturbed or have ulterior motives, they stay away. They do have spiritual powers and can influence our activity and behavior if they want to.

PART 3

The Dark Side

of Life

THE NATURE OF EVIL

U P TO THIS point we have been exploring the marvelous network of celestial beings who guide our spiritual growth. Yet one aspect of life seems out of context with this spiritual splendor. This is the idea of evil spirits, the devil, or Satan.

Every culture has had its own concept of evil or the devil. In Genesis, there is the famous temptation of Adam and Eve by evil—personified by the snake—in the Garden of Eden. While the Hebrew Bible mentions Satan by name only in the book of Job, the idea of evil permeates Jewish mystical and religious thought. If we turn to noncanonical Jewish writings such as the Book of Enoch, we find a dominant theme of good and evil. In that apocalyptic story, there are fallen angels called *watchers* who are led by a dark being known as Samael, often associated with Satan. The fallen Archangel Samael becomes a theme of evil in the Talmud.

If we go back further, we discover that Zoroastrianism laid the groundwork for our modern understanding of good and evil. They called the evil one *Angra Mainyu*, the antithesis of the divine Ahura Mazda. Zoroastrian belief in good and evil was an important development in spiritual thought, as it taught about personal responsibility. It was an act of empowerment for people to realize they had a choice in life to align with either divine or evil powers. Their actions made a difference. The lessons of good and evil are a teaching tool of morality. People were not simply pawns in the hands of the gods.

The concept of good and evil is center stage in Christian theology. Here, Satan is the antagonist in the great drama of human life. In the Christian concept, our spiritual destiny of heaven or hell is determined by which spiritual force we align ourselves with. Islam has its belief in evil. As a monotheistic religion, it shares much with the Judaic/Christian concepts of evil. In Islamic theology, Satan is known as *Shaytan*, or "the rejected." In Hinduism, there is no concept of a single devil who is the source of all evil, but there are many evil spirits and demons known as *asuras*. Asuras are the antithesis of the angelic suras. Hindu theology identifies many classes or races of asuras, including *danavas* and *rakshasas*, to name just two.

In more recent times, humanity has questioned the concept of the devil. Some believe that the entity we call Satan is really our own creation—there is no such thing as the devil, only the evil we create ourselves, and that we personify evil as the devil so that we can better deal with the dark side of our own nature. As always, metaphysics has a very definite insight into this age-old question. I hope to put to rest some confusion relating to this difficult subject.

To understand the problem of evil and the devil, we must bring into play several spiritual concepts. The first is the concept of the One. Clearly, if there is only one divine power in the universe, there cannot be a power opposed to it. According to the law of the One, there cannot be two ultimate sources in creation, God and a devil. There can be only God. The second principle to consider is free will. We are all creations of God, but it is our choice to express that divinity or not. And the third concept is the differentiation between an actual spiritual being called "Satan" and evil actions.

EVIL AS A BEHAVIOR

Metaphysics takes several different approaches in understanding evil. There is an esoteric definition of evil as "an inherent quality of matter resistant to the divine impulse." In this interpretation, while physical matter is born of the spiritual life, ironically, of itself, it resists the promptings of spirit. This philosophy has made many devout people mistakenly think that physical matter itself is evil—hence physical life is bad, something to be negated in preference to the spiritual life. We see the extremism that some ascetics have taken in denying themselves basic physical needs as a reflection of this belief.[1]

Certainly, all of us on the spiritual path can recognize the inherent challenges of physical life. We may feel the desire to pursue the spiritual life, yet we can feel that the physical life is the antithesis to that spiritual impulse. But this does not mean that material existence is bad or not spiritual. What we must remember is that the resistance we face in physical form is what makes us strong. If we see the physical as *part* of the spiritual, rather than something contrary to the divine, then we start to

---

[1] In *Kingdom of the Gods*, Geoffrey Hodson eloquently compares this philosophy to the ancient symbol of the Scarab. To quote Hodson:

> All evil, and in consequence all human sorrow, springs from this heresy of "separateness" (Ahamkara). . . . As the scarab beetle encloses the seed of its life in a ball of mud, so it would seem, does Beelzebub (the devil), also named Lord of the Scarabs, enshroud the monad (human soul) of men in material vehicles. Having performed its enclosing function, the scarab rolls the ball of mud to a sunny spot and leaves it to its own devices and to the influence of the sun. Ultimately the egg hatches and brings forth larva which becomes the winged scarab, in its turn parent of further eggs. Beelzebub, in its esoteric meaning, may perhaps be regarded as a personification of that impulse. . . . That is probably why the scarab was sacred in Egypt.

spiritually master the physical. The physical pulls are not something to succumb to, fear, or avoid. They are something to face and master. Conquering physical resistance not only elevates one's soul, it transforms physical matter as well.

This brings us to another interpretation of evil or Satan as the "adversary." In this definition, the purpose of Satan and the evil impulse is to test humanity's spiritual strength and devotion to God. This is the theme that runs through the book of Job. We see this challenge in our everyday life. Sometimes our worst enemy can be our greatest opportunity. It forces us to muster up courage and strength that we thought we never had. If everything came easily, we would not be challenged and therefore would not grow. It is when we are challenged by some adversarial force that our true colors shine forth and our souls are tempered by the spiritual fires we are going through. In all mystical stories, there is a great adversary the hero must conquer. We are all heroes in our own life and must not shrink when adversarial situations present themselves.

These are all important interpretations of evil. I would like to emphasize another interpretation that is intimately connected to our evolution and work with the spiritual hierarchy—*evil as a behavior.* What is an evil act? We know when we see something terrible that goes beyond comprehension; we call it evil. Murder is certainly a terrible act. We qualify murder, however, depending on the reason for murder. If we kill in self-defense, it is not the same thing as premeditated murder. We look upon a crime of passion differently than cold-blooded murder. But if the murder is particularly heinous, we call it evil. The root of the word *evil* comes from Middle English; it is associated with the words *up* and *over* and means "exceeding due measure" or "overstepping proper measure." So, evil can be described as *excessive* destructive behavior.

Now the word *sin* comes into play here. There is a definition of sin that means "off the mark." If we are meant to spiritually grow and un-fold the divine potential within us, then every act we perform that helps us in this goal, we call "spiritual" or "constructive." Every time we per-form an act that takes us away from this goal, we call "destructive" or "sinful." Making mistakes is a natural part of the growing process. We're all bound to sin, or "miss the mark," at one point or another. This does not make us sinners in a basic sense or imply that our souls are bad. It just means we need to get back on track.

These kinds of mistakes are something completely different from evil acts. *Evil acts are a deliberate misuse of spiritual principles for selfish ends.* In other words, you have to willfully and knowingly commit acts that you know are against divine or natural laws to be committing something evil. An evil act is deliberately perverting spiritual laws. Evil acts are the true anathema to the soul. By doing an evil act with conscious knowing, you are cutting yourself off from your spiritual source, and the act you commit will obviously be very destructive, because there will be no Divine Light in it.

THE STORY OF SATAN

Evil is a behavior that exists, whether the devil does or not. However, we still have left part of our question unanswered. If evil exists, does Satan exist? Is there really a force that operates on such a diabolical level? As sad as it is to say, and without trying to create a sense of fear or para-noia, Satan does exist. And not only does he exist, he has legions work-ing under him.

To better understand what is meant by Satan, we have to step back and explore some of the intricacies of the spiritual hierarchy. As we have learned, there are twelve celestial archangelic leaders working to uplift humanity. Yet, in addition to these twelve celestial archangels, there are also twelve *planetary* archangels who are *counterparts* to the celestial archangels. These counterparts are not as evolved as the celestial archangels but are splendid in their own right and answer to the twelve celestial archangels. These planetary archangels have their own responsibilities and play an essential part in the evolutionary process. Interestingly, these archangels go by the same names as their celestial counterparts. For example, as there is a celestial Archangel Michael whom we pray to when calling on the Light, there is also a planetary Archangel Michael who works behind the scenes and helps us in our evolution.

One of the twelve celestial archangelic leaders is Archangel Lucifer, or "the morning star." As we saw in chapter 7, the celestial Archangel Lucifer is a glorious archangel in his own right. In addition to this celestial Archangel Lucifer, there is his planetary counterpart. This planetary Archangel Lucifer was splendid as well and very involved in the development of humanity. He had several jobs to do, including going to the netherworlds to help lift up the lower entities, to try to awaken them and bring them back into the Divine Light.

As the story goes, these lower entities formed an idea about how great it would be to convince a being like Archangel Lucifer to leave God and join them. These entities began to worship Lucifer. They told him that he was greater than God and that he could become God himself. You might say they "wined and dined" him. Through a series of events, Lucifer was beguiled by the planetary entities and began to believe that he could be greater than God.

The spiritual hierarchy warned Lucifer that of course he could not supersede God, but he became so entranced by his own splendor that he disconnected from God. At the same time, this planetary Archangel Lucifer and his agents had been given a difficult but important assignment connected to the blossoming of humanity. In his self-entranced state, he refused to fulfill the divine work that had been assigned to him. This was the dramatic fall from heaven. In truth, the celestial Archangel Lucifer has not fallen. He remains in the heaven worlds. It was the planetary Lucifer who fell and became known as Satan. The worst part of the whole thing was that not only did this archangel fall, he managed to bring down one third of his spiritual legion with him.

There are several references to this fatal fall in religious and mystical literature. There are the haunting words from the Gospel of Luke in which Jesus said, "Behold, I saw Satan fall like lightning from heaven."[2] There is poignant reference to the fallen Lucifer in the book of Isaiah, which speaks of him as the "son of the morning" who, through pride, tried to "raise his throne above the stars of God," but instead was brought down to the "depths of the pit."[3]

There is a tradition found in the Babylonian Talmud about the "Primeval Ones" who refused to participate in the creation of humankind and were destroyed by God. The story of the Fall of Satan is found in the Qur'an. After he refused to prostrate before Adam, and was therefore expelled, the spirit Iblees swore to God that he would do his utmost to mislead humankind. It was then that he came to be known as "Shaytan" (Satan), and his followers from among the jinn and humankind as "Shayateen."[4]

---

[2] Luke 10:18.

[3] Isaiah 14:12–15.

[4] From the Qur'an: [7:11] We created you, then we shaped you, then we said to the angels, "Fall prostrate before Adam." They fell prostrate, except Iblees *(Satan)*; he was not with the prostrators.

The Test Begins

[7:12] He said, "What prevented you from prostrating when I ordered you?" He said, "I am better than he; You created me from fire, and created him from mud."

[7:13] He said, "Therefore, you must go down, for you are not to be arrogant here. Get out; you are debased."

Satan is an extreme example of walking away from the light. Even though he has yet to turn around and walk back into the Divine Light, he is still part of the One. But since he cut himself off from his spiritual source, he cannot tap the universal life energy directly. His power lies in his ability to *steal* spiritual light from others for his own end. And he does this all too well. The story of Satan is an extreme case of evil because he is committing these acts with full knowing and intent.

This tragedy in the spiritual unfoldment of creation was *not* part of the divine plan. God did not design this to happen. It was an act of free will. This shows that even at the level of an archangel, there is always freedom of choice, even if the choice is a terrible one. The actions of Satan and his angels threw the whole spiritual plan off-kilter. God and the spiritual hierarchy had to compensate for what happened, and have done so beautifully, but it created new challenges and has slowed the whole unfoldment process down.

This is why spiritual protection is so important to you. It helps keep these types of vibrations away, because the satanic forces cannot stand someone who is strong in the Divine Light. Always remember, Satan and his forces have no power over you unless you permit them to have it. By aligning yourself with the Divine Light, you give them no opportunities to influence you. Fortunately, you do not have to directly concern yourself with Satan. God has assigned many wonderful beings to deal with the satanic forces. That is not your job. Your job is to keep yourself a clear channel of the Divine Light.

DEMONS AND ENTITIES

Satan doesn't work alone. Unfortunately, he has many working with him. He has created his own pseudo-hierarchy, with him at the top.

Remember, these spiritual beings may have fallen, but they still possess the intelligence and knowledge they have accumulated. If the purpose of the spiritual hierarchy is to serve God and the divine plan, then the goal of the satanic hierarchy is to serve Satan and their own selfish ambitions. They see God and the spiritual hierarchy as the enemy who must be overturned.

The Kabbalah teaches of a demonic hierarchy known as the ten inverse Sephiroth (emanations).[5] For our present study, I would like to put our attention on two broad aspects of the satanic hierarchy: demons and entities. As it is extremely rare that you would come in contact with Satan himself, it is the demons and entities that may try to interact with you in some way. They often attempt to disturb or disrupt your life when they can. This is not to say they succeed, but it is something you have to be on the alert for. I have had many encounters with lower forces, and the challenge is very real. My mentor Inez spoke eloquently on the subject of Satan and aptly commented that one of the greatest feats the lower forces have done is to convince many that they do not exist.

Demons are fallen angels. These were once glorious members of the spiritual hierarchy. Before the fall, they were angels working under the then planetary Archangel Lucifer. These fallen angels are of varying orders and abilities. They are now the administrators of the satanic plan. They are skilled in their dark crafts and answer to Satan himself.

Entities are human souls who were once high up the spiritual ladder.

---

[5] As S. L. MacGregor states in his book *The Kabbalah Unveiled*: "The Demons are the grossest and most deficient of all forms. Their ten degrees answer to the decad of the Sephiroth, but in inverse ratio, as darkness and impurity increase with the descent of each degree. . . . Their prince is *Samael*, SMAL, the angel of poison and of death. His wife is the harlot, or woman of whoredom, ASHTH ZNVNIM, *Isheth Zenunim*; and united they are called the beast, CHIVA, *Chioa*. Thus the infernal trinity is completed, which is, so to speak, the averse and caricature of the supernal Creative One."

They were working in the spiritual realms with the angels and archangels. When the titanic struggle began, like many of Lucifer's angels, they took sides with the satanic forces. Some entities have redeemed themselves and turned back to the light, but many have stayed in their fallen state. Entities are the type of lower forces we are most likely to encounter.

Demons and entities are attracted to negativity. When people lie, cheat, steal, hurt, or kill, this can attract the lower forces. These forces are harassing, argumentative, vindictive, clever, and organized; they love to create friction and cannot be trusted. They incite people to violence, abuses of sex, drugs, drinking, smoking, and avarice of money. They encourage crime, corruption, bad habits, and perversions of all types. They will try to cloud the mind and judgment as well as stir the emotions out of control. They hate those in the light. They despise the family unit and try to break up homes and happy lives. Wherever there is good, they try to destroy it to serve their purposes. They direct their evil in all areas of life: financial, political, social, educational, business, scientific, artistic, medical, religious, and the metaphysical.

They know how to work together well in their common goal. Their bond, however, is not based on love as it is with the spiritual hierarchy— it's based on mutual ambition. They have been promised spiritual powers and gifts beyond what they have earned. In some ways, Satan has been able to grant certain transitory gifts to those who follow him. Fortunately, this ability is diminishing, which is one of the reasons that the satanic hierarchy is losing ground. Satan is simply not able to keep the same kind of promises as before. Slowly, his circle of influence is diminishing as many are turning back to the light. In the end he cannot hope to succeed, but he would rather bring everyone down with him than admit defeat, and this is what makes him particularly dangerous.

WHY DOES GOD ALLOW
SUCH EVIL TO EXIST?

This is the question that many have asked through the ages. It is not so easy to answer, as we simply don't have all the answers. There are several things, however, the Holy Ones share with us. First, we must remember that Satan is still in the archangelic kingdom even though he has fallen in stature. His demons are still in the angelic kingdom, as the entities are in the human kingdom. They were part of the hierarchal structure of our evolutionary plan, and it is not easy to simply cut that off. For example, we may have a family member who has committed a terrible crime, but that person is still a family member. We must also remember that even though the demons have forfeited their spiritual position and power, they still have their intelligence intact and use that intelligence to their advantage. As the saying goes, "They have fallen from a greater height than you and I have yet reached."

Perhaps the single biggest reason God has permitted the lower forces to exert influence in human affairs is as a testing ground for us. While their presence creates greater resistance and danger, they also offer greater opportunity to grow. If you can meet the challenge that these lower forces present, you can become extremely strong and sturdy in the Divine Light, more than you otherwise would have. Since the forces cannot influence you unless on some level that influence was permitted, it's a test of your resolve to stay in the light.

Renouncing evil is part of your spiritual maturity. This is a test that every soul must eventually pass. We saw this test with Jesus, who was tempted by Satan in the desert. It was beautifully illustrated in the story of Siddhartha, who was tempted by Mara just before reaching enlightenment and becoming the Buddha. In fact, every soul, before fully claiming enlightenment, must pass the test of evil. The lower forces will attempt to seduce the aspirant with any possible weakness. If all your weaknesses are tested and you can stay strong, they are no longer weaknesses. You have demonstrated that you would not use the blessings of God for selfish ends, and you have proven yourself ready for the higher life.

A PERSONAL ENCOUNTER

The most challenging encounter I have had in my life with the satanic forces was an encounter with Satan himself. I was in my late twenties and already had the extraordinary visitations of celestial beings. I felt well-acquainted with the spiritual hierarchy, very loved and supported by them. One day, I was reading alone in my home, when I looked up and saw a man standing in front of me. He was about ten feet away. I couldn't tell at first if this was a vision or visitation, or if someone was actually in the house, because he appeared very flesh-and-blood. He was tall and strikingly handsome, and he presented himself as benevolent.

He smiled and humbly said, "I'm a lieutenant of the Higher."

When he spoke, I was able to tune in to his aura somewhat. It appeared at first to be almost Christlike, with strong flows of light. But the vibration I picked up was the most chilling I had ever experienced, so I was very apprehensive. I thought it might be a lower spirit, but I had never encountered one like this before. I didn't know what was going on, but I was very on my guard.

"I don't believe you," I challenged him.

"You have to believe me," he replied innocently.

As this exchange was going on, I was silently calling on my angelic teachers for help. I needed their guidance and support to reveal to me what was happening. Confused or masquerading spirits had appeared to me before, and the angels were always there to help. Now I needed them more than ever.

As I sent the signal for help, I realized they were already present. There were a group of angels protecting me by surrounding this being from the spirit worlds. Then they flashed in the picture who this was. It was a shocking moment, and I felt great apprehension and dread. This was my first time having a one-on-one encounter with a malefic force such as this. Even with the angels there, my first thought was fear that he wanted to hurt me.

Of course, he was well aware that I was now on to him, so he quickly dropped his benevolent demeanor. He now became aggressive and hypnotic.

"I want you to follow me," he said.

The starkness of this declaration took me by surprise. An unanticipated indignation sprang in me. "Not on your life. I know who you are!" I replied.

He looked at me intently, saying, "Worship me and I'll give you everything."

At this point I could see more clearly the circle of angelic beings surrounding him. I knew I was protected but remained extremely alert as his hypnotic power was considerable, even with the help of the angels. I tried to deflect his trancelike energy.

"What do you want with me? There are so many others." I really was wondering why he was bothering with me.

In a disgusted tone he replied, "I have them already. It's you I want!" It was chilling to realize he had absolutely no respect for those already under his spell.

Then he tried to flatter me. "As high as you think you are, you're even higher!" I knew I was a developed soul, but what he said came as a surprise. I was to find out later that it was true. I was further up the spiritual ladder than I had originally thought. So he was right, but not for the right reasons.

He then started projecting the pictures of what I would receive if I followed him. At this time, I knew I was destined to be a teacher, but I had no idea how it was going to happen or what shape that teaching career would take. Satan started projecting pictures of my being a very successful world teacher, adored, wealthy, and influential. The way he projected these thought images was compelling. This was a lifestyle I had not imagined for myself. Yet, I confess, the images were intriguing. They made me look so flattering, and it seemed like I was still doing good with my spiritual gifts. What made this even more compelling was that I sensed that that these were not empty promises—he could actually make these things happen if I followed him. The fear of him hurting me now changed to a deeper fear that I might actually succumb to his will.

At that moment of bewilderment, a magnificent angelic being came very close to me. He gave me a divine vision of what would happen if I did what Satan asked. It would have been disastrous. I would become a false prophet, a black magician. I would lose my connection to the Higher and God. I would pervert my spiritual talents for ambitious ends. They showed me that that was what Satan really wanted. It wasn't me at all—it was my spiritual gifts that he wanted, for diabolical ends. The angel flashed pictures of people being hurt and misled because of me, while I falsely claimed it was all in the name of God. I would completely waste and destroy my life along with many others. It was terrifying. The angel showed me how, when I finished this life, I would end up in the lower netherworlds on the other side, completely emptied of my spiritual position and forfeited of my mystical gifts. They even flashed the long, difficult road it would take to redeem myself from such a transgression. It was a gruesome scenario.

My reaction was complete shock. Yet I knew that what the angel showed me was completely true. The full scope of this encounter was becoming clearer. Satan was still at his full offensive, now trying to displace the images the angel had given me. What was adding to the menacing energy was that during this part of the encounter, Satan was presenting himself as if he were God himself granting these gifts and the Holy Ones were the enemy. It was a completely upside-down picture, but he so believed it himself that it convolutedly made his demonic appeal more convincing.

"Come now. Follow me," he insisted.

But now I was resolute. I refused to succumb to his suggestions no matter what the cost. The angels directed the light more strongly at him and I gradually saw through the fake, camouflage aura he put on and started to see his real aura, which was unbelievably dark and menacing. It was also clear that the handsome form he had presented himself in was not his real form at all. The Holy Ones chose not to show me what he really looked like. I was grateful for that, as it would have been too much for one encounter.

He did not advance, as the Holy Ones were preventing that, but he continued to be aggressive in his energy and tone, trying to plant ideas in my head to turn me his way.

"I'll never worship you," I declared.

"You're a fool!" he said.

"I only worship the Christ," I proclaimed.

Saying this seemed to really infuriate him. "Then I'll make you suffer!" he retorted.

He became vindictive, realizing I was not going to comply. The Holy Ones soon took him away and the encounter was over.

My blessed angelic teachers sent light to help me calm down, as I was shaken by the ordeal. They said to me, "Thank God you were aware of what was going on." Only now did I fully realize this was a test. This was my trial to see if I could be swayed to use my spiritual gifts for selfish ends.

The experience lasted barely five minutes and there was more that happened that I cannot share. In fact, this is the first time I am sharing this story in this detail, again at the urging of the Holy Ones. I do this not to scare you, but to let you know that Satan is real. He is not all-powerful and doesn't have carte blanche to do whatever he likes, but he does exist.

The experience was sad and unsettling. Up to this point, my spiritual experiences were so ecstatic, and this was very sobering, to experience such evil firsthand. It affected me for some time. In a way, you could say it was a loss of spiritual innocence. I was always on the cautious side, but now I became even more cautious. It is this cautionary note I wish to impart to you. The spiritual path is so exciting and wonderful that you can mistakenly think the whole world shares your excitement and that everything labeled spiritual is in fact spiritual. This is simply not the case. There are evil forces at work. You must be careful, as there are many pitfalls on the path. It is part of your test to be tempted by the dark side at some point, and to learn to choose the Divine Light.

The good news is that passing such a spiritual test makes you much stronger. In my case, this experience actually brought my spiritual gifts to a new height, and my determination to walk the path of Divine Light deepened. As far as Satan's declaration to make me suffer, he did try to cause my death a couple of times. But the Holy Ones protected me each time. And this is something I wish to share with you. The satanic forces will say things to lure you or scare you, but their words are empty if you stay in the Divine Light. I'm not saying they don't have power or intelligence—they do. But if you stay in the light of God, you'll be fine. The lower can't touch you if you stay strong, alert, and in the light.

THE POWER OF PROTECTION

What can you do to protect yourself from these negative influences? First, understand that it is not you that the lower forces are ultimately after. It's the spiritual hierarchy. We are the battlefield. Since they have cut themselves off from their spiritual source, the lower forces have to steal divine power from others to succeed in their plans. So what they want from us is our spiritual light.

The most valuable thing you possess is not your fame, money, power, or influence. It is your Divine Light. You have earned it through your every good word, thought, act, and deed. The light within your soul is what gives power to your consciousness. It gives you the energy to do anything. It gives you the ability to climb the spiritual ladder and enjoy life to its fullest. The lower forces recognize how valuable Divine Light is and will do anything to get it.

The lower forces, however, can't simply take the light from you. You have to open up to that lower influence on some level. The truth is that no negative energy can enter your aura unless you permit it to happen. If you were able to keep yourself in an absolute pure state of consciousness, the lower could not touch you. The problem is that we don't live in a perfect world, and we are not yet perfected, so this does open up the possibility for negative influences.

Here are three tips for staying protected from negative influences:

1. Use Protective Light
2. Connect with Your Higher Self
3. Call on Your Angelic Teachers

1. Use Protective Light

Keeping protective light around you is one of the best things you can do to keep negative influences away. Spiritual protection is so important. Just as you lock your home or your car for safety, it's important to keep the protective light around you. The spiritual being who is assigned the job of protection is Archangel Michael. Work with him and the angels of protection. Every soul has two or three angels of protection working with them. This is not all at the same time, but they come when the need arises. They work with you whether you are aware of them or not. When you work with them more directly, they can make a better connection. The angels of protection place the protective light in your aura and help to maintain the spiritual connections with the divine.

You also have angelic bodyguards. These are angelic beings who work to reinforce the protective light and work with the angels of protection to ward off evil advances, as well as alert you to dangers and physical distresses.

The spiritual power ray that works very well for protection is the golden ray. This is a dynamic power, and a ray the Higher uses when surrounding you in protective light. Here is a wonderful protective exercise that you should use regularly. Begin by standing up and holding your arms out, parallel to the ground. Close your eyes and envision a golden bubble of light surrounding you, just beyond your arms' reach. Then say the following prayer:

MEDITATIVE PRAYER WITH THE GOLDEN
BUBBLE OF PROTECTION

Heavenly Father/Holy Mother God, under the direction of Archangel
Michael and the angels of protection, encircle me now in a golden
bubble of protective light surrounding me in seven
flows of this holy power.

As you say these words, envision the light enveloping you seven times in a clockwise motion. Hold this thought for a moment to feel the power being established, and you are done. I recommend this protection before every meditation, and at least once a day to maintain your protective light. If you feel you were upset by something or feel a pending danger, again you can reinforce this power. Once you have done the exercise, it's established and you don't have to think about it.

2. Connect with Your Higher Self

As human souls, we all have temptations. By raising your consciousness to your Higher Self, you can rise up out of temptation. Every soul on earth has a Higher Self. This is seen in the aura as a radiant point of light about two feet above the head (see chapter 14). When you put your attention here, you have raised your consciousness above human toils and troubles. And you have raised your consciousness above the lower demonic influence. The lower forces can't touch your Higher Self. They try to stop you from reaching into that Higher Self, but once you are there, you are truly "under the shadow of the Almighty."

The key with effectively reaching into the higher nature is not getting caught in disturbing mental and emotional conditions because this holds you to those levels, making it difficult to reach into higher states of consciousness. And here is where you can be deceived the most subtly—through wrong thinking. If someone wallows in sadness, anger, hatred, or self-pity, they can unintentionally open up to the influence of the lower energies. I'm not saying every time you have an angry outburst, for example, this will open you up. But persistent negative activity can attract lower energies. So staying in a positive state of consciousness is an essential elevating and protective tool.

3. Call on Your Angelic Teachers

In addition to the angels of protection and bodyguards, you can always call on your teachers. Your angelic teachers are the front line of support on a day-to-day basis. If there is something you are not sure about or something you feel uneasy about and you need guidance, then call on your angelic teachers for illumination. They will reveal to you any possible malefic influences.

In closing this chapter, let it be said that the time period when Satan can affect our lives is nearing its end. For a long time, there has been an extraordinary effort by the hierarchy to turn things around. In the New Day that is fast approaching, the spiritual hierarchy will claim full keys to this earthly kingdom and can begin guiding this planet and the entire evolutionary process as it was meant to unfold. The Holy Ones have conveyed the message to stay very close to the Divine Light in these last days of spiritual purging. They have cautioned that there may be rough times ahead, but the Divine Light will prevail. You can do your part by living the spiritual life as best you know how, and let God do the rest.

PART 4

The Tools

of Perception

CHAPTER 12

THE PSYCHIC AND DIVINE WORLDS

N THIS SECTION, we will explore the process of spiritually interacting with the Holy Ones through such means as clairvoyance
and telepathy. The ability to perceive and communicate with the
spiritual hierarchy is one of the defining characteristics of a truly
illumined soul. Yet clairvoyance and telepathy are some of the most
misunderstood and misused aspects of all spiritual study. In my own
case, my clairvoyance was awakened at age three. I was also having
mental communications with divine beings from the other side about
the same time, but it was many years before I was a *trained* clairvoyant
and could harness my gifts and consistently communicate with the
Holy Ones. I had to earn that right through many years of dedication
and service. Even today, I am still deepening my relationship with the
Holy Ones.

Interacting with the spiritual hierarchy falls under two broad categories of experiences: the psychic and the divine. To understand how to
interact with the Holy Ones and avoid potential dangers, I need to step
back and give you a crash course on the difference between the psychic
and divine dimensions of life. Many people in metaphysics do not realize

there is a difference. They consider the two to be the same, when there is actually a great difference.

As we look at these two dimensions of life, please remember: You do not need to perceive the Holy Ones to work with them. They are already working with you. Understanding them—including them in your life, meditations, and prayers—is the first step to direct communion. Yet even if you are not clairvoyant or telepathic, understanding the dynamics of these spiritual tools is essential in connecting with the Higher. And it's especially important for those who have had contact or are working with someone who claims to be in contact with the Higher.

Gifts like clairvoyance are not for the simply curious, because spiritual perception is not just about seeing the Higher—an interaction with a divine being is a transformative, creative experience. Several dynamics are going on at the same time, which is why it's such a sacred moment when one is having a genuine interaction with a celestial being.

The ability to communicate and interact with the Holy Ones was one of the most sacred acts in the ancient world. This practice of theurgy, or "divine action," was the time when the mystics interacted with celestial beings. The Neo-Platonists called this ability *theophany*, which means "appearance of God." The mystic Helena Blavatsky gave one of the best definitions of theophany as "communication between the gods or God and those initiated mortals who are spiritually fit to enjoy such intercourse." She went on to say that to be truly able to communicate with divine beings required a holy, sanctified life. As she writes, "Knowledge of the inner meaning of their hierarchies and purity of life alone can lead to the acquisition of the power necessary for communication with them. To arrive at such an exalted goal the aspirant must be absolutely worthy."

To reach this place of communion, the initiate had to go through many trials and tests to prove worthy. If there was any self-interest or ulterior motives involved, the candidate would have to wait until such desires were tempered and the soul was ready for such an experience. The dangers connected to misuse of spiritual powers were great. If one turned clairvoyant abilities to selfish ends, what was once selfless service to the divine would turn into black magic. The initiate could end up invoking evil spirits, either unintentionally or with deliberate intent. The holy practice of theophany could turn into sorcery.

There are no shortcuts to the mystical experience. Building your character and developing your intuition are your keys to experiencing the Higher. Eventually we will all experience the Holy Ones in our own time.

THE PSYCHIC REALMS

Let us start our exploration by looking at the psychic world. The word *psychic* comes from the Greek word *psyche*, which can have two meanings. It can mean "pertaining to the mind" as in the word *psychology*—the science of the mind. Or it can mean "pertaining to the soul," or animating life principle. This was the original metaphysical use of the term *psychic*. A person's psychic nature was their inner essence. Some saw psychic energy as a type of spiritual fluid that pervaded the universe and animated all living things. As time went on, the definition changed. Today the common definition of *psychic* denotes the talents or phenomena that appear inexplicable by physical laws.

The modern understanding of psychism came into Western consciousness prominently in the 1800s, with the rise of spiritualism, which was very popular in Europe and the United States. (Of course, psychic phenomena are not limited to Western culture. In India, there are many demonstrations of psychic feats. Many practices of the shamans are psychic in nature as well.) Two famous figures were the Fox sisters, who performed various psychic feats. Spiritualistic groups practiced séances, materializations, contacting spirits through mediumship, trance mediumship, and other psychic activities. A key goal in the spiritualistic movement was the desire to prove that there was an existence beyond this physical world. They confounded many in the scientific community with their psychic phenomena, performing feats that could not be explained with material scientific understanding. Spiritualism appealed to those who wanted to see some kind of sign that there really was a world beyond the physical.

The psychic energy gets its power from the dimension of life known as the *astral planes* or *astral worlds*. The astral worlds are the next realm of life from the physical. The word *astral* comes from the Latin word for "starry." The astral planes are the hereafter. When we cross over from earth to the other side through the portal we call death, we cross over to the astral planes. The astral worlds, then, are the closest nonphysical dimensions of life to the physical.

These astral worlds are multidimensional. There are seven distinct astral levels or planes. Within each of these levels are seven subplanes, comprising forty-nine gradations of astral matter. These astral planes are in ascending order of development, with the first astral plane being the most primitive and the seventh astral plane being the most developed. When each of us crosses over to the other side, we will gravitate to one of these astral planes, depending on how much spiritual power we have accumulated during our time on earth.

The astral worlds are the stepping-stone to the divine worlds. They are the dimensions where we learn to acclimate to the heavenly vibrations. They are where we assimilate our earthly experiences, get spiritual instruction, and grow in Divine Light. They are the planes we go to when we make our transition from this earth, and the planes we come from when we incarnate on earth.

We are linked to this astral world even while we are here in physical experience. When we incarnate on earth in physical form, we bring with us our astral body. This astral body is supporting our physical body during our incarnation. Our astral body is our connecting link to the astral worlds. When we die, we drop the physical and completely withdraw into the astral body and return to the astral worlds. So this means that while we are on earth, we are encased in astral as well as physical matter.

The *psychic world* is the term we use when referring to our connection and influence with the astral planes while we are on earth. It is our awareness of this astral support that we call *psychic*.

When handled in a balanced way, the psychic can help us acclimate to nonphysical environments. The psychic part of us is important to our evolution. It helps acquaint us with the inner life. The psychic is the way to prepare for the spiritual. Much of our intuition starts in the psychic. The psychic world takes us out of the mundane, everyday existence. It is a sensationalistic world. Through the psychic dimensions, we can see spiritual colors, connect with souls who have passed on, get predictions, talk with spirits, produce psychic phenomena, and so on.

When you have your spiritual awakening, it's the astral part of you that the Holy Ones first awaken. The celestial beings stimulate the astral part to stir you on the spiritual path. This is why it is so easy to mistake the astral for the divine. However, once you are spiritually awakened, the Holy Ones then encourage you to break through the psychic and start connecting with your higher, divine nature. This sets your feet on the mystical path. The soul now learns to completely rely on the divine for support.

Although the psychic helps you in your spiritual journey, the thing to remember is not to rely on the psychic for your spiritual guidance and growth. The psychic world has a limited range of expression. Though that range is greater than the physical, it is not nearly as powerful as the divine/etheric realms. In addition, the astral realms are of mixed vibrations. There are evolved and unevolved levels of consciousness. This means that information from the psychic channels alone may or may not be accurate. It is not easy to distinguish what aspect of the astral the information is coming from. And if you are not careful, you can unintentionally open up to the lower aspect of the astral, which can cause a lot of trouble for you.

We are all psychic in one way or another. It's part of our makeup. It is not difficult to be a psychic, per se. What it requires is a certain talent that a person either is born with or learns to develop, but *being a psychic does not require spiritual advancement.* Trained psychics are not necessarily more spiritually developed than you are. Now there are some very good people who are spiritual and also are working on the psychic level. Naturally, these souls are working on a higher order, yet psychic activity draws its power from the same astral realms of life, whether it is psychic clairvoyance, channeling, or something else.

When you are operating from the psychic level, you are not connecting with your Higher Self. This is why the celestial beings want you to connect with your divine powers, which can steer your psychic and physical selves. In other words, there is a place for your astral/psychic gifts. God has given them to you for a reason, but you don't want to build your spiritual foundation on them. Just as you do not want to depend entirely on the limited perspective of the physical, you do not want to depend on the limited point of view of the psychic either. *You want to connect with your divine nature first.* Through your divine nature, you will incorporate everything else.

Rising up from psychic influences is a daunting task. There is a tremendous psychic bombardment going on each day of our lives. It takes a lot of spiritual power not to be affected by it. Yet one of the most important things you can do as a spiritual student is learn to control the psychic part of you.

There can be a glamour and excitement to having psychic powers. You experience unusual things, and that can be intoxicating. And here is where you must be careful not to base your judgment on these experiences. I have seen more than one student's ego bloat because of psychic visions they had. They started to feel more advanced than others, and this hurt their spiritual growth. Do not fall into the psychic trap. I jokingly refer to the trappings of the psychic as "the circus floor," because psychic phenomena can be like the diversions of a circus carnival. Whatever your psychic experiences may be, bless them, but pursue your spiritual growth first.

THE DIVINE DIMENSIONS OF LIFE

If the psychic is not the divine, then what are the divine dimensions of life? As your soul evolves through the various dimensions of the astral worlds, you eventually work your way off the astral planes altogether. You then prepare for the next step in your spiritual evolution—entering into the heaven worlds. The heaven worlds are the divine realms of consciousness.

The heaven worlds are the source from which the physical and astral worlds were generated. This means that all of the spiritual light, guidance, and inspiration that flows from the divine source first flows through the heaven worlds to reach you. These are the realms that guide your spiritual evolution. They are spiritual headquarters. It is from the heaven worlds that the angels, archangels, and celestial beings do their work for humanity. The heaven realms are the source of true spiritual knowing. These are the realms from which you make the direct connection to the divine. Yet you don't just jump from this earth plane to the heaven worlds by being good—you *grow* to heaven through a steady process of evolution.

The heaven world that is the next step up from the astral planes is known by the mystics as Spiritual Etheria. The heaven worlds of Spiritual Etheria are a place of Divine Light and power where there is no darkness or unevolved planes of consciousness. The angels and archangels work from Spiritual Etheria to connect with us. This tells us that we already have a connection to the spiritual etheric realms. It is this connection that allows us to receive the Divine Light and love from the Holy Ones. While everyone has this divine connection, when you start consciously working with this part of you, you greatly deepen your connection to the Holy Ones and the celestial planes from where these divine ones come.

Even while in the physical/astral existence, you have this direct link to your divine nature. This link is your Higher Self. Your Higher Self is working with you regardless of whether you are aware of that connection. As you make the effort to consciously connect with the higher nature, you make a direct link with divine realms and all that is part of the divine, including the spiritual hierarchy.

The divine path is the only path to eternal life. The psychic cannot give you that. Only the divine path can. By connecting with the spiritual first, you avoid letting the psychic rule you. I know it takes more time and effort to develop your spiritual powers, but I can tell you—as someone who has developed both the divine and the psychic—there is no comparison. The divine rewards *far* outweigh anything the psychic can give.

Your divine self is in direct connection with the God flow. All your answers and guidance will be entirely accurate and part of your spiritual unfoldment. You want to receive your guidance directly from Spiritual Etheria. That beautiful Higher Self is the key to connecting to the divine you. So why settle for the psychic when you can have the spiritual? There is more effort to reach the divine, but the rewards are far greater. Why stop at the sixth floor when you can go to the penthouse? There is no need to be smitten by the allure of the psychic world when the divine world calls on you. The choice is yours.

TRANSCENDING THE PSYCHIC

As you are aware by now, this is not a book about psychic development. The goal is not to teach you to be a psychic or medium. If you are seeking those experiences, this is not the book for you. The purpose of the metaphysical work is to help you to *transcend* the physical and psychic and connect directly with your divine nature, which is supreme.

There are several keys to transcending the psychic belt. Here are two very effective tools.

1. *Refuse to Be Mesmerized by Psychic Phenomena*

It is very easy to get caught up in the experiences of the psychic world. My mentor Inez Hurd used to caution her students, saying, "Do you think that because you can see spiritual colors and your fellow students cannot that you are better or more developed? If so, then you had better take a close look at your personality ego."

If you are having psychic visions, bless those experiences as a sign that you are on the right track, but don't try to make too much of those experiences or try to analyze their inner meaning. They are only spurs to urge you onward in your spiritual journey. If you become entranced by these experiences, you can actually slow down or retard your spiritual growth. In my teaching, students sometimes become discouraged because they have not had psychic experiences, while others have. I continually remind them that this is not the measure of spiritual development.

The Theosophist William Judge eloquently states the dangers of what he called psychic "intoxication" in his book *Vernal Blooms*. To paraphrase Judge:

> When a student starts upon the path and begins to see spots of light flash out now and then, or balls of golden fire roll past him, it does not mean that he is beginning to see the real Self. . . . Nor are psychical splashes of blue flame, nor visions of things that afterwards come to pass, nor sights of small sections of the astral light with its wonderful photographs of past or future . . . any proof that you are cultivating spirituality. The liability of being carried off and intoxicated by these phenomena is to be guarded against . . . the result is an intoxication that produces confusion of the intellect . . . because he was drunk with this kind of wine. . . . The astral planes, which is the same as that of our psychic senses . . . has to be well understood.

The Indian yogi Sri Aurobindo called the psychic belt the "intermediate zone" and warned of its dangers in a letter published in 1933. Here is a quote from that letter:

This is in fact an intermediary state, a zone of transition between the ordinary consciousness in mind and the true yoga knowledge. One may cross without hurt through it, perceiving at once or at an early stage its real nature and refusing to be detained by its half-lights and tempting but imperfect and often mixed and misleading experiences; one may go astray in it, follow false voices and mendacious guidance, and that ends in a spiritual disaster; or one may take up one's abode in this intermediate zone, care to go no farther and build there some half-truth which one takes for the whole truth or become the instrument of the powers of these transitional planes—that is what happens to many sadhaks and yogis.[1]

The answer to these dangers is to simply take psychic experiences in stride, but keep your attention on the divine; that is one of the biggest keys to transcending the psychic.

2. Work Directly with Your Higher Self for Guidance and Direction

Without question, your Higher Self is the key to transcending any intermediate or disturbing aspects of the physical/astral influences and reaching directly into the divine part of you. Your Higher Self is in direct communion with the divine. It is always there for you and always reliable. Make the connection to the Higher and you can reap the benefits of the divine life. As you work with the Higher Self and the Divine

---

[1] Letters on Yoga, Part 3, Section 3, "Experiences of the Inner and the Cosmic Consciousness," Subsection 5, pages 1039–46.

Light, you are greatly quickening your evolution. (See chapter 14 for a full description of the Higher Self.)

Here is a meditative prayer to stay clear of the psychic belt by reaching into the divine part of your nature.

MEDITATIVE PRAYER TO TRANSCEND THE PSYCHIC

Heavenly Father/Holy Mother God, I ask that the Holy Ones down-ray the pure white light of God to all levels of my consciousness to give me the power to transcend all false allure, intoxication, infatuation, delusions, and illusions connected to the psychic/astral world. I proclaim my allegiance to the divine through my Higher Self Point of Spiritual Knowing as the only source of true accurate wisdom and illumination. I refuse all false pictures of the psychic, lower self and claim my Higher Self completely. I ask that my Higher Self bring my psychic and physical natures under its guidance, balance, and control. May the Holy Ones who work with my divine nature guide and direct all facets of my life. I ask this in love and utmost humility. So be it.

CHAPTER 13

THE MYSTERY OF CLAIRVOYANCE

O NE OF THE biggest questions I am asked as a clairvoyant is, "Can I become clairvoyant, too?" Clairvoyance is an area of spirituality that holds one of the greatest mystiques. It is one of the areas that separates the believers from the nonbelievers, an area of wonderment for those who are clairvoyant and those who wish to be.

The answer is: Yes! Of course, you can learn to develop your clairvoyant powers. No one becomes clairvoyant without careful study and training. As with any talent or gift, it doesn't just happen. You earn the right to be clairvoyant through your own efforts, usually through lifetimes of development. Whether you will open that gift is a matter of determination and training.

Without a doubt, clairvoyance is a wonderful thing. The ability to see beyond the physical realm while in a physical body is exhilarating. And of course, clairvoyance is the tool to fully perceive and interact with the celestial hierarchy. When used properly, clairvoyance is an integral part of your spiritual growth. Yet, as with many other aspects of the spiritual world, there is much misunderstanding about clairvoyance and exactly how it works.

The word *clairvoyance* comes from the French for "clear seeing." It relates to the ability to perceive into the realms of life that are beyond the range of physical sensing. Many terms have been used for this gift: the sixth sense, the third eye, the seer, the mystic, and so on.

In this chapter, it is not my goal to teach you how to be clairvoyant. No book can do that. In my own case, it took many years of steady application and study before I became a trained clairvoyant and could use this gift to help others in their spiritual journey. It is important, however, to become acquainted with your spiritual senses, because you are using these senses now, even if you have not yet developed your clairvoyant gifts. They are part of your spiritual apparatus and are making a contribution to your spiritual growth and relationship to the hierarchy.

Clairvoyance is a by-product of your spiritual evolution. As you focus on your spiritual development, clairvoyance will open in its time. Clairvoyance is an intricate subject because it requires a sophisticated understanding of your spiritual anatomy, including your auric composition and your subtle bodies that support your physical form, as well as various spiritual forces at work in your consciousness. For our purposes, the attention will be focused on how clairvoyance relates to experiencing the Higher, yet even in this introduction there are several things to consider.

The process of perceiving and interacting with the Holy Ones works in several possible ways. These methods of celestial interaction include the following:

Intuitive and Inspirational Tools

1. Intuitive promptings
2. Inspirational promptings

Mental Tools

3. Mental visions given by the Higher

4. Mediumship and channeling

5. Etheric mediatorship (not mediumship!)

Perceptual Tools

6. Psychic clairvoyance

7. Mystical clairvoyance

We will also explore two dangers and misrepresentations of the clairvoyant experience that you need to be keenly aware of:

1. Self-induced hallucinations

2. Visions and clairvoyant experiences induced by evil spirits

INTUITIVE AND INSPIRATIONAL PROMPTINGS

Without question, intuitive and inspirational promptings are the two most common connections you have to the Holy Ones. Your intuition is the divine talking to you. Every day, you receive intuitive promptings from the divine, regardless of whether you are aware of them. In the same way, the divine regularly inspires you with new ideas to help you in your spiritual journey. We will look at intuition at the end of this chapter and at inspiration in chapter 16, as they are the most immediate and essential ways to connect with the divine.

MENTAL VISIONS GIVEN BY THE HIGHER

Mental visions of the Higher are not actually clairvoyant experiences, because you are not using your spiritual senses. These are blessings the Holy Ones give to inspire, teach, or acknowledge a spiritual height you have achieved. Visions can appear to be clairvoyant experiences, because during such visions you can "see" Divine Light, angels, and other Holy Ones. You can be given extraordinary visions of the inner worlds, pictures of future events, or insights into current events.

True mental visions are life-changing events. You feel like the divine has given you a glimpse of eternity, and in many ways they have. During a mental vision, the Holy Ones raise your consciousness and directly inspire the mental part of you with whatever they want you to experience. During these visions, the spiritual senses are not active at all. The images are directly impressed on the mind along with a heightened level of awareness. Note that although mental visions of the Higher are wonderful, you are not actually seeing the Holy Ones. You are being given a living vision of them.

In the aura, visions can be seen as gorgeous enlightened thought-forms blessing the recipient. These visions can happen at any time but are given rarely. The Holy Ones do not do this often, as it would be overpowering and could easily mislead the soul into thinking he or she has already reached the spiritual pinnacle.

MEDIUMSHIP AND CHANNELING

Mediumship is a type of astral/psychic telepathy with spirits from the other side. The idea is that a spirit sends mental messages to the medium, who is able to pick up the thoughts and communicate them to others. It's a very popular form of spirit communication. The National Spiritualists Association of Churches defines a medium as "one whose organism is sensitive to vibrations from the spirit worlds and through whose instrumentality, intelligences in that worlds are able to convey messages and produce the phenomena of Spiritualism."

To understand mediumship, we need to understand a little how telepathy works. Metaphysics teaches that thoughts are not confined to the brain. True thinking is an activity of the mind, but the mind and the brain are two distinct and different things. The brain is the physical *instrument* of the mind! The mind impresses the brain with ideas and, as those ideas register in the brain, we pick up those ideas as thought. So it feels like the brain is the thinker when, in truth, it is not.

In the aura, the mental center—or mental chakra—is the nucleus of your conscious, thinking self. Right now, everything you are thinking is radiating a spiritual energy from the mental center corresponding to the quality of your thought. As the mental center impresses the brain with mental currents, you pick up those currents as thought.

These mental currents can travel. For example, if you are thinking of someone strongly, you can send a thought current to that other person. If that person is sensitive to that thought, they can pick it up! This mental transference happens all the time, but not many people are consciously sensitive to this telepathic communication. In the same way, you can receive thoughts from others who may be projecting their thought currents to you. These thoughts could be constructive or destructive. This gives an idea of just how powerful your thoughts are and how important it is to be mindful of the quality of your thoughts, as well as how important it is to be aware of the kind of thoughts you accept from others.

This mental exchange is going on from one mental consciousness to another, while both souls are in physical life. In the case of a medium, you are dealing with psychic communication. A medium has learned how to access the psychic/astral part of their mental consciousness and is able to pick up astral thoughts. So mediumship is astral/psychic telepathy (see Figure 13.1).

The most common form of mediumship is with spirit guides. Since spirit guides are enlightened human souls, this makes them ideal at helping to bridge the link between the spiritual hierarchy and the aspiring soul. The spiritual hierarchy can work through spirit guides to inspire and uplift us.

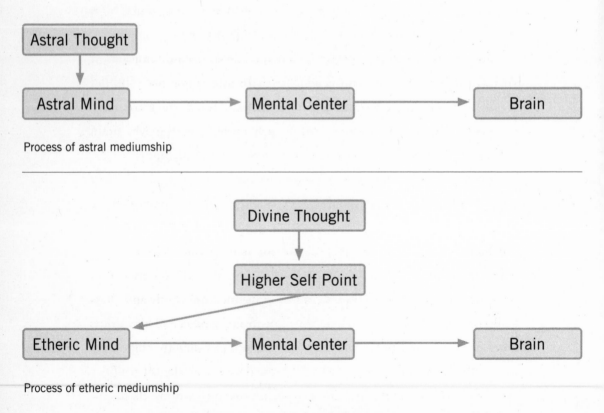

Process of astral mediumship

Process of etheric mediumship

FIGURE 13.1. *Astral and Etheric Telepathy*

As far as other aspects of the spiritual hierarchy, such as the angels and archangels, they can occasionally use mediumship as a channel of communication. The astral mind is sensitive enough to pick up signals from the celestial levels to a certain degree. However, since this communication is not coming through the Higher Self, the medium can confuse the message. In general, it is not common that an angel or archangel would speak directly through a medium, as the mechanism of mediumship is not their regular line of communication.

This brings up the point that since the medium is not working through the mystical nature, most often they cannot confirm what spirit is actually coming through them. They can ask, but there is no guarantee that the answer is accurate. To help lessen the possibility of miscommunication, good mediums often get to know specific spirits and work regularly with them because they are familiar with their vibration.

The other facet of mediumship is channeling. Today, the terms *channeling* and *mediumship* are often used interchangeably, with maybe slight differences. Historically, channeling is a form of trance mediumship—or trance channeling.

In a trance medium session, the channel goes into a hypnotic state and, many times, is completely unaware of what is actually happening during the session. The channel has become an empty vessel for the spirit from the other side. Once the trance state is established, an entity from the other side takes over physical control of the medium's body and physically communicates through the medium to the audience. This spirit is known as the "control." This way, the audience can directly communicate with what is hoped to be an enlightened soul from the other side.

For those who cannot communicate with the spirit worlds, this seems like a wonderful opportunity to directly commune with the other side.

These trance sessions are usually dramatic, which adds to the whole effect. The medium's body and voice can take on an entirely different demeanor as this other entity comes in. Almost always, the promise is that an advanced soul, or even a famous person, comes through during these sessions. In actuality, as with mediumship, you cannot confirm who is coming through during these sessions because, unless you are clairvoyant, you cannot actually see the control.

Trance channeling is a type of hypnosis. But in this case, the hypnotist is not a physical person—it's a spirit from the other side. The control accesses the medium through a process of hypnotizing the astral mind. This spirit or control depresses certain keys in the subconscious of the trance medium, and this is how the trance sessions are conducted.

The same benefits and challenges that apply to mediumship apply to trance mediumship. But in this case, there is an added risk, because the trance medium is a completely passive player in the process. With mediumship, the medium is still in control. He or she can stop the session at any time or decide what part of the astral communication to share. But with trance mediumship, the control is in charge. There is a physical assistant to support and help the medium during the trance session, but still the spirit is in control.

Spirit guides can communicate through these channels if they wish to, but it is my understanding and experience that, with rare exceptions, other members of the spiritual hierarchy do not. There are simply too many risks involved and other far more effective channels of communication open to them.

ETHERIC MEDIATORSHIP
(NOT MEDIUMSHIP!)

Mediatorship is a form of telepathy with the divine. In contrast to mediumship, a very different spiritual process is going on. As mediumship is a communication from the astral mind, a mediator is working through the *etheric* channels of communication. Just as you have an astral counterpart, you also possess an etheric counterpart. These counterparts have been called bodies, but I prefer to call them *templates* (see Figure 13.2). Your etheric template is extremely powerful. It is part of the connection to your divine self. Communication at this level is the mystical communication. This is the method of communication of the Holy Ones. All the great prophets, sages, rishis, and mystics commune with the Higher through etheric mediatorship.

What makes mediatorship so powerful is that, among other things, it involves a direct connection with the Higher Self. This brings you into a direct knowing of whom you are dealing with, because the spiritual being must reveal their vibration to open the lines of communication. Less evolved spirits cannot reach into these channels, so there is no chance of drawing on lower energies.

Of course, mediatorship takes longer to develop than mediumship. The aspirant must go through many levels of development before being entrusted with this etheric form of communication. But it is worth every effort and sacrifice, as you are truly communing with the divine in the fullest sense of the phrase. I can tell you that all mental communication done with the Higher to write this book was done through etheric mediatorship.

During the mediatorship experience, you are in a heightened level of

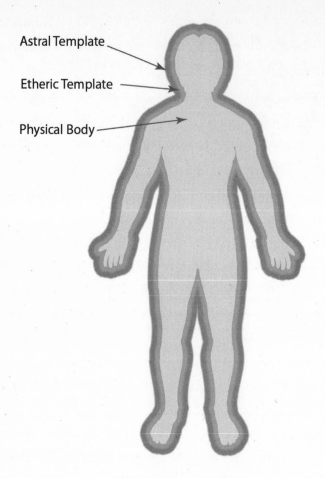

Astral Template

Etheric Template

Physical Body

FIGURE 13.2. *The Etheric and Astral Templates*

awareness. You are actually in the consciousness of the Holy Ones for the time they are sending you their enlightened thoughts. This is an exhilarating experience. A famous example of this mediator relationship was the dynamics of the man Jesus and celestial Lord Christ (described in chapter 8). For the time Jesus was the emissary for Lord Christ, he was not being a medium or channel for Lord Christ; he was a mediator. He was in the actual celestial consciousness of the Christ and in full awareness of His presence. There was no question in Jesus' mind what was going on and whom he was dealing with. This was what made that relationship so powerful and why it was easy for the uninitiated to mistake Jesus for the actual Christ.

This same type of divine relationship went on with the famous Orphic, Delphic, and Elysian mysteries of ancient Greece. The great Egyptian mystery teachers, as well as the Hebrew mystics and prophets, made their celestial connections through the etheric channels. The inspired teachings of every religion and metaphysical teaching through the ages was done by this means.

Etheric mediatorship is meant for everyone. It is part of the process of your becoming a mystic. As you continue to develop yourself spiritually, you will eventually build this bridge to your etheric nature and your communion with the divine will reach a marvelous plateau.

PSYCHIC CLAIRVOYANCE

Clairvoyance is a different process from telepathy. As telepathy involves the mind, clairvoyance involves the senses. Clairvoyance does not operate by itself. It is part of an intricate *set* of senses we possess. In actuality, we have *eighteen senses* in all! Each has its place in our spiritual development. These senses break down into three areas: five physical, five astral/psychic, and eight spiritual senses. Let's start with the psychic senses.

To understand psychic perceptions, let's review the five physical senses. We all know we need physical senses to operate effectively in the physical world. Without them, we would have no awareness of our physical surroundings and would not be able to survive. So the five senses are our way of interacting and communicating with our environment and with other people.

As wonderful as our physical senses are, they have a great limitation. They cannot perceive into the spiritual dimensions. This shortcoming has caused a great debate among humanity. Some people question the reality of the spiritual life because they cannot sense it physically. And here is where they make a great mistake. *The five physical senses were not designed to perceive the spiritual dimensions.* That is not their job. No matter how hard we try, the physical senses cannot pierce the veil of matter, as they are composed of that physical matter themselves.

In order to perceive into the spiritual realms, you must use senses that are designed for just that purpose. This means that when someone is having a genuine experience of the Higher, they are not seeing the Holy Ones with their physical eyes—they are using their inner senses. As part of your spiritual anatomy, you have this entire set of senses. For some, these inner senses are active, and for others they are latent and need to be developed.

The five astral senses are the connection to your astral counterpart. As we have seen, while the soul is here in physical life, not only are you encased in physical matter, you are also encased in astral form. This astral form is a duplicate of the physical form. This astral counterpart helps support the physical and maintain a connection to the astral dimensions while you are in physical life. It has many jobs and is very connected to health and well-being. This astral counterpart has a similar composition to that of the physical, which means it also possesses the same set of senses. The astral senses cover the same areas as the physical ones: sight, sound, taste, smell, and touch. However, the astral senses are more powerful than the physical senses. We can see farther and hear much better in the astral than we can in the physical. The astral senses operate at a higher frequency, which is why they can tune in to the astral world while the physical senses cannot.

What many people do not realize is that you are connected to your astral senses right now. As we explored, when the astral influences the physical, we call this *psychic*. So, when someone is psychic, that person *has a conscious connection to the astral senses while in a physical body*. This is psychic clairvoyance.

The astral senses are always in operation, but not all of us have developed a conscious connection with the astral apparatus. The same rules that apply to the psychic world apply to our psychic senses. They have a limited range of expression compared to the etheric senses and are not the ones to rely on for your spiritual growth. The information and perceptions may or may not be accurate, because the psychic vibration is mixed. This is why it is not recommended to focus on developing your psychic senses once you are on the metaphysical/mystical path. If you find you are having psychic visions, that is wonderful, but be careful not to base your judgment on those experiences.

It is possible to see celestial beings through your psychic senses. Angels and archangels and other divine ones can reveal themselves to your psychic vision if they wish to. They don't do this often, as they prefer to work through the mystical channels of perception. The most common psychic experiences with the spiritual hierarchy are with the spirit guides. Another common form of psychic interaction is with loved ones and souls who have passed on to the other side. I have had many visitations this way, and the interaction almost always happens on a psychic/astral level. Sometimes the interaction happens most unexpectedly. I remember having a visitation from my father after he had passed on. He died young and I missed him. I had seen him on the other side, so I knew he was doing well, but I still felt sadness at his passing. One time, he appeared in our living room sitting in his favorite brown armchair. He had a playful smile and wanted me to know he was there and was doing fine.

This interaction happened entirely with psychic sensing, since he was in his astral body.

Other types of psychic interaction are not so pleasant, and those are with lower spirits. Since they are in their astral forms, they will try to reach you through the psychic channels. They can impersonate and masquerade as benevolent beings and can fool those who are unaware. Without question, this is one of the most important reasons to be careful when dealing with psychic clairvoyance.

Through psychic perceptions you can see spiritual colors. These colors are not exactly the Divine Light. It is a type of reflection of the Divine Light known as the astral light. The astral light is beautiful to see and can be quite stimulating, but again it must not be confused with the Divine Light itself. Through astral senses you can hear astral sounds and smell astral smells. Again, these experiences are the stepping-stone for the mystical experience. The soul realizes through these experiences that there is most definitely a greater life beyond the physical realm.

MYSTICAL CLAIRVOYANCE

In addition to the physical and astral/psychic senses, you have the spiritual, or mystical, senses. The spiritual senses are in a class by themselves. God gave you these senses for a very great purpose—to open you up to the divine life. Just as you need your five physical senses to perceive and operate in the physical world, you need the spiritual senses to perceive and interact with the spiritual world.

You have eight spiritual senses. Five of these senses are the spiritual sight, sound, smell, taste, and touch. These senses are connected to your *etheric counterpart* or *template*. The etheric template is similar to the astral counterpart in that it is also a duplicate body to the physical. However, it is much more powerful than the astral, being made up of etheric atoms, which are extremely potent. This etheric counterpart has its own set of chakras, which are the chakras so well described (sometimes symbolically) in yogic literature. This is important because, in addition to the sensory mechanisms, the etheric chakras play an important part in the mystical experience.

In addition to these five senses, there are an additional three senses that are solely connected to the chakras. These senses are known as the spiritual "sensing," "feeling," and "knowing"—the knowing of how you know.

These eight spiritual senses are your God attributes. The *God seeing* is the clairvoyance of the mystic. You need spiritual vision to see the full aspects of your aura and to truly perceive the celestial beings. There is the *God hearing*, also known as *clairaudience*, where you hear the spiritual voice of the celestial hierarchy, the music of the spheres, and so on. The spiritual taste, smell, and touch connect you to the inner worlds in a very real and tangible way. As ethereal as these senses are, they also have the ability to keep the mystic well-grounded, so that the celestial experiences don't overpower or unbalance the soul. These senses are truly exhilarating. To taste the celestial ambrosia or smell ethereal roses makes one feel like heaven is here on earth.

Then there is the *God sensing*, also called *clairsentience*, where you have the high intuitive powers of what the divine is communicating to you. This sense truly opens your heart to God. The *God feeling* is where you get into the spiritual ecstasy of the God presence. Physical pleasure is only a shadow compared to the God feeling. This sense keeps the desire nature focused on the divine. Most important, you have your *God knowing*, also known as *claircognizance*, where you know God is there regardless of what the world may show you. This is the most important and mystical sense of all. It is also the last and most difficult sense to be awakened. Many people confuse this sense with your intuitive powers. While your intuitive nature is extremely important, intuition and claircognizance are not the same at all. I tell people that if I had to choose one spiritual sense, it would be the God knowing.

It is through the mystic senses that the spiritual hierarchy truly interacts with you. When I learned to awaken the full breadth of the mystic senses, it was as if a whole new world opened up. I became completely enveloped in the spiritual hierarchy and experienced them in a whole new way.

The spiritual hierarchy works primarily through the mystical part of your nature, because this is the part of you they can identify with and relate to. The genuine metaphysical teacher or guru does their great work through the mystical senses. This is the tool of theophany. The wonderful part is, even if you have not yet awakened your spiritual senses, the Holy Ones will still prompt you through these sensory mechanisms and you will pick up the signals unconsciously. This is yet another reason why it is so important to include the Holy Ones in your meditations and spiritual work. It is also why you do not need to see the Holy Ones to interact with them. By genuinely reaching out to them, you are stimulating all the spiritual senses.

Your spiritual senses are a wonderful part of you. When they are in full operation, there is no question as to your purpose and the true nature of life. At some point in your spiritual development, your spiritual senses will unfold in all their glory, if your desire is strong enough.

God has given you a tremendous spiritual arsenal. You are not meant to walk blindly through life, without understanding. God has given you the tools to operate with full awareness and spiritual knowing, but you have to build this awareness through the way you live your life. Your success in this work lies not in the seeing of the Holy Ones, but in the living. If you are *living* the spiritual principles, all these other aspects will fall in line. Yes, spiritual vision is wonderful, and I hope that it is an experience all of you will have in this life, but it is not nearly as important as your spiritual growth.

SELF-INDUCED HALLUCINATIONS

It is easy to get caught up in the excitement of clairvoyance, but one must be keenly aware of some dangers. And there are very real dangers. My goal here is not to scare you, but to encourage you to tread carefully. True clairvoyance is a natural by-product of your spiritual development. Work on your spiritual evolution, better yourself, help others, and this gift will open in its time. There is no simple road to developing these gifts.

I have counseled many people who thought they were clairvoyant and in communication with the Holy Ones when, in fact, they were not. It was something they had created in their own mind out of a deep desire to have such an experience. These are hallucinations and can appear real. If the intention is strong enough, it is possible to create a mental image of the desired experience. It doesn't mean you are schizophrenic, but it can mean that you have gotten carried away in the desire to reach spiritual heights. This is particularly possible in a group setting when one can get caught up in the frenzy of the moment and, without realizing it, work oneself up into a type of self-hypnosis.

Stephen Isaac expressed very well the danger of self-induced hallucinations in his book *Songs from the House of Pilgrimage*. He was the husband of the famous clairvoyant Flower Newhouse, whom I had the good fortune to meet. In this quote, he is talking about her clairvoyant gifts, and how her students wanted to duplicate those gifts for themselves before they were ready.

> It was a gift she attained gradually under the close supervision of many teachers and required lifetimes of preparation and purification. . . . The young student is grossly unrealistic to expect it sooner for himself. Unfortunately, his keen wish for this prize can arouse unconscious forces capable of simulating such contacts, much as dreams are created during sleep. These projections from the unconsciousness, mistaken for authentic receptions, reinforce his ego's desire to "be somebody spiritually" and a flood of counterfeit experiences follow.

The other type of self-induced hallucination is more elusive. In this scenario, the person is already psychic and has had genuine psychic experiences. This excites the mental faculties. Sometimes the ego gets involved and, in the desire to repeat the experience, the person unintentionally invents images of the Holy Ones from their own unconscious mind. Because they have had a genuine experience, they can make this illusion very convincing. If you are having a spiritual experience and are not sure if it is real, ask the Holy Ones to reveal the truth. If it is not real, ask the divine to release the false images.

The bottom line is to make it your aim to work with the Higher, rather than to see the Higher. The seeing will happen in its own time. The slow, steady approach to clairvoyance is the winning hand.

VISIONS AND CLAIRVOYANT EXPERIENCES INDUCED BY EVIL SPIRITS

There is another aspect of the counterfeit spiritual experience that must be mentioned, and this is the influence of evil spirits. Since psychic experiences are part of the astral world, and evil forces work on the astral level, there is a danger that by opening up to the psychic influence, you can unintentionally open up to the lower forces. I don't have to tell you how terrible this can be. These malefic spirits are cunning. They have spiritual powers, so they can present themselves in a benevolent light and even perform psychic phenomena, including conducting healings. This, of course, is not to help, but to deceive souls. The tip-off is their vibration. If you are pure in heart, regardless of how they present themselves, you will feel uneasy, and this is an indication that something is potentially off. Immediately call on the divine for help.

Another tip-off is if you are asked to do something that goes against your nature, or if you feel coerced in any way. In any genuine spiritual experience, you naturally will feel excited and elated, yet at the same time you should feel very clearheaded and grounded. Any sense of disconnect or feeling ungrounded is a warning sign. In all my spiritual experiences, I have never felt "out of it." I have always felt empowered by the Holy Ones—always.

DEVELOPING YOUR INTUITION

It is the destiny of each of us to come into a direct knowing of the spiritual hierarchy, yet until you awaken that mystical part of you, how do you build a stronger conscious connection to the divine? There are several tools the divine gives you to start using right now. The greatest keys to building your direct pipeline to the Higher are your powers of intuition and inspiration. We will look at inspiration in chapter 16. Here, let us focus on that magical process called intuition.

What is intuition? It has been defined in several ways. Perhaps it is best to start with what intuition is not. Intuition is not the intellect, although the mind is keenly involved in the intuitive process. Intuition is not an emotion—it is not the instinctual nature either, although both of these aspects of your consciousness come into play with intuition.

Intuition is a perceptual prompting. During an intuitive prompting, the Holy Ones are blessing your divine senses. Even though your spiritual senses are not yet open, they are still active. There is an unconscious connection to these sensory mechanisms. The Holy Ones use this connection to reach you. So even if you are not yet a mystic clairvoyant, your dormant clairvoyant faculties are being used by the divine, urging you upward on the spiritual path.

During an intuitive prompting, you may get a sense or feeling about something. You cannot rationalize why you are reacting this way. This is the intuitive part of you speaking. For example, you may walk into a person's home and feel very uneasy. For some reason you feel disturbed being there. The home itself may be pleasant to look at and well appointed, but the vibrations do not feel right. What is happening here is you are picking up stimulus from the divine senses on an unconscious level. You perceive something, just not with your physical senses. This is intuition in action. You get these promptings every day. Unfortunately, and too often, many ignore these promptings because they may not make "logical" sense. In truth, they are logical—you just can't always identify them that way because you are not consciously aware of the means through which you picked up the perception.

It is important not to confuse intuition with the dynamics of your mental and emotional nature. For example, you may be emotionally upset about something. Maybe someone triggers that emotional distress in you. You feel upset by what happened and get a "bad feeling" about that person, but that is not intuition. That is an emotional reaction. Intuition, on the other hand, is objective. It is not contingent on how you feel at a particular moment. This means that to be an effective intuitive, you must have a balanced and impartial mental and emotional nature.

The more you build up your aura and consciousness, the more easily the Holy Ones can reach you through intuition. Right now, there is a spiritualized part of your consciousness through which the Higher can connect and communicate. You may not be fully aware of these aspects of your consciousness, but they are there. Through intuition, the Holy Ones activate these developed parts of your consciousness.

The intuitive approach is not the sensationalistic approach that characterizes psychic experiences. Generally speaking, the soul following the intuitive path will not have psychic visions or experiences. Intuition starts quietly. It is that still small voice within. We all get these intuitive promptings, but too often we cloud this voice with our own human wants. Yet when you get into the stillness, you can hear it speak. This means the intuitive path requires greater faith and steadfastness. It may not be as phenomenal as the psychic approach at first, but eventually it bears the greatest fruit.

For those who are psychically inclined, I doubly recommend the intuitive approach. By building intuition, you are developing a steady, stable consciousness and helping your psychic senses as well. If you are psychic and can balance your intuitive side, you have the best of both worlds.

PRACTICING INTUITION

Many ask, "How do I know if what I am getting is intuition from the Higher or simply me?" It is a valid question. And the only answer is: You won't know until you apply the prompting you are getting. Intuition must be tested in action. There is a trust factor with intuition. Through application, if things work out, you know it was an intuition. If it doesn't, you're still ahead, because you tried and you will learn from the experience. You'll apply that experience next time. Intuition gets better with practice.

Also, intuition sustains itself. In other words, you may get a surge of excitement from your own impressions that is not necessarily coming from the Higher. This surge of excitement is temporary and usually dissipates quickly. This is not intuition, but what could be thought of as impulse. Intuition can be exciting too, but also has a type of calm strength.

To cultivate this attitude of "calm strength," it is important to quiet the mind of cluttering thoughts. As part of becoming still and receptive, follow through on all of the light work recommended in this book. Building up the power in your aura has the effect of raising your consciousness into higher dimensions of awareness, which brings you more in tune with intuition. As part of this work, make sure you are making a strong connection with your Higher Self.

All the Holy Ones help with intuition, yet when you are trying to build your intuitive powers, the Lord of Wisdom Light (Lord Christ) is the celestial being to call on, along with your angelic teachers.

MEDITATIVE PRAYER TO STRENGTHEN INTUITION

Heavenly Father/Holy Mother God, I ask under the direction of Lord Christ and my angelic teachers to down-ray the pure white light to my Higher Self Point of Spiritual Knowing to activate all of my divine senses, especially the spiritual seeing, hearing, sensing, feeling, and knowing. May this white light bless my etheric template, my mental center, and all levels of my consciousness, to bring me into greater awareness of my intuitive powers. I ask under Archangel Michael and the angels of the golden ray to strengthen me with courage and faith that I listen to the divine prompting me and have the courage to act on the intuitive promptings I receive. I thank thee that this is so. So be it.

PART 5

Communing with the Divine

CHAPTER 14

CONNECTING WITH THE HIGHER

ONE OF THE great joys of being a spiritual teacher is observing the Holy Ones interacting with students. I remember one time a student had lost her job. It was unexpected, as she was excelling at the company she was working at. But there were changes and she was suddenly let go. The experience left her shaken and worried, which showed up as a gray energy in her aura. She made some attempts to find work, but after a couple of months of not finding a job, she was getting very discouraged.

One night in class, we were working with the golden ray for inner strength and courage. I saw an angelic being objectify himself right in the room very near to her. He was not even an arm's length away. He was behind and above her, about three feet. She had no idea that this angelic being had come so close. Generally, the angels do their work from a distance, which is very effective in itself, but this Holy One decided to do a direct healing. He projected a beautiful ray of golden light to her, and the energy flowed into her aura, especially her mental and heart centers. He worked slowly and carefully so as not to disturb her or cause her to unconsciously resist the process, which sometimes happens.

The group meditation lasted about ten minutes, but the angelic being stayed with her for almost half an hour, steadily blessing her. I could see negative energies leaving and her aura brightening with the golden light.

She left that night feeling uplifted, as if a weight had been taken off her. After this spiritual interaction, she was able to maintain a more optimistic approach to her situation. This is not always the case. Sometimes, the Holy Ones give extraordinary blessings, but the recipient is so stubborn and set in their way of thinking and feeling that they end up re-creating the disturbing energies again. This makes the job of the Holy Ones more difficult. But in this case, the woman had intuitively received the message that she needed to take a more proactive approach to remedy her situation. She realized she had allowed herself to fall into a depressed state and was not really utilizing the spiritual powers she was calling on. Her persistent worry dissipated, and fortunately she did not reenergize that old condition. About three weeks later, a new job opened up for her.

In this section, we will look at practical techniques to include the Holy Ones in your life and spiritual work. The primary tools we will be working with are meditation and prayer, or *meditative prayers*. Meditative prayers are an extremely effective way to reach the Holy Ones and interact with them. Through meditative prayers you can receive Divine Light and power, guidance and direction, and inspiration and blessings.

YOUR HIGHER SELF POINT OF SPIRITUAL KNOWING

The master key to communing with the Holy Ones is your Higher Self. The Higher Self is the link to becoming one with God, and it is the link to connecting with and receiving from the spiritual hierarchy. The Divine teaches that they perform three quarters of the work in any spiritual interaction. They step down their vibration to meet you. As their energy is so exalted, they need to temper their vibration so as not to throw off your energy field. But they also teach that you have to do your part. You have to do one quarter of the work and step up your vibration to meet theirs. You cannot simply approach them steeped in the consciousness of your troubles and concerns. You have to make the effort to step out of that consciousness and be in a state of mind where you are receptive to the divine guidance and direction. The meeting of the minds is your Higher Self.

What is your Higher Self? It is a perfected part of your consciousness that does not embody itself in physical form when you incarnate in material life. The Higher Self remains in the spirit realms, connected to the divine source, and acts as a link among God, the Holy Ones, and your evolving soul. It is this spiritual counterpart that the spiritual hierarchy can relate to and work with to support you.

In the aura, the Higher Self looks like a radiant golden sun about two feet above the physical head. Its formal name is *The Higher Self Point of Spiritual Knowing* (see Figure 14.1). It is sometimes called the eighth chakra. It radiates beautiful golden-white rays of light. By remaining above the head, it does not mix with the element of the human aura. And this is its great benefit to you. By being outside the human aura, it remains in a state of perfection, perpetually supporting and uplifting your soul upward in its ascent. All of the Divine Light and inspiration you receive first flows to this Higher Self Point before reaching you. Without the Higher Self, you could not grow spiritually.

The Higher Self Point is the place where you commune with the spiritual hierarchy. The divine beings cannot descend lower in consciousness than the Higher Self, so you have to make the effort to get into a higher state of consciousness to relate to them more directly.

FIGURE 14.1. *The Higher Self Point of Spiritual Knowing*

Connecting with your Higher Self is part of a beautiful sequence of activity that goes on every time there is a genuine interaction with the divine. This sequence of activity is part of the meditative process we will explore in chapter 15. It can be thought of in the following way:

- Raising your consciousness to your Higher Self
- Uniting and becoming one with God
- God sending what you need to the spiritual hierarchy
- The spiritual hierarchy sending to you the light, guidance, and inspiration

In any spiritual interaction, you first unite with your Higher Self. Then, in that higher nature, you unite with your divine source—God. Then you interact with the Holy Ones who administrate the light and power from the divine source to you (see Figure 14.2). The act of reaching out

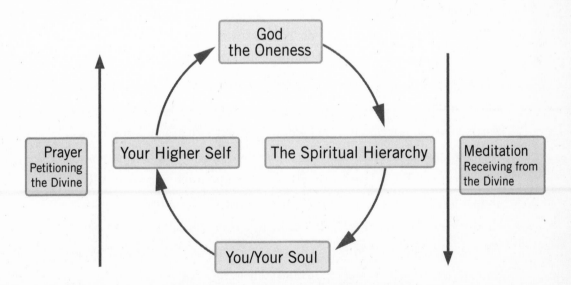

FIGURE 14.2. *Relationship of You and the Divine*

to the divine is called prayer, and the act of receiving from the divine is called meditation.

CALLING ON YOUR ANGELIC TEACHERS

Although there is a host of loving and supportive celestial beings, the Holy Ones you will work with the most are your angelic teachers. What makes the teachers so important is that they are orchestrating the interaction with the spiritual hierarchy. They are the fulcrum upon which rests the balance of the divine interaction.

You have a special connection to the angelic teachers. They are assigned to you by the divine to guide your evolution. On average, you will have two or three teachers assigned to you. Some people have more as they grow in the light or are on a particular mission. Teachers change depending on what is going on in your life. They have specialties, so you often attract a teacher according to the type of need and activities going on in your life.

Angelic teachers are not with you every minute of every day. But they are there more often than you think. It's their job to help you grow. These teachers know your purpose in life and spiritual potential. They know your karmic debits and credits. They know your strengths and weaknesses. In many ways, they know you better than you know yourself. The angelic teachers work intimately with other aspects of the spiritual hierarchy. They work strongly with your guardian angels as well as the Divine Energy angels. Spirit guides work under the teachers, taking their direction from these celestial beings. And of course the teachers take their direction from Holy Ones more advanced than themselves, so you are always getting the exact kind of help that you need.

Some have asked if there is a "master teacher" who coordinates all the other teachers and oversees your entire evolution. The answer is yes. Each of us has what might be called a master teacher. This celestial being is not an angel or even an archangel. It is a spirit from the Unnamed Sacred Eleventh Kingdom. Master teachers love us dearly and carefully guide the grand plan of our purpose and destiny. While you can acknowledge this celestial being in your meditations, the divine prefers the attention focused on the angelic teachers.

To start connecting with your teachers is not difficult. To feel closer to the teachers, begin by simply acknowledging them. Express your love to them for all that they do for you. Do this during meditation and also throughout the day, so you build an awareness of your teachers on a consistent basis, whether you are in meditation or not.

Many people have asked if I could name their teachers. They ask this because they think in terms of getting to know a person, putting a face and a name to a presence. I understand the desire to personalize the Holy Ones, but they do not work like that. They do not want you to think in terms of a form or a person. They want you to think in terms of vibration and light. So it is not necessary to know who they are or their names—*they* know *you*. At this point, it doesn't matter if you see or hear them. What matters is that you know they are there and feel and sense the promptings they are giving you.

I'd like to point out here that even though you may not see your teachers, it does not mean you cannot intimately work with them. The teachers want to connect with you. They want you to see them. They love you and are doing everything in their power to help you come up into your true spiritual self where you *can* commune with them.

As you connect better with the teachers, you will feel and know their presence. They come in on such a beautiful vibration. At times, you may smell a wonderful fragrance and wonder where it comes from—and it will be them. Most of all, you will notice a positive change in your pattern of activity. As you go about your business, you will feel you are working in cooperation with the Higher, and you will have greater success in your pursuits. And yes, if you are steadfast in your spiritual growth, there will come that day where you behold the teachers more directly.

THREE WAYS THE HOLY ONES CONNECT WITH YOU

In connecting with the Holy Ones through your Higher Self, they will approach you in one of three ways:

1. *The Holy Ones project blessings from their celestial domain.* There are celestial realms of great splendor and beauty in the spirit worlds, and the spiritual hierarchy can target spiritual energy and inspiration from these realms directly to us. It is extremely effective and efficient. They direct divine power to your Higher Self Point, and from there the energy flows into your aura and consciousness. You can't clairvoyantly see the Holy Ones in this scenario, but you can perceive the magnificent light rays they are sending.

   This is a particularly common technique for the leaders of the spiritual hierarchy. As they often work on a collective level, this technique is extremely effective at sending spiritual light and blessings. Some have misunderstood this to mean that these beings can be in more than one place at the same time. This is not true. They can project their consciousness to more than one place at a time, but they are still one great spirit.

2. *The Holy Ones come around but stay some distance above, projecting their blessings to the Higher Self.* In this scenario, the celestial beings are on the earth plane but do not directly mix into the human vibration. They are close but, again, project the spiritual power directly to the Higher Self. Most often they are not clairvoyantly visible this way. This approach is often used in healing work, when the divine wants to make a deep connection. It is also seen in meditative prayers when the soul is making a strong connection with the divine.

3. *The Holy Ones objectify themselves to where you are as a visitation.* Seeing a celestial being in close proximity is, without question, a dramatic experience. While Holy Ones do come close to us during meditations, objectifying themselves in the same space is not their usual method. When they do objectify themselves, they often pick unexpected times to do this. Sometimes it's done in great need. Other times, it's a blessing they wish to bestow. It can happen when a strong healing is needed or special spiritual work is being done. Even with visitations, they will work with your Higher Self to make the actual connection, but then they can work directly in any area of your consciousness they wish.

GUIDELINES FOR WORKING WITH THE DIVINE

As we explore the various ways of connecting with the Higher, here are some additional guidelines to keep in mind.

- *The Holy Ones are your support, not your servants.* Do not try to make the Holy Ones do the growing or solve your problems for you. They are there to support your growth and participate in the divine plan. This means you need to put aside selfish desires when it comes to the Holy Ones, and take responsibility for your part in the divine plan.

- *Acknowledge your own self-worth.* You are an essential part of life. When done sincerely, you have every right to call on the Higher for support. It doesn't matter what has happened or what you might have done. The Holy Ones are there for you in moments of triumph and in moments of disaster.

- *The Holy Ones are not God.* They are not ubiquitous and do not have unlimited powers, even though their powers are extraordinary. And they are not infallible. It is said that every once in a great while even the angels need to be reprimanded.

- *The Holy Ones cannot infringe on your human will.* Earth is a spiritual schoolhouse, and we are all students. The Holy Ones are our teachers as well as friends and fellow spiritual travelers. They do many things on our behalf but are limited by how well we cooperate with the divine plan. When we are in step with divine support, things flow smoothly. When we are stubborn and adamantly refuse to cooperate, this weakens our spiritual foundation.

Sometimes the Holy Ones have to step back and let us make mistakes—sometimes big mistakes. This is all part of the growing process. It does not mean they do not love or care for us. It simply means, from our human perspective, we cannot always understand the divine reasoning that goes on in the celestial planes. Sometimes, bad things happen as part of the expression of free will. If we did not have this freedom of expression, the spark of life would be stifled. We cannot judge the Holy Ones. Our job is to do our best and trust in the greater forces of life.

Once in a while, there are exceptions when the Holy Ones will directly involve themselves in human affairs. It is my understanding that during the height of the Cold War there were times when the Holy Ones had to step in and prevent what could have escalated to a nuclear exchange. Had they allowed this to happen, the effects would have been too devastating to imagine.

The Holy Ones also cannot infringe on karma. Many things going on in your life are the result of past actions—karma—or the law of cause and effect. It is the job of the Holy Ones to manage karma. But, like free will, they need to let our karmic tests play out or we would not learn and grow. As much as possible, they help to alleviate karmic burdens, but they can't interfere in karmic energies playing out. In truth, without the help of the Higher, we could not resolve our karma. They love us dearly and are keenly aware of humanity's sorrows and trials. They do more than we can possibly imagine to help us through life's challenges.

CHAPTER 15

THE HOLY ONES AND
THE HIERARCHY OF
DIVINE LIGHT

THERE WAS A man named John in one of my classes who was very dedicated in his spiritual work and wished to advance spiritually. He was in his thirties, on the serious side, handsome, yet single. He was an architect and showed a lot of promise in his career. He had been studying with me for about five years. I could see in his aura that he was already an advanced soul but had not quite reached his full potential. He was very sincere and was working with the spiritual hierarchy in his light work. He meditated diligently and was particularly good at applying the light in his daily life.

One day in class, we were meditating with the purple ray of peace. This power ray is under Archangel Uriel. While the light was coming in, I could see the angelic beings working with us. Then, unexpectedly, Archangel Uriel objectified herself in the room. No one could see her but me, yet clearly the class was enraptured by this meditation. She moved very close to John and started working with him directly. I saw her go into prayer, and a tremendous white light down-rayed from her higher nature to his aura, especially his mental center. Everyone was getting blessed, but she was focusing on John. He did not know who was working with him but was clearly uplifted by the blessing. She stayed for about five minutes and then left, but I could clairvoyantly see the illumination in his aura from her blessing.

That experience turned out to be a breakthrough moment for him. It led to a new level in his spiritual pursuit, an initiation into a new level of consciousness. It led to a mystical experience in which he clairvoyantly saw, for the first time, the angels. He saw four angelic beings in prayer sending him light as an acknowledgment of his dedication and progress. His attitude and life changed after that experience. His faith deepened and his determination increased. In his case, this meant that he would soon reach his spiritual potential. For each person, we reach our potential either early in life or later, sometimes much later. It all depends on our karmic chart and what we are to accomplish. In John's case, he already came in developed, but he needed to cross this spiritual bridge so that he could move forward and fulfill his purpose.

His career as an architect blossomed and he became very well-known for his residential property designs. He married a wonderful woman and had two lovely children. He became successful in his professional, personal, and spiritual life. All along, he had the potential for all of this, but it happened because of his dedication to put his spiritual development first. He eventually finished his studies with me and expressed his gratitude for all that he received. He continued to have occasional experiences with the angels and kept up his light work and meditations. It was wonderful to see him succeed and how that blessing from Archangel Uriel was the turning point.

One of the most essential ways you will work with the Holy Ones is by calling on Divine Light. The celestial beings are part of a hierarchy of Divine Light. As there are degrees of Holy Ones, there are degrees of Divine Light. This hierarchy of light forms an energetic template that fuels all of creation. The Holy Ones are "stationed" within this order of light, and this is what gives them their spiritual power and authority. For example, Archangel Michael is a celestial being in the archangelic kingdom. He also holds the station and responsibility of his office as a guiding force for humanity. To accomplish this, he embodies a spiritual power ray in the hierarchal order of light. One day, he will go on to other experiences, and another archangel will take his office and duties.[1]

This brings us to a central question: What is Divine Light? It is not physical light. Although it is clairvoyantly perceived with colors and hues, it is not a form of electromagnetic energy at all. Divine Light is the conduit of consciousness. It is how God transmits the various attributes of the divine life to you and all creation. Right now, you are in the process of elevating and expanding your consciousness. The Divine Light is what gives you that higher consciousness. Light and consciousness walk hand in hand. The more light you earn in your aura, the higher in consciousness you climb. Because Divine Light is imbued with divine consciousness, it is often called a "living light." So receiving Divine Light is much more than being blessed with pretty colors. These are living powers that are transforming your awareness.

There are many different types of spiritual energies to call on, because there are many differing attributes of God that you must embody,

---

[1] There is a fascinating correlation of this hierarchy of light in the Vedas. In the Vedas, there is the reference to 33 *crore* gods. A *crore* can mean 10 million, which would indicate that 330 million divine beings are working for humanity. Yet the word *crore* comes from the Sanskrit word *koti*, which can also mean "host" or "class," indicating 33 classes of divine beings—a clear reference to a divine order.

We also find in the Vedas the reference to "the protector of the Go." Classical Sanskrit defines *Go* as "cow." Here is the root of the Hindu reverence for the cow. This in itself is not strange, as many ancient societies revered cattle, being that cattle were such an important part of their daily life. Yet in the Vedic Sanskrit, which is a much older form of Sanskrit than what is in use today, the word *Go* can also mean "light." This gives a completely different interpretation of the expression "protector of the Go"—protector of the light. The Indian mystic and teacher Sri Aurobindo called it "the cow of light." When you put together the *crore* with the Go, you find a clear reference to a divine order of light.

including love, peace, balance, wisdom, motivation, and prosperity, to name just a few. For each attribute of the Divine Light, there is a spiritual being who is the administrator of that light and power. Each Holy One has their unique power and talent.

THE FULL SPECTRUM OF DIVINE LIGHT

In this book, we will primarily be working with the individualized Divine Light rays that can help you in so many aspects of your life. Yet before delving into these energies, let's step back and look at the full spectrum of Divine Light to better appreciate the spectacular power you are invoking.

The hierarchy of light breaks down as shown in Figure 15.1.

The Primordial Ray of God Absolute

The first spiritual ray out of which all other Divine Light rays come is the Primordial Ray. This ray emanates from God Absolute. All creation is under its power. The attributes of all the spiritual rays of creation are embodied in this staggering primal power. This ray powers all consciousness. It is the light of lights. All creation bathes in this light and we benefit from its essence every day.

The Seven Rays of God the Almighty

As this Primordial Ray filters down to God Almighty, it becomes the Seven Rays of the Almighty. Much has been written about these rays. The metaphysician Alice Bailey was particularly eloquent on the subject. The Seven Rays form the energetic template of the entire divine plan

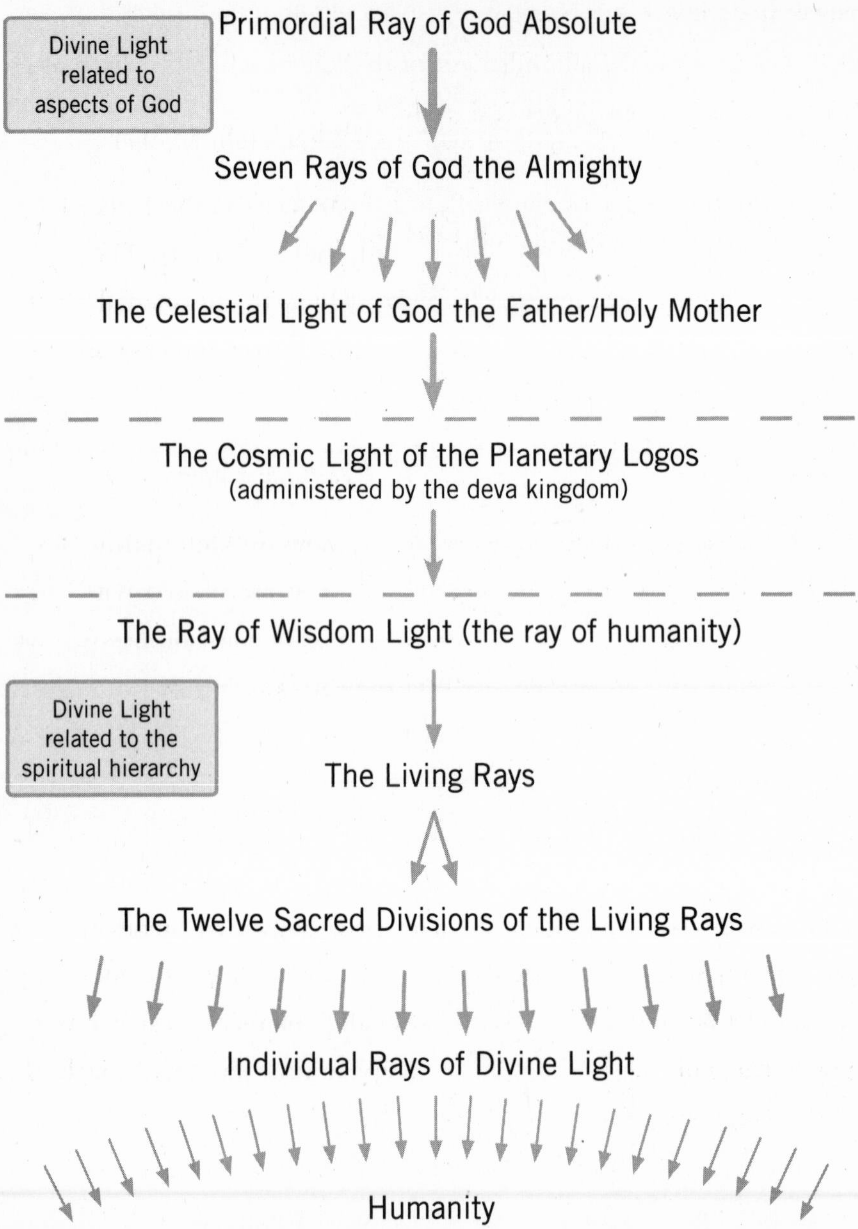

| Divine Light related to aspects of God | Primordial Ray of God Absolute |

Seven Rays of God the Almighty

The Celestial Light of God the Father/Holy Mother

- - - - - - - - - - - - - - - - -

The Cosmic Light of the Planetary Logos
(administered by the deva kingdom)

- - - - - - - - - - - - - - - - -

The Ray of Wisdom Light (the ray of humanity)

| Divine Light related to the spiritual hierarchy | The Living Rays |

The Twelve Sacred Divisions of the Living Rays

Individual Rays of Divine Light

Humanity

FIGURE 15.1. *The Hierarchy of Divine Light*

under God Almighty. Through these seven rays, each of us is given the power to complete our purpose.

The Celestial Light of God the Father/Holy Mother

This is the power ray of creative life. It is under God the Father/Holy Mother, which means it has a dynamic and magnetic quality. This power ray is the guiding force urging us to return Home to our celestial parents as mature souls. It is the source of our creative power and expression.

The Cosmic Light of the Planetary Logos

This is the ray of evolution on earth. The various divisions of this power ray have been known as the *ascension rays*. You are blessed with these energies when you are initiated into a new level of consciousness or have strengthened your current level of divine awareness.

The Wisdom Light Ray of Humanity

As the Divine Light enters this phase of expression, now you are dealing with powers that are stations of light for the spiritual hierarchy. The Wisdom Light Ray is under the celestial Lord Christ, also known as the Lord of Wisdom Light. It is the ray of all humanity on earth. It is the power that is urging you onward to complete your journey through the twelve kingdoms.

The Living Rays

The Wisdom Light Ray breaks down into two basic dynamic/magnetic powers. These rays are connected to the "objective expression of the creative life." The custodians of these powers are the Holy Ghost and Holy Spirit. These rays are helping you to realize the divine plan. They are a source from where the angels and archangels receive their guidance and direction.

The Twelve Sacred Divisions of the Living Rays

These twelve rays are the energetic "stations" of the twelve celestial archangels. From these rays come forth the many Divine Light rays that we receive and work with every day.

Divine Light Rays

These are the diverse rays that bring in specific attributes of God and the spirit life. There is an angel of Divine Light who is responsible for each of these rays as they receive it from the archangels. We will be working a great deal with these Divine Light rays. They represent the various levels of consciousness, and we are meant to call on these energies daily.

THE POWER OF MEDITATION
AND PRAYER

Meditation and prayer are the two most important tools for communing with the divine. Meditation is receiving from God. Prayer is petitioning God—it is a giving out. In your work with the Higher, you will do both through meditative prayers. They are a type of supplication to the divine. In this type of meditation, you are making a specific request to the Higher and then receiving the blessing that the divine wishes to give you. You may ask to be blessed with the spiritual power of love or abundance. Or you may petition the divine to receive illumination or balance. The beauty of meditative prayers is that you are focusing your mind and consciousness on the spiritual quality and consciousness you are requesting, which keeps the mind alert and focused during meditation.

To begin, choose a quiet place to meditate. You want a place away from noise or anything that can distract your attention. Since meditation is your one-on-one time with God, you want your consciousness completely focused on making your connection with the Higher. A bedroom or private office can work very well.

Reflect upon what it is that you are requesting of the divine. Are you looking for guidance, love, peace, or illumination? All of these things are wonderful, but you want to be selective, so that you can make a strong connection. Each attribute of God comes in on its own power ray, so, by being specific in your request, you will be more effective in the results. Don't overdo it. I would recommend working with no more than three or four energies in one sitting, as this way you give yourself more time to absorb these powers and implement them. Don't stress if it is not clear what to request of the Higher. If you are not sure, ask divine intelligence to guide you.

Begin by sitting in a chair with your feet flat on the floor and your back straight. (See the Appendix for a more complete description of the aura meditation technique.) In this type of meditation, it is not recommended to have your legs crossed, as in the lotus position. The energy will be coming down from your Higher Self above your head and flowing through you like an electrical current, so you don't want to "cross the wires" by crossing your legs or inhibiting the flow of energy in any way. (Figure 14.1, page 254, for an illustration of the meditative pose.)

You want to be in a relaxed state of mind, yet alert and awake. Take a couple of deep breaths to feel your body moving in rhythm with your mind and soul. As you feel relaxed, envision the divine lovingly surrounding you. See a golden bubble of protection around you. It is important that you are spiritually protected when doing any type of meditation.

Then put your attention on your Higher Self Point two feet above your physical head. See this point as a radiant golden sun above your head. As you place your attention on the Higher Self Point, let go of all of your earthly worries and concerns. They do not exist in this divine place. You're on sacred ground now and you want to feel completely connected to the divine. Feel part of your consciousness as actually in that Higher Self. Feel that Higher Self Point pulsating with light and power. It's joyful and reverent just to be there.

As you are putting your attention on this Higher Self Point, recite out loud this invocation (it's recommended that you memorize it):

INVOCATION TO CONNECT WITH THE HIGHER SELF POINT

Heavenly Father/Holy Mother God, I raise my consciousness into Thy consciousness where I become One with Thee. I ask to receive that which I need and that which I need to know now.

In your Higher Self, feel the union with the divine. Feel the evolutionary link connecting you and the Holy Ones to God and the Oneness of life. In this beautiful meditative state, you feel at Home. You are in your rightful place in the universe. Your life has purpose and your consciousness is refreshed and renewed to fulfill that purpose in even more beautiful ways.

You are now ready to begin your meditative prayers. Follow the ones offered in this book to get a feel for how they work. Then you can include your own inspired meditative prayers. These are like personal confessions to the divine. They are an art as much as a science. In your meditative prayers, let your mind open and speak your heart to God.

When making your request, envision the beautiful power of light that you are calling on down-raying from the divine source to your Higher Self Point. See the Higher Self Point activated in a burst of light. Then from the Higher Self Point, envision this light showering you like a waterfall of light. It bathes your entire aura, your body, your chakra points—all levels of your thinking, speaking, activities, actions, and feeling. Give permission for this light to touch every part of you.

Hold still to feel the light blessing you. Feel your consciousness being raised up with the spiritual quality you are requesting. As you are doing this, feel the closeness of the Holy Ones themselves. They are right there with you, loving and supporting you. Their very presence is elevating and exciting. You welcome them into your consciousness. Tune in to their God-filled presence. Their presence empowers you, fills you with love and reverence. Your compassion expands. You feel boundless in your spiritual expression. You know in your heart that whatever challenges or tests present themselves, with God and the Holy Ones, you can meet them all and master them. With God, anything is possible.

In finishing your meditation, express your gratitude to the divine for what you have received. Gently come back into your earth consciousness empowered with the God light. Feel refreshed and grounded. You want to be very grounded in the light, because you must now take the holy blessing given and put it into active life. You must use the power granted to fulfill your potential and purpose.

When starting out, I recommend meditating for fifteen to twenty minutes a day. Yet what is more important than the length of a meditation is the depth of your meditation. When you finish a meditation, you should feel different from when you started. In these meditations, it is not expected to see the light or Holy Ones, but to sense or feel their presence. And even if you do not sense the Higher, this does not mean the Higher is not there. It is your devotion and dedication that draws the Holy Ones close to you.

WORKING WITH SPIRITUAL BEINGS AND DIVINE LIGHT

Now that you have the technique of working with Divine Light, you are ready to begin your meditative prayers. In the following prayers, you will be making requests of specific divine beings to bring in the spiritual power associated with them. You can call on the light itself, without including the Holy Ones, yet by invoking the presence of the divine ones you are greatly increasing what the Higher can give you.

Please remember that meditative prayers are requests, not commands. You cannot say for sure what spiritual being will respond and what you will receive. But if you are sincere, the divine support will be there and the meditation will be a blessed experience.

In calling on Divine Light, the Holy Ones you will primarily be working with are:

Lord of Wisdom Light (Lord Christ)
Archangel Michael

Archangel Gabriel

Archangel Uriel

Archangel Raphael

Divine Energy angels

Of course all celestial beings work with spiritual energy, yet these celestial leaders have particular responsibility for sending light to you and want you to call on them.[2]

DIVINE LIGHT UNDER THE LORD OF WISDOM LIGHT (LORD CHRIST)

The Lord of Wisdom Light is responsible for the radiant pure white light. The white light is an uplifting energy. If you are feeling burdened by troubles and cares, the white light can lift you out of that unenlightened consciousness. Because of its purity, it's a redeeming energy to bring parts of your consciousness back into the light. The Holy Ones themselves most often come in on the white light. It's a strong power for building up intuitive and clairvoyant skills.

MEDITATIVE PRAYER WITH THE PURE WHITE LIGHT

Heavenly Father/Holy Mother God, down-ray unto me under the direction of Lord Christ and the angels the pure white light to equalize, align, center, and attune all levels of my consciousness into the divine Oneness. Raise my consciousness into the highest level I am capable of reaching at this time.

---

[2] For a fuller explanation of the attributes of Divine Light, please refer to my books *Change Your Aura, Change Your Life* and *The Healing Power of Your Aura*. These books complement the light work with the Holy Ones very well.

DIVINE LIGHT UNDER
ARCHANGEL MICHAEL

Because of his many duties, Archangel Michael is responsible for sending several divine rays, including the following:

The orange-red flame of purification

The golden ray of wisdom light and protection

The carnation-red and ruby-red rays for vitality

The bright orange ray of motivation and enthusiasm

The lemon-yellow ray of concentration

The Orange-Red Flame of Purification

The orange-red flame is the purifying ray for your aura and consciousness. While walking this earth, you are immersed in a sea of spiritual energy. Spiritual purification is essential to release the unenlightened energy you may pick up or that you may generate yourself. Michael and his ministers of light are masters at releasing these negative energies from your aura.

MEDITATIVE PRAYER WITH THE
ORANGE-RED FLAME OF PURIFICATION

*Heavenly Father/Holy Mother God, down-ray unto me under the
direction of Archangel Michael and the angels of purification the
orange-red flame of purification to release all black and gray
atoms—all unenlightened energies from my aura and
consciousness—and dissolve those negative
energies in the mineral kingdom to
be reconstituted in the light.*

(Follow up this meditation with the blue-white
fire under Archangel Gabriel.)

The Golden Ray of Wisdom Light and Protection

Not to be confused with the Wisdom Light Ray of humanity, the golden ray is the great dynamic power of God. If you need more confidence, courage, faith, willpower, illumination, or any of the dynamic attributes of God, this is the ray for you. It is an indispensable ray in giving you the strength to fulfill your spiritual purpose.

MEDITATIVE PRAYER WITH THE GOLDEN RAY OF WISDOM LIGHT

Heavenly Father/Holy Mother God, down-ray unto me under the
direction of Archangel Michael and the angels of wisdom light the golden
ray, so that my aura and consciousness may be filled with all the dynamic
attributes of God—including wisdom, courage, strength, confidence, and
faith. I ask that this dynamic power give me the strength I need to carry
out all the inspiration and intuitive promptings the divine blesses me with.

The golden ray also brings in the strong protective powers. This not only is good for physical protection, but is essential in protecting yourself from other people drawing on your aura and spiritual power.

MEDITATIVE PRAYER FOR PROTECTION WITH THE GOLDEN RAY

Heavenly Father/Holy Mother God, down-ray unto me under the
direction of Archangel Michael and the angels of protection and the
bodyguards the golden ray of protective light. May it surround my
aura seven times in a gold bubble of protection. May I be strong
to affirm this protective power in all facets of my life.

The Carnation-Red and Ruby-Red Rays for Vitality

The carnation-red ray is a wonderful vitalizing power. It gives you energy and stamina. If you are physically, mentally, or emotionally tired, then this is an essential energy to work with. This energy is essential for those who are very active physically.

MEDITATIVE PRAYER WITH THE
CARNATION-RED RAY OF VITALITY

Heavenly Father/Holy Mother God, down-ray unto me under
the direction of Archangel Michael and the angels of vitality
the carnation-red ray of energy—revitalizing, reenergizing,
and remagnetizing all levels of my consciousness.

The ruby-red ray is a deeper color than the carnation-red ray. This energy is also an energizing power, but it works more quickly than the carnation-red ray. Think of it as a spiritual booster shot. It does not have the sustaining power of the carnation-red ray. It is not recommend for use near sleep time, as it could keep you up!

MEDITATIVE PRAYER WITH THE RUBY-RED
RAY OF QUICKENED VITALITY

Heavenly Father/Holy Mother God, down-ray unto me under the
direction of Archangel Michael and the angels of vitality the deep
ruby-red ray of vitalizing energy. I ask for the power as
a spiritual booster shot, giving me quick energy
to the full degree of my need.

The Bright Orange Ray of Motivation and Enthusiasm

The bright orange ray (not to be confused with the orange-red flame) is a fascinating power. It is the energy of ambition. In spiritual work, ambition is sometimes downplayed, yet you need to be ambitious to complete your spiritual purpose in life. This energy brings in a wonderful motivating power to propel you to action. It also brings in enthusiasm, which is needed if you feel discouraged or something has dampened your spirits.

MEDITATIVE PRAYER WITH THE BRIGHT ORANGE RAY OF MOTIVATION

Heavenly Father/Holy Mother God, down-ray unto me under the direction of Archangel Michael and the angels of the bright orange ray the energy of motivation, enthusiasm, and organization into all levels of my aura and consciousness, encouraging me to reach higher and fulfill my highest good. May this light inspire me to be ambitious and to use my talents and power to their fullest extent.

The Lemon-Yellow Ray of Concentration

The pristine lemon-yellow ray brings in powers of concentration. If you are studying or learning new material, this ray is needed. It also helps if you need more emotional focus or more focus in your daily activities.

**MEDITATIVE PRAYER WITH THE
LEMON-YELLOW RAY OF CONCENTRATION**

*Heavenly Father/Holy Mother God, down-ray unto me under the
direction of Archangel Michael and the angels of the lemon-yellow ray the
energy of concentration and focus to stimulate my intellect and all levels of
my consciousness so that my entire aura is more alert and focused.*

DIVINE LIGHT UNDER
ARCHANGEL GABRIEL

Gabriel is a diverse archangel in that he works with a variety of spiritual
powers. Archangel Gabriel is responsible for several rays:

The blue-white fire of new life force and healing

The emerald-green ray of balance and harmony

The turquoise ray of prosperity

The powder blue ray of inspiration

The electric-blue ray of talent

The royal blue ray of determination

The apple-green ray of spiritual growth

The Blue-White Fire of New Life Force and Healing

The blue-white fire is one of the most potent spiritual powers the divine
gives us. It is sapphire blue with flows of white light and other energies
intermingling. It has been said by the Higher that if you have time to
work with only one ray, you can't go wrong with this energy. It brings
in new life force. So after working with the orange-red flame to release

old energies, you want to follow up by replenishing your aura with the blue-white fire.

MEDITATIVE PRAYER WITH THE BLUE-WHITE FIRE OF NEW LIFE FORCE

Heavenly Father/Holy Mother God, down-ray unto me under the direction of Archangel Gabriel and the angels of the blue-white fire the electrifying life force of this holy fire. I ask that it charge and recharge all levels of my consciousness, refreshing every facet of my aura and being.

The blue-white fire is the single greatest healing ray there is. If you are in need of healing, you want to work a great deal with this power.

MEDITATIVE PRAYER WITH THE BLUE-WHITE FIRE OF HEALING

Heavenly Father/Holy Mother God, down-ray unto me under the direction of Archangel Gabriel and the angels of healing the blue-white fire to restore perfect health to my mind, body, and soul. May this light touch into all the cells in my body, bringing them into thy health consciousness.

The Emerald-Green Ray of Balance and Harmony

The emerald-green ray is the power of balance and harmony. It is indispensable to keep the various facets of your life and consciousness moving harmoniously together. If you feel that something has upset or unbalanced you in any way, work with this ray. It helps to bring you into the divine rhythm so you feel in better sync with the Higher. It's too easy to get caught up in the chaotic rhythms of our daily lives, and this power can keep everything in divine perspective.

**MEDITATIVE PRAYER WITH THE EMERALD-GREEN
RAY OF BALANCE AND HARMONY**

*Heavenly Father/Holy Mother God, down-ray unto me under the
direction of Archangel Gabriel and the angels of balance the
emerald-green ray of balance and harmony to steady all
levels of my consciousness—mind, body, and soul—
in divine rhythm and harmony. May I walk
in sync with divine rhythm.*

The Turquoise Ray of Prosperity

The turquoise ray brings in the consciousness of abundance and prosperity. This is a favorite energy to work with, as it can help lift you out of poverty consciousness or any sense of lack or limitation, and bring you into the awareness of God's unlimited supply.

**MEDITATIVE PRAYER WITH THE
TURQUOISE RAY OF ABUNDANCE**

*Heavenly Father/Holy Mother God, down-ray unto me under the
direction of Archangel Gabriel and the angels of prosperity the turquoise
ray of abundance and supply to bless all levels of my consciousness
with God's unlimited wealth. Release me from any sense of lack
or limitation—any poverty consciousness—and help me
to tune into God's infinite abundance.*

The Powder Blue Ray of Inspiration

The powder blue ray of inspiration brings in the high original creative ideas. If you are an artist or inventor, this is the power that can quicken your inspirational flow. At the same time, this power is important for anyone who is seeking fresh inspiration in their life.

MEDITATIVE PRAYER WITH THE
POWDER BLUE RAY OF INSPIRATION

Heavenly Father/Holy Mother God, down-ray unto me under the direction of Archangel Gabriel and the angels of inspiration the powder blue ray of inspiration, blessing me with original creative ideas that are uplifting and elevating. May I feel open in all levels of my consciousness and receptive to divine inspiration.

The Electric-Blue Ray of Talent

Inspiration and talent are two different energies in the aura. Inspiration brings in original ideas, and talent is the skill to carry out those ideas. In your creative endeavors, you need to be building up both. The electric-blue ray is the power of the actual creative skill or talent a person possesses. It is peacock blue. You build up this power as you develop your creative skills, whether in the arts, the sciences, or wherever you are directing your creative talents.

MEDITATIVE PRAYER WITH THE
ELECTRIC-BLUE RAY OF TALENT

Heavenly Father/Holy Mother God, down-ray unto me under the direction of Archangel Gabriel and the angels of creative power the electric-blue ray of talent to help build up my skills and creative abilities. May it especially be directed to the magnetic division, where the creative power in my aura is expressed.

The Royal Blue Ray of Determination

The royal blue ray of determination is a powerful energy that also brings in devotion and loyalty. If you feel that your dedication to the divine wavers at times, this is the energy to bring in to help reorganize your priorities.

**MEDITATIVE PRAYER WITH THE ROYAL BLUE
RAY OF DETERMINATION**

*Heavenly Father/Holy Mother God, down-ray unto me under the
direction of Archangel Gabriel and the angels of determination the royal
blue ray of devotion and determination, to deepen my dedication and
loyalty to God. Help me to stay steady and follow
through on the things I need to do.*

The Apple-Green Ray of Spiritual Growth

This energy is light green. It's known as one of the "pearl luster" colors. It shimmers and has almost an opalescent quality to it. This energy is seen in the aura of someone who is making strides in their spiritual progress. Calling on this power can help accelerate your spiritual progress and give you a fresh outlook on life. It works very well with the powder blue ray.

*Heavenly Father/Holy Mother God, down-ray unto me under the
direction of Archangel Gabriel and the angels of spiritual growth the
apple-green ray to inspire and elevate me in my spiritual journey.
I ask this energy to refresh my soul so that I feel ready to
take the next step in my spiritual evolution.*

DIVINE LIGHT UNDER ARCHANGEL URIEL

Archangel Uriel brings in the magnificent magnetic energies of the divine life:

The deep rose–pink ray of spiritual love
The purple and violet rays of peace and tranquillity

The Deep Rose–Pink Ray of Spiritual Love

This is one of the most essential rays to work with. You could not get through this life without a great deal of love. Love is the bond that holds creation together. It is through love that you experience the Oneness of life. This ray is essential to feel closer to God and the spiritual hierarchy. It is an indispensable energy to call on if you are feeling lonely or unloved. It's a great healing energy in any relationship discord, or if you simply want to feel closer to someone. This ray brings in the many qualities of the magnetic attributes including compassion, joy, kindness, and tenderness. It's a wonderful complementary energy to the dynamic golden ray. There are many attributes of this ray, hence many angelic beings under Uriel who work with this power.

MEDITATIVE PRAYER WITH THE DEEP
ROSE–PINK RAY OF SPIRITUAL LOVE

Heavenly Father/Holy Mother God, down-ray unto me under the
direction of Archangel Uriel and the angels of love the deep rose-pink ray
of spiritual love to fill my aura and consciousness with God's eternal,
unconditional love so that I may be more loving, kind, and compassionate.
Release me from any sense of loneliness or sadness and fill me with
God's eternal joy. May this loving light bring me in close
communion with God and the spiritual hierarchy.

The Purple and Violet Rays of Peace and Tranquillity

The purple ray brings you into the deep spiritual peace. If you are restless, hyperactive, agitated, or irritated, this energy can bring you into the divine stillness. It's a wonderful ray to work with if you are in grief. If you feel like you are carrying the world's woes on your shoulders, this energy can help you relax and let go, placing all your cares in God's loving hands.

MEDITATIVE PRAYER WITH THE PURPLE RAY OF PEACE

Heavenly Father/Holy Mother God, down-ray unto me under the
direction of Archangel Uriel and the angels of peace the deep purple ray,
filling my soul and consciousness with the peace of God, bringing me
into the silence of peace and the peace of silence, releasing stress, and
letting me feel like I have not a care in the world except
to relax in the arms of the divine.

The violet ray is a lighter shade in color than the deep purple. It is a gentler version of the purple ray and brings in tranquillity and serenity. It's excellent for the nervous system if you are stressed and feel pressured at work or home.

MEDITATIVE PRAYER WITH THE VIOLET RAY OF TRANQUILLITY

Heavenly Father/Holy Mother God, down-ray unto me under the
direction of Archangel Uriel and the angels of peace the gentle violet
ray of serenity and tranquillity, quieting my nerves and
relaxing my mind, body, and emotions.

DIVINE LIGHT UNDER
ARCHANGEL RAPHAEL

Archangel Raphael works with the silver ray of divine intelligence. You may ask why Raphael is responsible for only one ray and the others more. This is because of the many applications of the silver light. This ray quickens your spiritual perception. It keeps you awake and alert in all facets of your spiritual pursuits. The soul can too easily become complacent and fall asleep, spiritually speaking. This ray keeps your awareness sharp. If you are trying to assimilate new knowledge, this silver light is extremely helpful. It is also a quickening energy. If you feel like you are stuck in "red tape" in some facet of your life, this energy can get things moving.

**MEDITATIVE PRAYER WITH THE SILVER
RAY OF DIVINE INTELLIGENCE**

*Heavenly Father/Holy Mother God, down-ray unto me under the
direction of Archangel Raphael and the angels of intelligence the silver
ray, releasing any areas of sluggishness and quickening all levels of my
aura and consciousness with greater powers of perception and awareness.
May I be alert and awake to the divine promptings and more aware of the
various energy rays the divine blesses me with. Help me to see more
clearly things as they really are, and not as I wish them to be.*

HOW THE HOLY ONES WORK WITH
YOU DURING MEDITATION

Now we come to a fascinating question: How do the Holy Ones work
with you during meditation? There is a most beautiful interaction going
on during your meditations, illuminating just how much the divine
loves and cares for you. As mentioned, the link to the entire meditative
process is your angelic teachers. Regardless of which holy being you are
calling on, it is the teachers who are coordinating the process.

During your meditation with the Holy Ones, several divine beings
are getting involved. This is because there needs to be a linking up of
consciousness, as the energy is being stepped down from the celestial
source to you.

The process works like this: During a typical meditation, two angelic
teachers come around you. They stay a good ways above you to maintain
the direct connection with the celestial realms. Below them are your
guardian angels. You have two guardian angels, one dynamic and the
other magnetic. Their job is to make sure the spiritual power coming

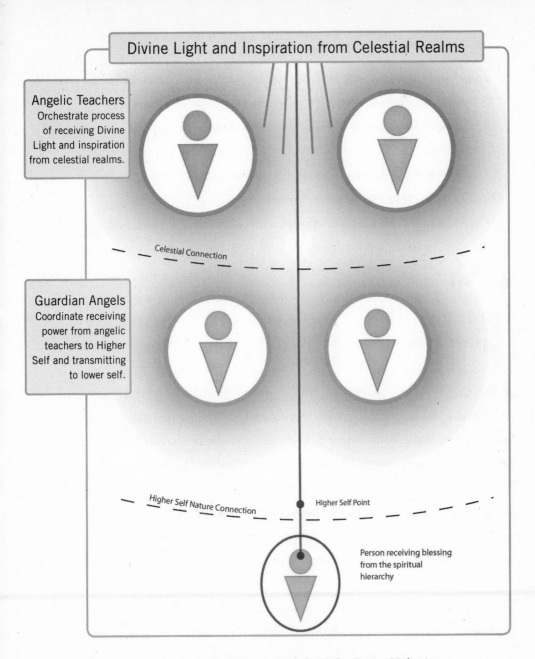

Divine Light and Inspiration from Celestial Realms

Angelic Teachers
Orchestrate process of receiving Divine Light and inspiration from celestial realms.

Celestial Connection

Guardian Angels
Coordinate receiving power from angelic teachers to Higher Self and transmitting to lower self.

Higher Self Nature Connection

Higher Self Point

Person receiving blessing from the spiritual hierarchy

FIGURE 15.2. *Connecting with the Higher During Meditation*

from the angelic teachers is accurately being transmitted to your higher nature, and from there to you. (See Figure 15.2.)

Above this entire configuration, the Holy Ones you are calling in your meditative prayers—the archangels and angels—are projecting the power from their celestial realms. This power appears like a beam of light descending down to your aura. The angelic teachers and guardian angels are coordinating this process to make sure it passes through all the various planes of consciousness to reach you.

Looking at all this support, you may ask if the divine comes to you like this every time you meditate. First, the meditation must be sincere and dedicated. It is harder for them to work with you if you are casual, distracted, or disturbed in your meditation. Second, they do this once or twice a day at best. They will also stay only as long as they feel they need to get the job done. The Holy Ones don't want you to "overmeditate" because they want you to put the light and power you are receiving into action. Meditation is the time to gather your spiritual power. Once gathered, you need to implement that power so it becomes a permanent part of your aura and consciousness. Some people meditate too much, thinking they will build up more power, but it doesn't work like that. You will receive what you need, and that is it. Then the Higher will wait and see what you do with the power they blessed you with. The more power you use, the more they will bless you with. In the same way, if you don't meditate enough, then it is harder for the Holy Ones to make this kind of connection.

What about people who do not meditate or are not on a spiritual path? Do they receive the blessings of the Higher in this way? The answer is yes, they do. The divine loves us equally whether we are aware of them or not. In cases where people do not take the time to directly commune with the divine, the Holy Ones will come when people are quiet and reflective to bless them with light and power. This tells us that even if you don't meditate, you need downtime to reflect and absorb. It's part of the balance of life. If you are too much on the go all of the time, the Higher still works with you, but not as much as they could otherwise. Of course, when you take time to meditate, that is the best method, because you are taking time for them, allowing the connections to be strong, and also strengthening your receptivity to them. Meditation is indispensable when you are on the spiritual path.

This is not the only way the divine reaches us. There are other methods, but this is one of the most common and effective ways to commune with the divine.

CALLING ON THE HIGHER OUTSIDE MEDITATION AND PRAYER

Meditation is not the only time to call on the Holy Ones for Divine Light. There will be times throughout the day when you will need the light but not necessarily be in a position to meditate. The Holy Ones want you to call on them throughout the day as the need arises. It's part of the divine experience. They are part of your life in and out of meditation. Your meditation time is a most sacred time to connect with the divine, but they are there to support you at all times and often offer assistance when you least expect it.

When calling on the Higher outside meditation, you are primarily calling on your angelic teachers for support. Remember, your angelic teachers are the link for the spiritual hierarchy, so by calling on them you will get whatever support you need. You don't need to raise your consciousness and go through the meditative process just described. Simply close your eyes, feel the Oneness, and ask your teachers for the help and the light you need. You can visualize the light coming down if you like. You can do this anytime. For example, say you are in the middle of a meeting at work and things are not going well. People's emotions are flaring up and you feel yourself getting sucked into that negative energy. Silently ask for help from your teachers, requesting, for example, the emerald-green ray to maintain your balance. Watch how your perspective will change for the better. Or if you are feeling low in energy in the middle of a strenuous activity, you can simply say something like, "Dear angelic teachers, I request the carnation-red ray to boost my energy levels. Thank you!" And feel that vital carnation-red ray power. It's that simple.

Calling on your angelic teachers during your daily activities helps to amplify your meditative work. It helps you to implement the power you are calling on and keeps you steady in the light. One of the most common things I notice with students is that they too often don't call on their teachers outside meditation. Acknowledging the divine during the course of your day can be one of the simplest and most effective ways to strengthen the bond between you and the Holy Ones.

CHAPTER 16

MEDITATIONS FOR GUIDANCE AND INSPIRATION

I N ADDITION TO working with the spiritual hierarchy to receive Divine Light, you can work with the divine to receive guidance and direction. In this way, the Holy Ones are acting as emissaries for the Divine Mind from which all inspiration and guidance come.

An inspiring story of the Holy Ones and divine guidance involves my co-author, Dimitri. When I met Dimitri, many years ago, he was in his twenties and had recently had a dramatic spiritual awakening. It changed his life, but he had not yet begun his spiritual studies. He came from an excellent home life and showed a lot of promise in a film career that he was just starting. He had a burning desire for metaphysics. However, I don't think he was yet aware of what it was like to live the spiritual life, as his background was foreign to metaphysics.

When we met, the first thing that impressed me was his higher nature. He had the most developed higher nature I had seen in a person's aura. Yet his lower nature, or "human aura," did not initially reflect this level of development. This told me he had a great deal of rekindling to do. This is not unusual, especially today. There are many who have developed their soul in past lives but need to reclaim that power in this life. Before meeting him, I had been told by the Holy Ones that I would meet someone who would play an instrumental part in the spiritual work I was doing. From that first meeting, the divine confirmed that Dimitri was that person.

We started working together and he took to the spiritual training quickly. The Higher had given him a few key insights as to his potential but not the full scope, so as not to overwhelm him. So he did not yet have a clear picture of the shape his future life's work would take. Before he could get to that place, there was much work to do to develop his soul's potential, and many tests to pass. I knew that he was the one, if he was successful in his training, designated to carry on the work of the Kingdom of Light Teachings after my tenure was finished.

To his credit, Dimitri made some decisions early on to redirect his life's path to pursue metaphysics more closely, but this was not easy, as his life was moving in a very different direction. This included letting go of some career opportunities to stay closer to the spiritual work. Switching directions meant changing, and potentially upsetting, many things. Not everyone is asked to do this, but for Dimitri, it was the right move.

Yet after making some sacrifices, when the "new life" and spiritual opportunities did not open right away as he expected, I sensed Dimitri was disappointed and bewildered. His passion for metaphysics remained strong, but he wondered if he had made a mistake in his career and personal decisions. Confusion ensued, as he was not sure which way to go. The work that was to come hadn't started yet, but he couldn't go back to his old life. I held the light for him but could not intervene much, as this was clearly an important lesson that he had to face on his own. Through this searching, he was meditating diligently, asking the divine for guidance and illumination. Yet the answers did not seem to be forthcoming.

One day, we were in meditation, and I saw Archangel Gabriel come in very close. He blessed Dimitri with a penetrating sapphire-blue ray. The sapphire blue is a concentrated healing power. I saw the light go to all levels of his consciousness, especially the mental part of the aura. Archangel Gabriel is the master healer, and it was incredible to watch him work. He especially gave Dimitri a mental healing to release confusion and wrong thinking. He felt very uplifted, and the distressed energy that was around him had dissipated. After that blessing, I could see that Dimitri's aura had brightened, and he was much more motivated. He was determined from the start, but this was a new level of commitment.

Gabriel's blessing was the beginning of the answer to Dimitri's prayers. He started to see things in a different light. He realized now that he was in this spiritual work for the long haul, and that he had to change his attitude. He had to be more proactive, work hard, and not expect quick results. This turning point started a concentrated period of spiritual training, which opened up new dimensions of the divine life and helped him reconnect with the developed parts of his nature. There were still difficult years ahead, as it took time for spiritual work to take root, but now he was fully committed. He pursued work that utilized some of his creative talents, yet would leave him room to develop his spiritual nature and long-term goals.

Today he has reached a marvelous spiritual pinnacle and is a spiritual teacher in his own right. As I look at his aura, I see that his lower self is now a beautiful reflection of his higher nature. He's made his own direct connection to the divine, and at the right time he will take over the work I have been doing for years. This is the power of divine guidance and direction.

When you go to the Higher for guidance, you are tapping into an extraordinary reservoir of knowledge and experience. The divine most often share this wisdom a little at a time. They do this so you have time to implement that wisdom before more is given. For example, you may ask the Higher what your purpose in life is. Perhaps you are confused and feel directionless. While they will give you inspiration, it would be rare for the Holy Ones to simply state plainly what that purpose is. The reason for this is that first—in your confusion—you may not fully appreciate or be ready for such straightforward answers, even though you are asking for them. Second, they want you to experience the moments of self-discovery where real growth comes from. Truth has no meaning until it lives in your heart.

What the Holy Ones most often do is give you the next step. They point your feet in the right direction. By doing so, they rekindle the inner knowing you already have. Then they will watch and see. Do you follow through on the inspiration given? Do you accept it and try it out? Or do you discard it? Once they see you implementing what they are giving you, more inspiration and guidance comes. If the inspiration is not used, they will keep trying or find another approach, but they will patiently continue to inspire you until you get the message.

Be careful how you approach the Higher. They are not there to tell you what to do, and they are not there to do the spiritual growing for you. They are lovingly there to help you reach your highest potential and purpose. As they are already aware of what you are meant to accomplish, every day they inspire you to realize your highest objectives. So the request you make for guidance or direction is more about you opening up to realign yourself with the divine plan.

A big question in working with divine guidance is this: How do you know if the inspiration is coming from the Higher, or simply from your own mind? Many people look for some type of sign or serendipity to confirm that they are on the right road. The truth is, you won't always know if the prompting you are getting is really coming from the Higher until you put it to the test. As with intuition, if the inspiration feels right, try it out. If you are making an honest appeal, the Holy Ones will answer your call. As you put it to use, you will quickly know if you are on the right track. If it was true guidance from the Higher, you will see the results and be encouraged to continue. And if it turns out to be your own voice, that's okay too. Learn from the mistake. Then next time you go to the Higher for help, you'll be a little smarter.

Please don't be discouraged if at first it feels like your request for guidance is going unanswered. Inspiration takes time to develop. The very effort you are making to connect with the Higher is strengthening that bridge. The key is consistency to include the Holy Ones in your decision-making process. Every time you reach out to them, they reach out to you and the spiritual bond deepens.

Here are some pointers for working with the Higher for guidance and direction.

Coming Up with the Right Question Is Half the Battle

Reflect on what it is that you want to ask the Higher. Try to do this in a dispassionate way. If you are frustrated, angry, or upset, it is harder to make a clear connection with the divine because your consciousness is colored by your feelings. Give yourself time to come from a calm, steady place.

Avoid conditioning your question. You have to leave the possibility that what you are asking for is not meant to be. For example, if you desire something very much and are asking for guidance, leave your options open for any possible answer, even if it is not what you want to hear. Some people think they can be clever and frame the question in the direction they want. Naturally, the Holy Ones can see your intention. You can't trick the Higher. The response you get will be in the way you put it out.

Have Your Question Ready

Once you decide what it is you are asking help on and have framed the question in an open way, write it down or have it clearly thought out in your head.

Raise Your Consciousness to Your Higher Self Point

Follow the invocation for raising the consciousness. As you do this, you are not thinking of your questions. You are first going to the Higher for the sheer joy of becoming one with the divine. Your concerns do not exist. You are going into meditation to feel the presence, to feel the Oneness of God. As you are in your Higher Self Point, feel the consciousness and beauty of the divine awareness and the Holy Ones making their connections with you.

Call on the Divine Light

The three spiritual energy rays that work very well in guidance and direction are the golden ray of wisdom light under Archangel Michael, the white light for illumination and upliftment under Lord Christ, and the silver ray of divine intelligence and perception under Archangel Raphael. In this case, you can bring the energies just to the Higher Self Point.

MEDITATIVE PRAYER FOR GUIDANCE AND DIRECTION WITH THE GOLDEN RAY

Heavenly Father/Holy Mother God, under the direction of Archangel Michael and the Divine Energy angels I ask for the golden ray of wisdom light to be down-rayed to my Higher Self Point of Spiritual Knowing. May this light illuminate my consciousness with divine understanding, guidance, and direction.

MEDITATIVE PRAYER FOR GUIDANCE AND DIRECTION WITH THE PURE WHITE LIGHT

Heavenly Father/Holy Mother God, under the direction of Lord Christ and the Divine Energy angels I ask for the white light to be down-rayed to my Higher Self Point of Spiritual Knowing. May this light reveal the power ray of God Mind, raising my consciousness to the highest vibratory level so that I am one with God Mind. I ask that the white light release any mental interference or unenlightened thinking in my consciousness.

MEDITATIVE PRAYER FOR GUIDANCE AND DIRECTION WITH THE SILVER RAY

Heavenly Father/Holy Mother God, under the direction of Archangel Raphael and the angels of divine intelligence, I ask for the silver ray to be down-rayed to my Higher Self Point of Spiritual Knowing. May this light quicken my spiritual reception so that I can clearly understand what the divine is saying to me.

Ask Your Question(s) to Your Angelic Teachers

Once you feel you have established your connection and feel you are in a clear and inspired place, then place your question on the altar of God. Surrender completely to the outcome. Be ready for whatever comes through, even if it is not what you thought it would be or wished it to be.

The celestial beings you will work with in guidance and direction are your angelic teachers. They are the ones directly responsible for helping you in your spiritual journey, and they are the ones who will respond to your call. They can access any aspect of the spiritual hierarchy to get the inspiration you need. In your request, and in all work with the divine, include the phrase, "According to divine law and love for the good of all concerned."

In making your request, you are laying down the desire of your heart. Of course, God already knows your needs, but by doing so you are letting the divine direct your actions. You are taking things out of your hands and putting them in God's hands.

Hold to Receive

After you have made your petition, get into the silence. Let your mind be as still as possible. Again, don't try to steer things—your mind is now the receiving station. Like a radio, you are trying to pick up the signals that the divine is sending you. The inspiration can come in any form. It could be a thought, an image, a sound, or a sense.

Give Your Gratitude

If you receive an inspiration, give your thanks. If nothing comes through, give your thanks and hold on to the knowledge that the answer will come in time. You have put the request out there and the answer could come at any time. Don't be disappointed if your answer doesn't come right away, but usually something will come if you are quiet enough to hear it.

Act on What Is Given

Once you get an inspiration, act on it. It is in the act of doing that your validation will come, and it can inspire more activity. Remain open and hopeful.

BUILDING YOUR INSPIRATIONAL POWERS

Inspiration is different from intuition. As we learned previously in this book that intuition is an unconscious activity of the spiritual senses. It's a perceptual tool that all of us are meant to develop as part of our journey to awaken the mystical senses.

While intuition is a perceptual experience, inspiration is an attribute of mind. Through inspiration, the Holy Ones are sending specific thoughts to you that they have received from the Divine Mind. They send these thoughts through your Higher Self to the etheric counterpart to your mental center. You will recall from chapter 13 that when a soul is in direct telepathic communication with the divine, this is called *etheric mediatorship*. Even if you have not yet built the conscious bridge to the divine, the spiritual hierarchy stimulates your etheric mind, which the mental/brain mind can pick up. We call this unconscious connection with the etheric mind *inspiration*.

The challenge is that your conscious mind is not always focused on the divine impulse. It's too often immersed in the mental activity of your own thoughts and the countless thoughts and mental bombardments of the world. Clearing your mind of mental clutter is essential to becoming more receptive to divine inspiration. You need to make room for fresh new thinking. If you feel you are not clearheaded, ask for the orange-red flame under Archangel Michael to cleanse your mind with the following prayer:

MEDITATIVE PRAYER FOR MENTAL CLEANSING WITH THE ORANGE-RED FLAME

Heavenly Father/Holy Mother God, under the direction of Archangel Michael and the angels of purification, I ask for the orange-red flame to be down-rayed to my mental center to release all mental confusions, illusions, and delusions—all mental bombardments and impingements, any unenlightened thoughts that I may have picked up or generated. Dissolve these black and gray atoms in the mineral kingdom in the light.

Then follow up with the rejuvenating power of the blue-white fire under Archangel Gabriel:

MEDITATIVE PRAYER FOR MENTAL REJUVENATION WITH THE BLUE-WHITE FIRE

Heavenly Father/Holy Mother God, under the direction of Archangel Gabriel and the angels of life force, I ask for the blue-white fire to be down-rayed to my mental center to

charge and recharge me with the celestial blue-white fire
of eternal life. I ask that my mental body be rejuvenated,
refreshed, and strengthened in the light.

To conclude this chapter, I would like to offer a meditative prayer with the powder blue ray under Archangel Gabriel. This is not so much for guidance and direction as it is for original thinking. It brings in new creative ideas. If you are inventing or creating anything new, this power is essential. I often see it in people's auras above the head, indicating that the divine is sending new ideas to that person. If you find that you are in a repetitive thinking pattern with no new ideas flowing in, the powder blue ray will help to open the inspirational channel.

MEDITATIVE PRAYER WITH THE POWDER BLUE RAY FOR NEW INSPIRATION

Heavenly Father/Holy Mother God, down-ray unto me under the
direction of Archangel Gabriel and the angels of inspiration the
powder blue ray of inspiration. I ask for new ideas and fresh
thinking to flow freely into my mental consciousness,
opening me to inspiration whenever it strikes.
Give me the courage to follow through
on the inspiration given.

As part of building up your inspirational power, follow through on all the energy work offered in this book. Building up the power in your aura has the effect of raising your consciousness into higher dimensions of awareness. Make sure you are building a strong connection with the Higher Self Point, as this is the gateway for all inspiration to flow through.

CHAPTER 17

A QUICK REFERENCE GUIDE TO THE DIVINE

THROUGHOUT THIS BOOK, I have done my best to offer you essential tools to working with the divine. These tools have been part of my teaching and personal experience for decades. Take the time to develop these tools, and your relationship with the Holy Ones will greatly deepen. As you have gathered, the study of the spiritual hierarchy is not a simple task. There are many things to learn. In this chapter, I would like to distill key points and offer a simple exercise so you can get started right away in your work with the Higher.

There are four basic goals in working with the Holy Ones we have looked at.

1. Recognition

You need to get involved with the Holy Ones. While they are always there for you, your attitude and attention are essential. As in any relationship, when you include them in your life, you build rapport and your effectiveness in working with them increases.

2. Understanding

The more knowledge you have about the Holy Ones, the better. Like any skill or art, you need to know what you are doing. Take time to understand which celestial being does what. If you are not clear whom to call on, always ask divine intelligence to guide you. Also be aware of the dangers of lower spirits. Don't take things at face value. Put every intuition or inspiration to the test, so that you recognize its value from your own experience.

3. Meditative Prayer

Meditation is the most intimate time to commune with the divine. Make meditation and prayer a daily practice, and watch the miracles unfold. Fifteen to twenty minutes per day is a great place to start (see chapter 15).

4. Intuition and Inspiration

Intuition is a perceptual experience and inspiration is a mental experience. These are two ways you will receive divine promptings. Building these skills leads to direct communion (see chapters 13 and 16).

STARTING WITH YOUR ANGELIC TEACHERS

Angelic teachers are the first celestial beings to start working with. They are the door to the entire spiritual hierarchy. They do not give you their names, but that doesn't matter in the least. They are there for you when you need them.

Here is a simple exercise to start working with your teachers right now:

- Sit upright in a comfortable chair, legs uncrossed.
- Envision a golden bubble of protective light around you. Take a couple of deep breaths and relax.
- Envision a golden sun above your head, about two feet (your Higher Self Point). Place your attention on this golden sun. Sense that it is filled with divine awareness. As you do this, you feel your consciousness elevating and your cares and concerns dropping away. You are in a sacred place of divine knowing.
- See a beautiful ray of deep rose-pink light showering you from this golden sun. As this Divine Light comes down, you feel a tremendous amount of love—unconditional love. This loving light blesses your mind, your body, and your soul. You feel thrilled, healed, and exhilarated in this holy power. As you receive this power, you sense that you are not alone. A magnificent angelic teacher is near you and is sending love to you. You feel very close to this divine being. You know you are loved and supported. You feel enormously grateful for the blessing.
- Hold in the silence for a few minutes to fully receive this blessing.
- Once again your attention goes to the golden sun above your head. You feel and sense the beauty and power of this sun even more deeply. You now sense that the angelic teacher near you is sending the pure white light to you. This white light is extraordinarily brilliant, yet not blinding in the least. You feel the angelic power coming on with the white light. It feels like the angel is right there in the room with you. This white light blesses all levels of your consciousness—your thoughts, feelings, words, and ac-

tions. Every cell of your body is receiving this white light. You feel even more elevated and united with the divine.

- In this mystical union, you feel safe and keenly alert. You open your heart and place one question, concern, or desire on the divine altar, asking that your angelic teacher bless, guide, and inspire you.

- Hold in the silence for a few minutes to wait for a response.

- Give your thanks for all that you have been blessed with. If you received an answer, do your best to implement what you received. If not, then hold to the knowledge that your answer is forthcoming and remain receptive.

- Return to your earth consciousness feeling very grounded. Once again, envision the golden bubble of protection around you.

- And that's it!

ROUNDUP OF THE SPIRITUAL HIERARCHY

Here is a quick reference to the members of the spiritual hierarchy we have been looking at in this book:

Leaders of the Spiritual Hierarchy

LORD OF WISDOM LIGHT (LORD CHRIST)—Leader of the spiritual hierarchy for humanity as a whole. He and his angels bring in the white light.

THE HOLY GHOST—Along with the Holy Spirit, this dynamic being is responsible for the execution of the divine plan and making sure humanity is in alignment with the divine laws of life.

THE HOLY SPIRIT—This magnetic being works with the Holy

Ghost in the execution of the divine plan. She works diligently to keep humanity on track spiritually, and is very involved with divine guidance and rightful direction.

Archangels—The Four Primary Leaders

MICHAEL—He is the senior archangel and is responsible for the dynamic powers of God, including the golden ray of wisdom light and protection, the orange-red flame of purification, the carnation-red ray of vitality, and the lemon-yellow ray of concentration.

GABRIEL—He brings in the healing powers, the prosperity energies, and the creative powers. Spiritual powers under Archangel Gabriel include the blue-white fire of new life force and healing, the emerald-green ray of balance, the turquoise ray of prosperity, and the powder blue ray of inspiration.

RAPHAEL—He is also a dynamic archangel and brings in the silver ray of divine intelligence to keep humanity awake and alert spiritually. His areas of expertise include business, science, and education. He works a great deal with divine guidance and rightful direction as well as quickening your spiritual perception.

URIEL—This magnetic archangel is responsible for bringing in the deep rose-pink ray of spiritual love and the purple and violet rays of divine peace. She works to keep us connected to the divine Oneness and keeps our relationships with others in a loving place.

The Eight Archangelic Specialists (part of the twelve archangelic leaders)

ZADKIEL—This archangel works with karma and the law of cause and effect. He works with the Primordial Ray to help administer the natural and divine laws of life to humanity.

SAMUEL—He administers the process of reincarnation. He works with the royal blue ray of truth.

SARIEL—This dynamic archangel works in the world of psychology, helping to maintain mental and emotional stability. He works with the spirit light, which helps us to release false desires and addictions and increase our desire to pursue the divine.

CELESTIAL LUCIFER—This celestial being, not to be confused with the fallen archangel who goes by the same name, is strongly connected to the development and maintenance of the physical body. He brings in spirit-substance, which helps to maintain the integrity of the physical atoms in the body.

HANIEL—She is a magnetic archangel and helps souls to make their jump from one plane of consciousness to another through the process of spiritual evolution. She works with the cosmic light, which assists in the ascension process of humanity.

RAZIEL—This powerful archangel works to uplift and refresh the soul, especially when it feels weary or burdened. He works with the Holy Breath to renew mind, body, and soul.

JOPHIEL—This lovely magnetic archangel works closely with Archangel Uriel. Jophiel works with the pearl-luster, pale-pink light of selfless love, to help souls release attachment and come into closer communion with unconditional love.

SANDALPHON—This dynamic archangel brings in the Holy Word of God. He works strongly with speech patterns and the spiritual tone that goes into the vibrated ethers.

Angelic Beings

CHERUBS—These angelic babies bring the energy of hope, optimism, and wonder. They come in with other angels and are full of the thrill of the angelic world.

JOY GUIDES—These angelic children are full of life and fun. They come around to lift your spirits and keep a smile on your face. Every soul on earth has joy guides that come around them.

DIVINE ENERGY ANGELS—These divine beings work intimately with the archangels to administer the various attributes and qualities of the divine powers.

GUARDIAN ANGELS—These holy angels maintain the divine connections and communications between the hierarchy and the human soul. They work closely with the teaching angels and take their lead from the teachers.

TEACHING ANGELS—These are the angels most strongly connected to humanity on a day-to-day basis. Each soul has assigned to him or her spiritual teachers who are the link to the entire spiritual hierarchy. It is essential to call on these divine beings daily for support and inspiration. There are many types of angelic teachers, each with their area of skill and expertise.

CHOIR ANGELS—Included within this group of angels are the nine levels of angelic support elucidated in the Judaic/Christian tradition (choir angels, choir archangels, principalities, powers, virtues, dominions, thrones, cherubim, and seraphim). These holy beings work strongly with religious souls and those striving to come up into their higher nature.

GREAT DIVINE BROTHERHOOD—These are the elite of the angelic world. They are the leaders of the angelic hosts and are strongly connected with the enlightenment process.

Human Support

CELESTIAL SPIRITUAL TEACHERS—These are human souls who have progressed beyond physical incarnations on earth and evolved to the high heaven worlds. These souls have similar duties to those of the angelic teachers but are not as developed. Celestial spiritual teachers are assigned to souls who are not ready to work with the angelic teachers and support those who have not yet awakened to their spiritual potential.

SPIRIT GUIDES—These are enlightened human souls who help make the connection with the angelic teachers. They are especially important for souls who have not yet found an earth-based spiritual teacher.

LIST OF DIVINE ENERGY ANGELS TO WORK WITH

There are many angels who work with the archangels and Lord Christ in sending light and power to humanity. These angels are in the category of Divine Energy angels. Here is a more detailed list of these divine ones.

Lord of Wisdom Light (Lord Christ)
Angels of Pure White Light
Angels of Revelation

Angels of Christ Light (ray of humanity light, Wisdom
Light Ray)

Archangel Michael

Angels of Wisdom Light

Angels of Illumination

Angels of the Orange-Red Flame

Angels of Purification

Angels of Protection

Angelic Bodyguards

Angels of Inner Strength

Angels of Motivation

Angels of Divine Will

Angels of Concentration

Angels of Energy and Vitality

Angels of Faith

Archangel Gabriel

Angels of the Blue-White Fire

Angels of Healing

Body Chemists

Angels of Balance

Angels of Creative Power

Angels of Inspiration

Angels of Determination

Angels of Devotion

Angels of Prosperity

Archangel Raphael

Angels of Intelligence

Angels of Communication

Angels of Finance

Angels of Business

Angels of Rightful Direction

Angel Mechanics

Angels of Science

Angels of Guidance

Archangel Uriel

Angels of Love

Angels of Peace

Angels of Compassion

Angels of Understanding

Sisters in Light (for newborn babies)

Archangel Zadkiel

Angels of Divine Justice

Archangel Samuel

Angels of Truth

Archangel Jophiel

Angels of Selfless Love

CHAPTER 18

WALKING WITH THE HOLY ONES

A s WE COME full circle in our exploration of the spiritual hierarchy, we have discovered a vast array of spiritual beings who work with us at every level of activity and consciousness.

Communing with the divine means connecting with your divine source through the spiritual hierarchy. The Holy Ones urge each of us to work diligently to build this bridge to the divine. Like any relationship, you have to put yourself in it if you want things to work. The love and care the divine expresses, and the power and wisdom the Holy Ones impart, are greater than can be fully understood. You can never fully repay all that they do for you, other than to be the expression of the divine and to be an example for others. As you let the divine flow through you, the divine blesses not only you but all in your life. Every time you reach into your Higher Self to commune, you bring back to your human awareness a part of that communion. This elevates your aura and consciousness. Then, as you live the truth the Holy Ones have blessed you with, your compassion increases and your soul evolves.

When you work with the Holy Ones, every facet of your life is blessed. Focus on your spiritual development, and your awareness of the Higher will unfold at the right time. What you want to do now is recognize the prompting that the Higher is giving you. You do not need your spiritual senses open to pick up the signals. Learn to interpret the intuition and inspiration the Higher are blessing you with.

Acknowledge the Higher every day. Feel their vibration and light rays. Call upon their help and support. Offer your love and gratitude for all they do.

Be patient. Just as you cannot climb the spiritual ladder overnight, you cannot build your mystical connection with the Higher quickly. Follow the spiritual steps you are inspired to take and that will lead you to the goal of spiritual union. Eventually, as you work with the spiritual hierarchy, the day will come when you behold the divine directly.

MEDITATING WITH THE SPIRITUAL HIERARCHY AND DIVINE LIGHT

The Higher Self Point

The Higher Self Point is twenty-four inches above the physical head and is the emissary for all the light and inspiration flowing from the divine source. It can be thought of as an eighth spiritual center and appears like a golden sun. All spiritual energy passes through the Higher Self to reach you.

The Four Key Spiritual Centers

There are seven spiritual centers, or *chakras*, within that are part of our spiritual anatomy. However, in working with spiritual energy, there are four key spiritual centers within the body that you will be using a great deal in your spiritual-light work. They look like golden spheres of light with beautiful light rays moving out of them.

1. *The mental center*: Located in the middle of the forehead, this is the nucleus of your conscious thinking self.

2. *The throat center*: Located in the middle of the throat, this center is the nucleus of your creative tone.

3. *The Hermetic center*: Located in the middle of the chest, this center is the nucleus of your personal affairs.

4. *The emotional center*: Located in the solar plexus area where the navel is, this is the energetic nucleus of your emotional nature.

Six Steps to Meditate with Divine Light

For a complete description of the process, please refer to my book *Change Your Aura, Change Your Life*. The six steps of meditation are provided here.

The six steps to down-ray light are as follows:

1. *Relax*: Do not begin meditation in a highly agitated state. Do your best to let go of your worries.

2. *Establish protection*: Envision a golden bubble of protection around you before beginning your meditation.

3. *Check your spiritual centers*: Make sure that your spiritual centers are moving clockwise, as if you are the clock.

4. *Connect with your Higher Self*: Put your attention on the golden sun above your head, and feel that you are in the divine presence.

5. *Down-ray the Divine Light.*

6. *Ground yourself*: After receiving Divine Light, give your thanks and let the light equalize throughout your body and consciousness before ending your meditation.

BIBLIOGRAPHY

Blavatsky, Helena. *The Secret Doctrine*. Pasadena, CA: Theosophical University Press, 1999.

Davidson, Gustav. *A Dictionary of Angels*. New York: Free Press, 1994.

Dionysius. *The Celestial Hierarchy*. Whitefish, MT: Kessinger Publishing, 2010.

Ehrman, Bard D. *Lost Christianities: The Battles for Scripture and the Faiths We Never Knew*. New York: Oxford University Press, 2005.

Guile, Rosemary Ellen. *The Encyclopedia of Angels*. New York: Checkmark Books, 2004.

Hall, Manley P. *The Secret Teachings of All Ages*. New York: Penguin/Tarcher, 2003.

Heindel, Max. *The Rosicrucian Cosmo-Conception*. Oceanside, CA: Rosicrucian Fellowship, 1988.

Hodson, Geoffrey. *The Kingdom of the Gods*. Adyar: Theosophical Publishing House, 1987.

Isaac, Stephan. *Songs from the House of Pilgrimage*. Escondido, CA: Christward Ministry.

Jones, Rufus. *Studies in Mystical Religion*. London: Macmillan, 1909.

Judge, William. *Vernal Blooms*. Whitefish, MT: Kessinger Publishing, 2003.

Kaplan, Aryeh. *Meditation and Kabbalah*. San Francisco, CA: Samuel Weiser, 1985.

Lovejoy, Arthur O. *The Great Chain of Being*. Cambridge, MA: Harvard University Press, 1964.

Sri Aurobindo. *Letters on Yoga, Vol. III*. Silver Lake, WI: Lotus Press, 1988.

Three Initiates. *The Kybalion*. New York: Penguin/Tarcher, 2008.

INDEX

Page numbers in *italics* indicate illustrations.

ABOUT THE AUTHORS

BARBARA Y. MARTIN is among the foremost clairvoyants and metaphysical teachers in the world. One of the first lecturers on the aura and the human energy field, she speaks across the United States and is cofounder of the renowned Spiritual Arts Institute, where she has instructed thousands on working with spiritual energy. Martin is the award-winning co-author of *Karma and Reincarnation*, *The Healing Power of Your Aura*, and the international bestseller *Change Your Aura, Change Your Life*.

DIMITRI MORAITIS is cofounder and executive director of the Spiritual Arts Institute. An accomplished teacher and spiritual healer, he is co-author of *Karma and Reincarnation*, *The Healing Power of Your Aura*, and *Change Your Aura, Change Your Life*. He lectures with Barbara Martin across the country.

ABOUT THE ILLUSTRATOR

HOWARD DAVID JOHNSON is a contemporary realistic artist with a background in the natural sciences and history. After a lifetime of drawing and painting, David's traditional art was exhibited in the British Museum in London in 1996, as well as in the Metropolitan Museum of Art and others. David's illustrations have made appearances in major bookstores as well as in magazines and educational texts around the world. For more information, visit www.HowardDavidJohnson.com.

ABOUT SPIRITUAL ARTS INSTITUTE

To contact Barbara Y. Martin and Dimitri Moraitis, and to learn more about classes, private aura consultations, workshops, books, and CDs, please write, e-mail, or phone:

Spiritual Arts Institute
P.O. Box 4315
Sunland, CA 91041
Email: Info@spiritualarts.org
Phone: 818-353-1716
Toll-free: 800-650-AURA (2872)
Or visit the institute's website: www.SpiritualArts.org

If you enjoyed this book, visit

www.tarcherbooks.com

and sign up for Tarcher's e-newsletter to receive
special offers, giveaway promotions, and
information on hot upcoming releases.

TARCHER
PENGUIN

Great Lives Begin with Great Ideas

Connect with the Tarcher Community

• • •

Stay in touch with favorite authors
Enter weekly contests
Read exclusive excerpts!
Voice your opinions!

Follow us

 Tarcher Books

 @TarcherBooks

If you would like to place a bulk order
of this book, call 1-800-847-5515.